GW00579178

THREE YEARS IN
THE LIBYAN DESERT

A BEDUIN SHEIKH.

THREE YEARS IN THE LIBYAN DESERT

TRAVELS, DISCOVERIES, AND EXCAVA-
TIONS OF THE MENAS EXPEDITION
(KAUFMANN EXPEDITION)

By J. C. EWALD FALLS

MEMBER OF THE EXPEDITION

TRANSLATED BY ELIZABETH LEE

WITH 61 ILLUSTRATIONS

DARF PUBLISHERS LIMITED
LONDON
1985

FIRST PUBLISHED 1913
NEW IMPRESSION 1985

ISBN 1 85077 080 8

Printed and bound in Great Britain
by A. Wheaton & Co. Ltd, Exeter, Devon

CONTENTS

CHAPTER I

PAGE

DISAPPOINTED HOPES I

Kaufmann proposes to explore Cyrenaïca, in North Africa—
Initial difficulties—The Tripoli question—Politics upset a scientific project—Our reserve project : the lost sanctuary of the
desert—The Menas expedition.

CHAPTER II

ON THE TRACK OF THE LOST CITY—PREPARATIONS FOR THE

EXPEDITION 9

From Athens to Alexandria—Captain Nicholas changes the pre-
scribed course—Old and new from the city of the Ptolemies—
The tomb of Alexander the Great—Schiess Pasha, a pioneer of
German research in Egypt—Preparations for the journey into
the Libyan Desert and the Menas expedition—Reception by the
Governor—Our equipment.

CHAPTER III

THIRTY DAYS IN THE LIBYAN DESERT 27

Departure of the caravan—Encampment at Haschm-el-Aisch—
Visitors to the camp : Amadeus Haydn, the negro Emperor's
grandson—I take my cousin for a hostile Beduin—Over the
desert tableland to Wadi Moghara—A forced ride by night :
twenty-two hours in the saddle—The petrified forest and the pass
of " Bab-Frankenfurt "—Sandstorm at Wadi Moghara—Bathing
and hunting at the Salt Lake—The negro grievance deputation
—To Kasr el-Gettajeh—Flight of the Beduin, Abu Sêf.

v

Contents

CHAPTER IV

PAGE

THE OASIS OF THE NATRÛN LAKES, OR THE "BALANCE OF THE
HEART"—IN THE MONKS' CITADEL OF THE NITRIAN
DESERT 61

The salt valley and the prehistoric Libyan Nile—We find bones
of old African fauna—Heathen and Christian sanctuaries of
Wadi Natrûn—Four strongholds in the sea of sand—Remains of
the "hundred monasteries"—A journey through the Natrûn
Valley—Sheikh Muftah loses the way—The first tents of the
Schuâbi—Arrival at Bir Hooker—Visit to Dêr Baramûs—The
monks take us for enemies—Cordial reception in the monkish
citadel—At the shrine of the "princes"—Wanderings through
churches and dungeons — Amba John of Abyssinia — The
monastery of the Syrians — Mangled library treasures — Dêr
Amba Bischâi—The salines—Ride to Dêr Makâr—The tomb
of the patriarch of the monks and the grotto of the forty-nine
Sheiks.

CHAPTER V

THROUGH THE LAND OF THE AULADALI—THE DISCOVERY OF
THE TEMPLE OF MENAS, THE "PRIDE OF ALL LIBYA" . 112

Departure from Wadi Natrûn—Muftah's "weakness"—Through
the land of the Children of Ali—Kom Marghab—*Fata Morgana*
—The Pasha deluded by the mirage—Story of the enigmatical
Sidi Melûnte—Arrival at the ruins of Karm Abu Mina—
Dangerous illness of the leader of the expedition—Eureka:
the holy city is found!—The Vineyard of Father Menas—
History of Menas—Departure and return of the caravan—
Strange farewell banquet in the casino at Mex.

CHAPTER VI

HOW THE BEDUINS EXCAVATED THE EGYPTIAN "LOURDES" IN
A CAMPAIGN LASTING TWO YEARS — A WALK THROUGH
THE MARBLE CITY 145

In front of Mamûr Markaz's house—Engaging a Sheikh—To
Karm Abu Mina for the second time—A rebellion among the
Auladali—The strangers are treasure-seekers—They intend to
build a Christian city—My housebuilding—Beduins as workmen
—A walk through the ruins of the Marble City—Our assistants
—Diplomatic intervention—The "German officers" signal to
German battleships.

Contents

CHAPTER VII

PAGE

MARIUT AND MARMARIKA : THE LAND AND THE PEOPLE . 186

The only real Arabs of Egypt—The Auladali and their branches —A German Christian boy the ancestor of the Senagra—Coast region, Gebel, oasis region—Caravan routes—The Dherb el-Hagg—Oasis routes—The land in ancient times—At the Gulf of Sollum—The Khedive's new railway—The Lake of Mariut— A ride along the dam at Orkan—From Bab el-Arab to Bahig, the station for the ruins of the city of Menas—To the future terminus of the railway at Mirsa Matru—The former capital of Marmarika.

CHAPTER VIII

JOY AND SORROW WITH THE SONS OF THE STEPPES . . 221

Christmas Eve improvisation—Divine worship in the tomb of Menas—Hail to the Kaiser !—Political unrest of the Beduins— The two Effendi are to be spared in the general massacre of the Christians—The Jôm dschûma—Fear of the European doctor —Resurrection of the negro Chêr—I win my horse Ibrahîm —The water caravan—A night attack—Siwi, the chief of the three faithful comrades — Visit of Europeans—Beduin panto-mime : jealousy—The iron donkey (Homâr hadîd).

CHAPTER IX

WITH THE VICEROY TO THE OASIS OF AMON—AN HISTORIC PROGRESS THROUGH THE DESERT IN THE STEPS OF ALEXANDER THE GREAT 262

Abbas Hilmi II of Egypt—The royal caravan—Why the Viceroy travels—The "crowned fellah" a title of honour—Table-talk in the desert—The Sultan's road, the Alexander route—Reception in the oasis of Siwa—The palm-grove men and their life—The Egyptian Governor—The prison as dark-room—Murder of the Mamûr of Siwa, 1910—Flora and fauna—Mud towns and troglodytes—The Oracle Temple and other classic ruins— Araschieh, the enchanted lake with Solomon's crown—From the Fountain of the Sun—Kasr el-Guraîschet — My ride to Zetûn—Return home—How Umm Sâd saved my cousin's life.

Contents

CHAPTER X

PAGE

RELIGION AND CUSTOMS OF THE BEDUINS   .   .   . 291

Natural piety and superstition—The world of spirits—How I
caught an Afrite—The ghost of the temple of Menas—" Saints "
of the Auladali—Dervish experiments—Primitive serpents and
scorpions—Mecca pilgrims—Mecca caravans in the interior of
Africa—The Senussi and Pan-Islamism—Sidi el-Mahdi, the mysterious lord of the desert—Wedding at Karm Abu Mina—
Birth and death in the desert—Hospitality and vendetta—The
Mâd—A nose for a nose—Haschisch smuggling—Slavery.

CHAPTER XI

BEDUIN AND FELLAH—THE RECLAIMING OF THE DESERT   . 332

The "ostraka" of the city of Menas—The lessons of the
excavations at Karm Abu Mina—The outlook for Mariut—A
far-reaching attempt of the Viceroy—Agriculture and Beduin
trade—Success on the borders of the Delta—How the Nile mud
changes the desert into a paradise—Fellah villages — The
rôle of the Beduins in the borderland—The awakening of the
Egyptian peasants.

INDEX   347

ILLUSTRATIONS

A BEDUIN SHEIKH . . . . . . *Frontispiece*

Facing page

THE TRIUMPH OF ST. MENAS 2

THE TRIAL OF ST. MENAS 2

THE EXECUTION OF ST. MENAS 2

IDYLL AT KARM ABU MINA. HERD-BOYS LOOK ON AT OUR
EXCAVATIONS 6

ST. MENAS, THE PATRON OF THE LIBYAN DESERT . . 16

SCHIESS PASHA STANDING BY A CAPITAL FROM THE ROYAL
PALACE OF ALEXANDRIA 16

MARBLE RELIEF. PUTTO WITH GARLAND OF FRUIT (CITY OF
MENAS) 24

KASR EL-GETTAJEH : ABU SÊF MEASURING THE RUINS . . 28

A ROCK WELL-CHAMBER IN THE DESERT . . . 32

RUSH CARAVAN IN THE DESERT OF MOGHARA . . . 36

INTERIOR OF THE WELL-CHAMBER OF BIR HASCHM-EL-AISCH,
SEEN FROM BELOW 36

ELUÂNI WITH A GOAT SUCKLING A GAZELLE . . . 40

FRONT VIEW OF KASR EL-GETTAJEH WITH EXCAVATED MARBLES
IN THE FOREGROUND 48

ix

Illustrations

Facing page

BEDUIN GIRL 52

KASR EL-GETTAJEH. PILLAR AND PRAYER NICHE IN THE
INTERIOR 56

PAGAN MINIATURE STELE WITH THE GOD HORUS (FROM THE
CITY OF MENAS) 64

DÊR ES-SURJÂNI, WITH THE MIRACULOUS TREE OF ST. EPHRAIM,
THE SYRIAN 64

SHEIK MUFTAH DABÛN SLAUGHTERS A GAZELLE . . . 72

SHRINE OF THE PRINCES (DÊR BARAMÛS) . . . 72

THE ABBOT (LEFT HAND LOWER FIGURE) AND THE PRIESTS
OF THE COPTIC MONASTERY OF DÊR BARAMÛS . . 80

VIEW IN THE PALM-COURTYARD OF THE MACARIUS MONASTERY
IN WADI NATRÛN 88

SALT EXTRACTION IN WADI NATRÛN 104

BEDUIN AND CHILD AMONG THE MARBLES OF THE HOLY CITY 112

A MENAS AMPULLA (FOURTH CENTURY) 116

A BEDUIN IN THE CENTRE OF THE RUINS OF THE CITY OF
MENAS AT THE TIME OF THE DISCOVERY . . . 120

BEDUIN TENT IN THE ANCIENT GARDEN LAND OF THE CITY
OF MENAS 128

COOKERY IN A FIELD OF ASPHODEL 128

BEDUIN HOUSE BUILT OF FREESTONE FROM THE BASILICA OF
SIDI JÂDEM, DISCOVERED BY THE EXPEDITION . . 136

EXCAVATION OFFICES (KASR A'BUMNA), WITH THE RUINS OF A
CHAPEL IN THE FOREGROUND 144

THE EXCAVATIONS OF THE CITY OF MENAS . . . 152

THE EXCAVATIONS OF THE CITY OF MENAS . . . 160

Illustrations

Facing page

THE EXCAVATIONS OF THE CITY OF MENAS . . . 168

YOUNG SHEIKH. SIDI SADAUI, OF THE TRIBE OF THE GNESCHAT,
THE OVERSEER OF OUR BEDUIN WORKMEN . . . 176

IN FRONT OF THE MAMURÌJE : BEDUINS WAITING FOR THE
DINNER OF MUTTON 176

BEDUIN WORK-GIRL AND BOY WITH HIS BASKET . . 184

BEDUIN CHILDREN ON THE STEPS OF THE EXCAVATION OFFICES 192

PINE CONE MOTIVE : MARBLE RELIEF FROM THE CITY OF MENAS 200

BEDUIN LOOM : WOMEN MAKING TENT CLOTH OF CAMEL'S
HAIR (KARM ABU MINA) 200

GIRL OF THE TRIBE OF SAMELÛS 216

THE EXCAVATORS IN A BEDUIN TENT 224

A ROOM IN OUR HOME. MENAS AMPULLÆ HANGING FROM THE
CEILING 232

INTERIOR OF AN ANCIENT TOMB 262

ROCK FORMATION AT MENSCHIJE 262

ABBAS HILMI II, KHEDIVE OF EGYPT 264

SCULPTURED LION FROM AMONIUM (FRANKFORT MUSEUM) . 264

THE OLDEST STATUETTE OF THE MADONNA (CITY OF MENAS) . 264

VIEW OF SIWA, FROM THE HEIGHTS 272

AÏN MÛSA (MOSES SPRING) 272

THE AUTHOR AT THE RUINS OF AMONIUM (UUM BÊDA) . 276

THE CITADEL OF SIWA A HUNDRED YEARS AGO . . . 280

THE DSCHEBEL EL-BEBEL, THE CITADEL OF SIWA AT THE
PRESENT TIME 280

xi

Illustrations

Facing page

IN FRONT OF THE MOSQUE OF THE SENUSSI AT SIWA : THE
HEAD OF THE SENUSSI MONKS AND THE GOVERNOR WEL-
COME ABBAS HILMI 284

THE MUD CITADELS OF THE CAPITAL OF THE OASIS . . 288

TOMB OF ABD ER-RAHMAN ON AN EMINENCE OF THE CITY OF
MENAS (THE INSCRIPTION IS IN THE FRANKFORT MUSEUM) 320

THE NABÛT AS FLAIL 332

IN THE OASIS OF THE FAYÛM : DRINKING AT THE JOSEPH SPRING 336

RELIC OF ANCIENT LIBYAN CULTIVATION : THE JOSEPH CANAL . 338

AULADALI REAPING WITH THEIR HANDS 338

DESERT AND METROPOLIS. THE ARAB CEMETERY OF CAIRO AT
THE EDGE OF THE DESERT. THE ALABASTER MOSQUE OF
MOHAMMED ALI IN THE DISTANCE 340

FLORA OF THE DESERT. NUÂR OF THE HATTJE . . . 344

Three Years in the Libyan Desert

CHAPTER I

DISAPPOINTED HOPES

Kaufmann proposes to explore Cyrenaïca, in North Africa—
Initial difficulties—The Tripoli question—Politics upset
a scientific project—Our reserve project : the lost sanctuary
of the desert—The Menas expedition.

THE object of the expedition in which my cousin,
Monsignor Kaufmann, of Frankfort, invited me to
take part was the early Christian ruins of Cyrenaïca,
in the Turkish Wilayet Barca. The mysterious
land into the interior of which we desired to penetrate is situated in the eastern portion of North
Africa, between the Mediterranean, the Sahara, and
Egypt, and has been less explored than the darkest
districts of Central Africa and the Great Desert.
The preparations for the expedition had lasted
for almost a year. In 1904 two documents had
been printed "concerning archæological and

Three Years in the Libyan Desert

scientific research in Cyrenaïca," and widely circulated among experts in order to obtain advice and assistance. It was stated that the chief aim of the expedition was "a journey to the Cyrenaïcan Pentapolis, partly in the footsteps of well-known men like Rohlfs, Camperio, Haimann and their companions," and also "to explore the wadis running from the plateau to the south, and for the first time to investigate a district in which there is every reason to suppose that there are not only some of the bishoprics mentioned by Synesius, but also, on the boundary of the fertile zone, large early Christian monasteries referred to by Procopius." Further, the special task of the expedition was to be a double one: "to make a scientific investigation of early Christian monuments, tombs, and sanctuaries, that had been only occasionally and superficially treated by earlier investigators, like Pacho and Smith-Porcher, and also to study archæological monuments of a secular character hitherto neglected," and secondly, to obtain geographical and topographical material through itineraries and the like.

The plan was approved by Professor Georg Schweinfurth, the Nestor of German African explorers, by Professor Viktor Schultze, the distinguished Professor of Christian Archæology in the University of Greifswald, Professor Furt-

THE TRIUMPH OF ST. MENAS.

Early Christian pyx in the British Museum.

THE TRIAL OF ST. MENAS.

An early Christian pyx in the British Museum.

THE EXECUTION OF ST. MENAS.

An early Christian pyx in the British Museum.

To face p. 2.

Disappointed Hopes

wängler of Munich, Professor Strzygovski of Vienna, Professor Harnack of Berlin, Professor Kirsch of Freiburg, Monsignor de Val of Rome, and the archæologist Kekule von Stradonitz, whose pupil Kaufmann was.

When we applied to the Foreign Office for a Turkish firman, we learnt that there would be difficulties about such an expedition, and also Professor Wilhelm Dörpfeld, the Director of the Imperial Archæological Institute in Athens, told us that in 1902 a Danish expedition had fallen through because permission could not be obtained for investigation and excavation in Cyrene.

Others, again, who sympathized with our project were Professor Supan of Gotha and the geographer Richard Kiepert of Berlin.

Two routes had to be considered for a journey in Cyrenaïca—the Egyptian, from Alexandria through Mariut and Marmarika, and the Turkish, from Tripoli through Bengasi. We chose the latter as the most promising, especially if we were unable to obtain the Sultan's firman and were compelled to travel disguised in Arab dress, when from the very beginning not only our lives but also the scientific success of our expedition would be at stake.

While we were making our final preparations, and when our instruments had been tested and our cases and trunks packed, events occurred which might easily have prevented the carrying out of the expedition : the death of Kaufmann's mother, and unfavourable news from Constantinople and Bengasi. Information came from the Bosphorus that under no circumstances whatever would a firman be granted for research in Cyrenaïca. It was also reported that even if the Sultan's permission were obtained, the Pasha, that is, the Wali of Bengasi, would strongly oppose any entry into the " Green Mountains," Dschebel Achdar—so the natives call the highlands of Cyrenaïca—since he would be held responsible for the life and safety of the travellers and was unable to furnish protection for them.

We had reckoned with the possibility that the diplomatic conditions which then prevailed in North Africa, where every explorer was suspected as a political emissary, would lead the authorities there to refuse their help, and on the other hand we knew that no speedy decision was to be expected from the Porte. Now came unfavourable news from Bengasi—the declaration of the Wali or Pasha, and a direct hint on the Egyptian side from the Imperial Ambassador, Freiherr von Rücker-Jenisch, that the inhabitants on the borders of Tripoli, who were especially fanatical, through the influence of the Mohammedan religious societies,

4

would render the life of a European traveller extremely insecure.

There remained then only one other possibility for us—to land in Bengasi as ordinary travellers, to remain there for a few weeks, to organize a modest caravan, and in native dress and at our own risk to invade the highlands of Barca. The slight knowledge of Arabic that we possessed at that time was a serious drawback. But the leader of the expedition reckoned on the assistance of the Franciscan mission stations, since a letter from the General of the Franciscan Order required all the Tripoli settlements to give the two explorers not only a kind reception and to show them hospitality, but also to further their plans in every way. This calculation, which appeared so plausible, was, as we experienced later, the most unfavourable possible, since in the course of centuries the missionaries in those districts—except in the ports, where the Maltese, Italians, and others had established their chief centres of work—had accomplished nothing. The hinterland was closed to them. If some man, bolder than the rest, ventured from the coast into the region of the Green Mountains, his enterprise was soon met by obstacles, and there was cause for rejoicing if, as happened a few years ago, one of them did not take the form of murder.

Three Years in the Libyan Desert

We were already in Tunis, where the Consul-General, Herr von Bary, received us in the kindliest manner, and our luggage was on the way to Tripoli, when difficulties arose both at home and abroad which definitely put an end to the Cyrenaïcan expedition, while, like a bolt from the blue, the whole political question of Italian interests in Tripoli was laid open. In 1905 it had become acute in regard to the harbour of the town of Tripoli. The diplomatists of the Mediterranean countries were more occupied with the old problem of the division of Turkish North Africa, especially Cyrenaïca, which fell within Italy's sphere of interest, than with the particular cause of the war, namely, to whom the newly built Turkish harbour of Berber Tripoli was to belong. The result was that, through the dispute thus enkindled, from April, 1905, all plans were ruined—those of the French firms to whom the harbour had long been handed over as well as those of the Italians, who claimed all rights for themselves.

Unfortunately, with the Italian " Difesa della Tripolitania " our Cyrenaïca expedition was definitely wrecked. The Turkish North African ports of Derna, Bengasi and Tripoli swarmed with spies, who, according to the situation of affairs, saw a representative of the spies of the enemy in every emissary of science, and kept all passengers on out-

IDYLL AT KARM ABU MINA. HERD-BOYS LOOK ON AT OUR EXCAVATIONS.

To face p. 6.

Disappointed Hopes

going ships from Tunis or Malta under observation. Consular and private advices confirmed all that we had already heard in Kairuan and Sfax, and so the wonderland that, according to Pliny, produced the basilisk, and in which the most mysterious medical plants of the ancient world grew, and sporadically still grow—I mean silphium, the dewdrops in which the ancients called the " tears of Cyrenaïca "—was closed to us.

Fortunately Monsignor Kaufmann had a reserve project. We proposed in case of ill success to cross over from Cyrenaïca into Egyptian territory, and to search for the lost sanctuary of Menas in the eastern part of the great Libyan Desert. Since, then, entrance into Dschebel Achdar and its hinterland was closed to us, we had all the baggage sent from Tripoli to Alexandria, paid a brief visit to Germany, and then travelled through Greece to Egypt.

We thus set ourselves to solve the second problem of the expedition : to rediscover the highly important, long and vainly sought early Christian sanctuary in the Libyan Desert, the tomb of St. Menas. There we were on Egyptian ground ; under the ægis of an administration regulated on modern principles, as is the case of Egypt since the English occupation, the difficulties could not be invincible. And this time we had rare luck, for the

7

Three Years in the Libyan Desert

discovery of the early Christian city of the desert and of the national sanctuary of the Christian Egyptians, which has rightly been described as a marvellous and fairylike event, surpassed our boldest expectations.

CHAPTER II

ON THE TRACK OF THE LOST CITY—PREPARATIONS FOR THE EXPEDITION

From Athens to Alexandria—Captain Nicholas changes the prescribed course—Old and new from the city of the Ptolemies—The tomb of Alexander the Great—Schiess Pasha, a pioneer of German research in Egypt—Preparations for the journey into the Libyan Desert and the Menas expedition—Reception by the Governor—Our equipment.

WE landed in Patras, and proceeded to Athens via Nea-Korinth, and the canal which traverses the most romantic scenery of Greece. We had only four days to spend in Athens in which to see the splendid temples, to admire the magnificent old churches, to visit the museums and the university. On St. George's Day there was a popular fête at the Lykabettos, and our last visit before our departure for Alexandria was to the tomb of Heinrich Schliemann, the excavator of Troy, Mycenæ, and Tiryns.

We embarked at the Piræus for Alexandria, and entrusted ourselves to a fairly ancient vessel which

9

bore the proud name of *Athene*. Although the good ship encountered neither storm nor accidents to its machinery, nor fire nor mutiny, she eloped with her passengers to the shores of Asia Minor instead of taking the regular prescribed direct route to Alexandria via Crete. The passengers had understood before embarking that such was the route to be followed, and it was to the interest of most of them that it should be adhered to. However, after a series of adventures we at last found ourselves being slowly piloted through the forest of masts of the Eunostos—the "harbour of safe return," which since 1871 has expanded into a large outer harbour—into the inner harbour, where we were to anchor near the warehouses and the arsenal. The vessel was lightly tossing up and down when the customary comedy of a landing in the East was played. A flotilla of small boats occupied by the most fantastic figures swarmed all round the *Athene*, ready to clamber up her wet sides and fall upon us. The impatience of the black, brown, and red adventurers was greater than ours. At last, after half an hour's wait, the yellow quarantine flag, which had been flown during the visit of the harbour authorities and the doctor, was slowly lowered, and the wild cats climbed up to possess themselves of the passengers' baggage.

A supple thick-set man, with sinister sparkling

eyes, a scanty bristly beard, clad in white up to his carelessly folded red turban, had evidently fixed on us. A painter would have been glad to paint the fellow, who suddenly stood there like Ahasueras and never moved an inch, but who would trust themselves to him? While agents, money-changers, hotel kawasses sang the praises of their houses, he told them in a decisive manner and in ponderous French, but, of course, without any commission so to do : " These gentlemen have engaged rooms in the Hotel St. George." Then he looked at us as if any disavowal on our part would be met with a blow. Monsignor Kaufmann laughed quietly, and said to me : " He'd do murder for a pound!" And so the incredible took place : we followed the man, who boldly swung himself on to the box of our carriage, to that Greek hotel, to the Xenodocheion of Hagio Georgios, situated in sight of the monumental " mixed court of justice," which settled disputes between foreigners and natives and in which some of the best German intellects are employed.

This strange person, who was named Mohammed, became in the course of time a faithful factotum, and in conjunction with the then proprietor of the Greek hotel, which we made our habitual quarters, indispensable to us. This Mohammed, so dreaded at first, became faithfulness and submission personified. Although we only employed him when we needed to make purchases in Alexandria, to procure tools for the excavations, provisions, etc., we were his "masters." At the times when he expected us, he would hang about the railway station all day long. He walked in front through the winding streets of Souks, the Oriental bazaar of the town, and shouting loudly made a way for us with his powerful fists. The motley, good-tempered natives only looked surprised when, to our great embarrassment, he stopped carts or rebuked a tradesman who ventured to demand from his "masters" the prices usually asked of tourists. Mohammed even appeared on board the Austrian steamer which, after three years of hard work, was to take us home again. At this last appearance in our service his wild eyes were sad, and when he had stowed away our luggage in the cabin, to the terror of the personnel he threw himself on the ground and plucked his beard—a farewell with tears !

The *Athene* arrived on May 11th, but our trunks and cases with the instruments and a part of the equipment of the expedition were still on the way from Tripoli to Alexandria. So besides the preliminary visits there was sufficient time for a cursory survey of Iskanderije, the city of Alexander.

On the Track of the Lost City

Its nearness to Cairo, the enchanted city of the Caliphs, which can be reached in a three hours' railway journey, has caused the successor to the ancient city of the Ptolemies to be merely a city of passage. The city has, of course, more interest for commercial men, for nearly three thousand steamers pass annually in and out of its harbour, and its exportation of cotton and fruit is always increasing. In summer, when the Khedive removes his court to Ras-el-Tin—opposite the ancient Pharos peninsula where once the wonder of the antique world, the celebrated lighthouse, far higher than the spire of Cologne Cathedral, rose into the air—and the ministerial and official world of Cairo goes into *villeggiatura* on the Eleusinian shore in the garden suburb of Ramleh surrounded by the sea, the life of the beautiful city becomes more animated. But the tourists and foreigners have then long departed from the land of the Nile, and certainly to their disadvantage. For after the Egyptian season, which lasts from November to April, the ancient land puts forth all its splendour ; and even autumn, when snowfields of cotton shine immeasurable beside the palms, has its own peculiar charm, one too little valued.

In population and extent Alexandria is gradually approaching its ancient golden age, when in the time of Augustus it had a population of half a

million. Indeed, as the days of the ancient Pharos,
the ruins of which, saved from earthquakes and
sea-storms, rose up masterfully in the Middle Ages,
are gone, so is the splendour of the temples and
of the classic architecture of the public buildings.
Every trace of the famous Gymnasium is lost,
and the actual site of the Museum and the
Ptolemaic Library, at the burning of which almost
a million manuscripts containing the written wisdom
of the ancient world were lost, is not known. In
the modern city of the natives and of the fifty
thousand " Franks," chiefly Greeks and Italians,
houses and villas have been erected over other
buildings. And the street traffic surges over the
sites of the Cæsareum and of that remarkable
theatre of which the sea formed the side scenes,
with a little crescent-shaped island in the background. On the site of the ruins of the Serapeum,
the sanctuary erected by the Ptolemies to Serapis,
ruler of the underworld, a single pillar of red
granite rises to the sky, the last remnant, which the
Emperor Theodosius had set up again as a victory
column of Christendom in memory of the destruction of the building. That " Pillar of Pompey,"
about 90 feet high, with its monumental pedestal
and its large Corinthian capital, is the modern lion
of the town. Schiess Pasha erected a smaller,
similar column with two figures of Sechmet, the

lion-headed war goddess, near the Government Hospital in memory of the victory of Omdurman and the conquest of Khartoum (1898). Like the Victoria Column, also erected by Schiess Pasha, it had its origin in the neighbouring royal palace of the Ptolemies, lying amid quiet gardens. Ismail Pasha, with great generosity, gave two fine obelisks of pink granite (improperly called Cleopatra's Needles) from the Temple of the Sun at Heliopolis, obelisks which the Emperor Theodosius brought to Alexandria, to foreign lands—one to London, the other to New York.

We were soon familiar with those parts of the town unfrequented by foreigners and less striking to the eye, and in the course of frequent visits the subterranean cisterns and catacombs claimed our special attention. The greatest attraction of that kind, Alexander's tomb, is unfortunately, on religious grounds, still inaccessible. Like all the royal necropolises of the Ptolemies, it is situated under the Nebi Daniel mosque, and tradition speaks of a wide subterranean passage that leads under the chief axis of the building to the royal tomb, which is recognizable externally on an eminence (Kom ed Dick). Since Schliemann's time, to whom Schiess Pasha was helpful, the possibility of excavation in that spot has been considered. A former guardian of the mosque and others had seen the gold mummy of Alexander in the catacomb. The rumour quickly spread, and when it came to the ears of Tewfik Pasha, the father of the present Khedive, the entrance to the royal tomb was closed up, and later effaced. The existence of a large subterranean annex in the neighbourhood of the mosque of the Prophet Daniel is absolutely certain, and was confirmed to me in a thoroughly determinative and trustworthy way. But the Ulemas will never permit Europeans to make investigations, and it will be necessary to employ force.

The most fantastic of all the stories hitherto put forward is that of a Greek whom Professor Thiersch of Freiburg mentions in an essay on the tomb of Alexander that appeared after this chapter was written. A Greek named Schillizzi, who was searching for antiquities, penetrated into the remains of the Nebi Daniel mosque. He descended into the depths of a catacomb corridor, and through a secret passage reached a worm-eaten wooden door. Through a crack he saw a glass case, and in it a dead man, whose head was crowned with a diadem of precious stones, and around whom lay manuscripts and papyrus scrolls.

It is very striking that Alexander, who was originally to have been removed to the oasis of Jupiter-Amon, but remained in the royal tomb of Memphis, and came thence to " his " town, accord-

ST. MENAS, THE PATRON OF THE LIBYAN DESERT.

Ivory panel from the throne of Mark, the evangelist.

SCHIESS PASHA STANDING BY A CAPITAL FROM THE ROYAL PALACE OF ALEXANDRIA.

To face p. 16.

ing to classical tradition, reposed in a glass coffin.
Augustus himself was among the Roman Emperors
who visited his tomb and placed a golden diadem
on the mummy, and it was Septimius Severus who
put sacred books from Egyptian temples into the
grave!

Among heathen cemeteries we may mention the
Greek rock necropolis near the bay of Anfûchi, on
the estate of Prince Tussûn, and the magnificent
Greek catacombs of Kom esch Schugâfa, the
chambers of which, with their picturesque mixture
of Egyptian and Græco-Roman decoration, we were
fortunate enough to study under the guidance of
their real discoverer, Schiess Pasha. What had
been found there, in addition to gifts, formed the
basis, or at least the most important part, of the
antiquities in the Græco-Roman museum of Alexandria. But unfortunately they are a very poor
representation of what might be expected in the
city of the Ptolemies. If, however, the sins of
omission of a town like Alexandria are to be partly
made good, it is owing to the energy of men like
Schiess Pasha and G. Botti. The latter was the
first director of the new museum. Under his successor and compatriot, E. Breccia, equally valued as
official and author, the collection has greatly improved, especially through occasional finds on sites
of buildings and streets, such as the discovery of a

Three Years in the Libyan Desert

Greek cemetery in the neighbouring district of El-Hadra.

The chief interest of the leader of our expedition lay naturally in the few early Christian remains of Alexandria. What we undertook in following up tracks in the precincts of both the ancient and modern city borders on the incredible. No bog was too deep, no field of stones in the desert too near the lair of the Beduin dogs, no wall could stand against our curiosity, and amusing episodes were not lacking. Unfortunately, our visits to the catacombs of Alexandria had no special result, although I myself brought home rich botanical booty and some geological specimens. During the excavations in Menas information was given us by a Beduin which threw light on the supposed situation of the lost cemeteries of early Christian Alexandria, a problem about the solution of which my cousin was specially eager. One day a Greek offered to sell us an early Christian bronze lamp, the inside of which was filled with earth. We were successful in finding the Beduin from whom he procured it, and he declared he had obtained the object from a relative who had formerly been "Ghaffir" at Sidi Gaber, a garden suburb of Alexandria. We were able, fortunately, to discover almost the exact spot where the guard's tent stood, but not the entrance to the Christian houses in

On the Track of the Lost City

the Sebel—a range of hills at El-Hadra—not even with the help of Beduins of the tribe in question. Excavations in that neighbourhood would certainly bring surprises, since the first early Christian cemetery found in Alexandria came to light in that chain of hills during the construction of the Cairo railway and was destroyed.

It was not, however, the old town that exclusively interested us. The modern town, that since Mohammed Ali had flourished anew, offered in the native quarter points of attraction not less strong. Even the European quarter, which has revived since the rebellion of Arabi Pasha and the occupation of the land by the English (1882), offered points of interest. It is focused round the large fine square with its equestrian statue of Mohammed Ali, where the most beautiful palaces are situated. But Alexandria derives its best adornment from the new harbour and fine quays, a work that owes much to the initiative of Schiess Pasha and is partly completed. It is built on a flat tongue of sand of the delta of the Nile, and in a few years will rank among the really fine harbours of the Mediterranean.

I have again mentioned the name of a man whose assistance greatly contributed to the success of the Menas expedition. Having once reached the country, everything lay in using the letters of introduction we had brought with us.

Three Years in the Libyan Desert

A fortunate fate led us to Dr. Johannes Schiess Bey, who effectually helped us where others would have deemed promises and dinner invitations all that was required. In Dr. Schiess, who later became Pasha, we found a pioneer of German research in Egypt.

"Tell his Royal Highness that Dr. Schiess makes no sort of distinction; he treats all alike!" Nothing better describes the man who was borne to the grave on February 25, 1910, amid the sympathy of the whole of Alexandria, than this reply given to the chief eunuch of the Khedive, who had been commissioned by his master to recommend a patient for special care. At that time Dr. Schiess was chief physician of the Government Arab hospital in Alexandria, an institution which he transformed into a model for modern Egyptian sanitation. We first met him in that place after he had held his post for nearly twenty-five years. His strong, rather thick-set figure, his decided, simple manner, did not conceal under the red tarbusch, the sign of the Egyptian official, the honest Swiss. Something of the freshness of youth lay on the slightly ruddy countenance and seemed to give the lie to the short white moustache, under which appeared, as always with the inveterate smoker, the cigar.

My cousin's purpose was to interest Schiess,

who then bore the title of Bey, in his quality as President of the Alexandrian Antiquities Commission, in the Menas expedition, and if possible to gain the moral support of the distinguished man.

The success was beyond all expectation. When Schiess had looked at our introductions and learned our plans, which included researches in the whole of the north-east corner of the Libyan Desert, where the mysterious lost sanctuary must be hidden, he rang for a servant and ordered the carriage to be brought round. He turned to me and said cordially : " Herr Falls, I admire your courage, and envy you your youth ; I am sorry that I cannot myself join this interesting expedition into the desert." And then came the important words : " I will do all that lies in my power to help you, but do not be too hopeful." He then invited us to drive with him to the museum and to call on the Governor.

Later we had the good fortune to know the man more intimately, and to see him at work in the laboratory, by the sick-bed, and under the palm-trees of his shady *villeggiatura* at Ramleh-Bacos. He had many reminiscences to give of the men who had worked in his laboratory— men distinguished for their investigations into plague and cholera, anthropologists, African explorers to whom he had shown hospitality ; men

Three Years in the Libyan Desert

like Virchow, Robert Koch, Schweinfurth, and Fritsch. His most important creative work was patent to the eyes when we walked through the barracks, tents, and wards of the Government Arab hospital, towering above the seashore on the ruins of the royal citadel of the Ptolemies, where Schiess first introduced Berlin disinfecting apparatus, modern instruments, in short, European scientific methods and hygiene, reforms of the utmost importance for the welfare of the whole of the Nile country.

Schiess Pasha was born in 1837 at Herisau, in the canton of Appenzell. It was intended that he should be a Protestant theologian, but he studied medicine at Basle, Berne, Paris, and Berlin. In Paris he often went hungry. A desire to see the world and a feeling for romance led the thirty-year-old doctor to the revolution in Crete. He travelled through the disturbed island on a commission from a Swiss-Italian committee to take help to the sick and wounded insurgents. There, so to say, in the saddle, he made the acquaintance of Elpis Melenas, the authoress, Baroness Marie Espérance von Schwartz, who was closely connected with the later history of the island. A year after, Schiess appeared in the brilliant suite of Ismail at the opening of the Suez Canal. The Khedive had invited him

22

to be present, and by his wish Schiess now remained in Egypt, the land which was to be so deeply indebted to him.

Division-surgeon in the military and civil hospital, Imperial Russian delegate to the Sanitary Council, physician-in-chief and director of the Arab hospital of Alexandria, such are the outward steps in the course of the life of the distinguished physician to whom Alexandria in 1897 paid the highest honour in summoning him to the head of her international composite municipality.

One day we met Dr. Schiess at his favourite spot in the hospital park, where now a granite tomb covers his bones, in an opening surrounded by trees, in the centre of which the ancient sarcophagus rests on a pedestal with four steps, flanked by rare early Christian pillars. His old friend, the President of the Council, had informed him that the Khedive purposed bestowing on him the dignity of a pasha. The democrat in him strove against it. "I am and shall remain Dr. Schiess," he replied, and his friends had great difficulty in persuading him to accept the honour. Exploration and antiquarian research greatly gained by the change.

Our reception by Mahmud Pasha Sidky, the Governor of Alexandria, who meanwhile has been transferred to a similar post at Cairo, was most

Three Years in the Libyan Desert

satisfactory. He occupied the old Government Buildings near the harbour, surrounded by a small army of officials, servants, and soldiers. Our business was inaugurated by the inevitable "Gawa" in pretty Arab coffee-cups. My cousin explained our plans in his best French, and the Pasha, who had already heard of them through Schiess Bey, immediately introduced us to Hopkinson Bey, now likewise Pasha, who was head of the police of Alexandria; the neighbouring parts of the desert were also under his authority. We could not have wished for a more intelligent and sympathetic man than Colonel Hopkinson. As an enthusiastic gazelle hunter, he had a great love of the desert, and until the conclusion of the later excavations, which he frequently visited with a military escort, he was a warm friend and patron of the expedition. "We do not wish you to be lost in the desert, Father Kaufmann," he said to my cousin, when we were studying the large map of the Libyan district in his office. It devolved on him to provide us with a military escort for our explorations. But my cousin thought it safer for us to travel in Arab dress without an escort; Hopkinson agreed, and our success proved him and us right. Hopkinson Bey gave orders to his subordinates in the police stations of Mariut to give us assistance. He placed at our disposal, without any expense to us,

MARBLE RELIEF. PUTTO WITH GARLAND OF FRUIT
(CITY OF MENAS).

To face p. 24.

military tents and other things from the Government stores useful to the expedition.

Meanwhile our cases had arrived from Tripoli, and we had to see about procuring provisions and the necessary equipment. As regards instruments, we had two aneroids, which the officer of the marine signal station of Fort Napoleon adjusted for us, compasses, thermometers, rain-gauges, surveying instruments—among them a very serviceable distance measure, which we later gave to Herr Kayser, the chief engineer of the Khedivial railway. Two excellent cameras, a Kodak and a Bentzin camera, formed a most important part of our equipment. It is to be noted that the films specially packed and prepared for the high temperature of the desert turned out useless, while ordinary films purchased in Alexandria, contrary to all expectation, kept in splendid condition. It generally happened that the specially prepared article was a failure. So it was a fortunate thing that no one had left his ordinary watch at home, for the " precision-watch " recommended by experts stopped being precise in the first days of the journey in the desert.

The Beduins laughed heartily at our " water-bags," the production of a well-known Berlin firm. They acted like filters. The water dropped—slowly, it is true, but without cessation—in spite of everything done to stop it, and the old goatskins used by the Beduins of Scripture saved our lives, and so contrasted with the poor product of civilization. It is possible that some evil spirit was against us. But in any case the traveller should be distrustful of improvements when equipping an expedition of this kind.

The usual tinned and preserved provisions were packed in practical, locked chests. Powder and shot for the Beduins and ammunition for our two double-barrelled guns and the revolvers were likewise carefully packed. Two pocket medicine chests, fitted according to the directions of Dr. Stendel, the staff-surgeon-major, and other medicaments, the selection of which was undertaken by Schiess Pasha, with directions for the treatment of well-known native illnesses, were to render us and others essential service. A compatriot from Hesse, Georg Ruelberg, the owner of the German pharmacy in Alexandria, helped us not only then with advice and deeds, but during the whole period of the excavations was a kindly counsellor. Vessels of all sorts, woollen rugs for the variations of temperature in the desert, and simple khaki clothes with which the fez was to be worn, and over which we wore the white burnous purchased in Tunis, completed our equipment, which was calculated to last a good month.

CHAPTER III

THIRTY DAYS IN THE LIBYAN DESERT

Departure of the caravan—Encampment at Haschm-el-Aisch—
Visitors to the camp : Amadeus Haydn, the negro Emperor's
grandson—I take my cousin for a hostile Beduin—Over the
desert tableland to Wadi Moghara—A forced ride by night :
twenty-two hours in the saddle—The petrified forest and the
pass of " Bab-Frankenfurt "—Sandstorm at Wadi Moghara—
Bathing and hunting at the Salt Lake—The negro grievance
deputation—To Kasr el-Gettajeh—Flight of the Beduin,
Abu Sêf.

At last the morning of our departure approached.
All details had been arranged with the Mamûr
Markaz, the police-officer of the district of Mariut,
situated west of Alexandria. Mahmud Effendi
Sidky—for he was a namesake and cousin of the
Governor of Alexandria—had procured Beduins
and camels for us, settled the price, and dispatched
the baggage and the rest of the military tents to
the last station of the Khedivial railway, then under
construction, which runs through the coast district
of the desert west from Alexandria. When we
left the carriage we were surrounded by a motley

crew of Auladali Beduins, who looked with curiosity at men and baggage, and when the Mamûr appeared, kissed his hand. Five camels lay ready, and our suite was to be sought among a group of Beduins taking leave of one another. A few days before our departure, Schiess Pasha had placed one of his officials at our disposal to accompany and assist the caravan. He was an amiable young man, whose heart, like ours, beat high with the anticipation of events. The Mamûr Markaz soon put a stop to the endless farewells of our future suite, the members of which had not paid the slightest attention to the arrival of their masters.

Meanwhile Monsignor Kaufmann and I sat down comfortably on the chests and tent-poles. "Muftah!" called the Mamûr, "Muftah!" and while he summoned the leader, the others came up and formed a circle of white figures, wrapped in the burnous, round the three of us. In their hands they carried the nabût, or slung the long Beduin gun over the shoulder.

When Muftah and his companions had come up, the Mamûr turned to us and said, taking the dignified personage by the arm, "This is Muftah Dabûn, the Sheikh; he is responsible for you with his life and his whole tribe." Muftah lifted his right arm to his brow and breast in token of respect, and Mamûr placed Muftah's hands in ours.

KASR EL-GETTAJEH : ABU SÊF MEASURING THE RUINS.

To face p. 28.

Thirty Days in the Libyan Desert

Then the remainder of the company—in contrast to the elderly Sheikh, all young men—greeted us. Eluâni Hamed, the descendant of a "saint"; Abd el-Al, son of an Arab from Wadi Dafne at Sollum, and also the Sheikh's son, Abu Sêf Sâle, "father of the sword." With the exception of the last, who, in spite of his terrifying name, was a spoilt child, and had never been more than a few days' journey into the desert, all our people were experienced and travelled persons.

As we wished to set out at once, the camels were saddled under the eye of the Mamûr. Every one helped, and so the matter only took an hour. Two young beasts were selected for us to ride. One beast carried four large water-skins, and the two last the baggage, among which there was room for another rider. The Beduins themselves would take turn about during a long march and mount one of the animals in order to get a rest. With the assistance of the Mamûr the fees were settled as follows: fifteen large piastres a day (about three shillings) for the leader, the same for each of the five camels, and only tips for the rest of the men. The keep of the men and of the camels was included in this small sum, which was not to be paid until the safe return of the expedition. The Sheikh asked for £3 in advance for his family, and my cousin gave it him through Mamûr Markaz.

Three Years in the Libyan Desert

At two o'clock in the afternoon the camels, laden and covered with soft woollen rugs, lay on their knees, and for the first time we boarded the ships of the desert. We tried to preserve our dignity in the sight of so many people. With a rolling motion the animals got safely on to their legs; a jerk of the back, and then a more violent one of the long stretched-out neck, and the three riders sat perched high in the air, and for the start the suite led them with a long leash. Just as we were leaving, two Europeans came to give us a farewell greeting : Miralai Kelham, inspector of police, and his wife.

The caravan steered through the centre of the scanty undergrowth of the hattje, the entrance to the desert, and very soon not a man was to be seen near or far.

Our programme was clear and simple. According to the historical sources, the sanctuary of Menas lay in the desert between Alexandria, Wadi Natrûn, and Marmarika. My cousin determined to go westward to the boundary of Marmarika, and thence south to Wadi Natrûn. Ancient remains, of which the Sheikh or some of the men had knowledge, or of the existence of which they told, were to be visited and examined, and for that purpose excursions right and left of the route were planned. The sanctuary itself was supposed to be in the interior of the desert, and therefore from Wadi Natrûn the whole of the portion known by the name of the Auladali Desert must be thoroughly explored, even if it became necessary to return once to the Nile delta in order to procure fresh supplies of provisions.

So we proceeded westward, and in order to train in men and beasts, for the first two days we only marched eight to ten hours, and on the day we started only five.

The first encampment was made about seven o'clock in the evening in the midst of the quiet hattje, near the two dozen palms of Schuêre. It gave us an opportunity of learning something of our people and their usefulness. The camels knelt down and, amid continual bellowings, allowed themselves to be unloaded. Chests, bags, tents, and skins lay scattered on the ground. When the camels were set free they could feed in the neighbourhood. But our chief threw himself on the ground and said the sunset evening prayer. No one was more delighted with this than we were, for we never imagined that it meant that for the Sheikh the day's work was ended. His prayer finished, he searched for dry wood in order to make a little fire, but did not trouble himself in the least about pitching the tents.

Thus Eluâni, the descendant of a Beduin saint, was a more valuable acquisition. He understood everything, and gave his two assistants plenty of work. Our own activity was limited to arranging the chests and getting the beds ready, that is, in spreading the woollen rugs on the ground in the long, low double tent. Then came a first attack on the provisions.

Darkness had long set in before we sat down near the fire on our folding chairs and warmed some unsweetened condensed milk. Our Beduins, en- camped on the other side of the fire, brewed the coffee we had given them on the hot ashes, Arab fashion; we had brought it with us in order to be able to entertain guests. Only Eluâni accepted the tobacco; the others, on religious grounds, were ab- stainers. To our great astonishment the conversa- tion of the young sons of the desert turned almost exclusively on their return home.

In imagination they pictured all they would have to tell, and how from far and wide men would seek their ancestral tents in order to hear their experi- ences. Although Sheikh Muftah had different thoughts, in his own way he shared the reflections of the others. He squatted on the ground a little apart, with crossed legs, and placed large and small stones in front of him. Each large stone represented a day, round which six smaller ones were grouped. When fourteen days had been laid out in this way—he thought the journey would last

A ROCK WELL-CHAMBER IN THE DESERT.

To face p. 32.

so long—he counted the small stones and thus reckoned the number of five-piastre pieces which he in his own person would earn for his service and his camels. As evidently he frequently reckoned wrong, he began the game of patience over and over again.

The silvery moon had long risen. My cousin fetched the route-books and diaries, and by the light of a lantern we began the journal of our travels, each from a definite fixed point of view. Our example had apparently a good effect on our third man, the assistant official whom Schiess Pasha had given us, who, so far, without parting with his double-barrelled gun, sat on his camp-stool blowing clouds of smoke from his short English pipe, now and then celebrating the wonderful stillness of the moonlight night with a poetical phrase. Now he fetched a large black portfolio, ink, and pen out of the tent and lighted a stearine candle. Then he wrote and wrote. We had trouble to make him join us when, about ten o'clock, we crept into the tent, changed our khaki clothes for sleeping-suits, and, after a brief prayer, crawled under the rugs, keeping near us our cartridge-boxes and guns as faithful sleeping companions.

Abd el-Al had the first night-watch. Gun in hand, he sat under the open sky immovable among his sleeping comrades, and looked towards the east, where at intervals of a minute the dim light of the lighthouse of Alexandria appeared like a kindly star. The night passed without disturbance.

Before dawn we were awoke by Sidi Muftah's prayer, "God is great and Mohammed His prophet!" It was not necessary to be sparing with water, since we intended to reach Hamam, the ancient meeting-place of the Hedscha pilgrims. In the keen yet soft morning air (the minimum thermometer did not go below 51° Fahrenheit during the night) we were in the saddle by 5 a.m., passed some small ruins of the Roman period, and reached Bir Hamam about 10 a.m.

At Bir Hamam, where the remains of an ancient town had been searched for, we were hospitably entertained in the tent of an Arab who declared, in well-turned phrases, that his house and property, (that is, his tent and his horse) were ours, but all the same could not withstand the temptation of demanding backschish for the milk we drank.

The next morning the caravan moved on in a north-westerly direction through the steppes. The camels went along bravely on the firm ground, apparently at the rate of about eighty steps per minute. The beasts and their riders understood each other, so that my cousin and I felt ourselves capable of longer independent excursions off the route, but we were always careful to return to the point of departure. We carried on a strap round our necks the official German route-book.

Some difficulty was made during the march through the desire of the camels to feed wherever they saw a suitable weed, safsaf, schije, or the like, a proceeding which appealed to Sheikh Muftah, since it saved him fodder. We had our animals so entirely under control that from our elevated seats we could risk a shot with the Kodak. Accompanied by the songs of the sons of the desert, we rode still in reach of the soft sea-breezes. The temperature, about 78° Fahrenheit, was pleasant, and on the gently rising ground from the low undergrowth of the hattje, single larger bushes lifted their heads. In the distance these sporadic bushes assumed an enormous size. They then looked like trees, but shrank when near to not much over a yard high. They were thickly covered with white snail-shells, which shone like fruit amid the green foliage.

Shortly before 10 a.m. the ridge of Haschm-el-Aisch appeared like a low range of hills at the foot of high mountains in the alluvial land of the pre-historic Nile delta. We passed a desert cemetery, a group of the longish Beduin grave mounds surrounded by large blocks of stone, and over all on an eminence a Sheikh's tomb. Whenever we saw the black ridge of a tent, Abd el-Al left the caravan and hastened towards it on foot, in order to convey our greetings, and naturally to be asked about the aim and purpose of our journey. Such was the ancient desert custom, and neglect of it would have been to court danger. If the Sheikh spied persons approaching, a thing his hawk's eye accomplished more infallibly than our binoculars, our escort quickly compared views, and one of the people, his long gun-barrel shining brilliantly in the sun, went forward, the caravan slightly lessening its pace, in order to see who it was. It happened that even mounted men suddenly changed their route when they saw our seven guns. In one case Muftah Dabûn thought it well for us to make a detour, and he justified it by declaring that the persons visible in the far distance were enemies of his family. We could never get him to tell us how he recognized them, although the Italian attendant helped out our Arabic, for we were fairly in-experienced in the practical use of the native tongue.

Bir Haschm-el-Aisch was reached at a quarter to three. It was a subterranean well-house in the ridge of hills of that name. The camels lay down on the stony ground covered with a fair amount of undergrowth. A tent was soon pitched, and by its side waved the German flag on a short pole. The

RUSH CARAVAN IN THE DESERT OF MOGHARA.

INTERIOR OF THE WELL-CHAMBER OF BIR HASCHM-EL-AISCH, SEEN FROM BELOW.

To face p. 36.

afternoon was to be employed in examining a large field of ruins that, according to the Sheikh, was situated in the immediate neighbourhood.

We here had a foretaste of the wells of the desert and their water. The goat-skins which had been freshly filled in Bir Hamam were to be reserved for the next day, and I desired to quench my thirst with the fresh water of the springs of the desert, and went off to the Bir, which was about a dozen yards from the tent. Bir Haschm-el-Aisch is a half ruinous old cave, with traces of plaster and some Arabic scribbling, as well as signs of caravans and individual travellers. Through a wide opening we clambered into the well-house, which was about twelve and a half yards long. A short narrow passage led from it down to the spring, a small mud cauldron in which, except in the rainy season, there was never more than a pailful of water, and when it was drawn off, it refilled in about a quarter of an hour. We soon became accustomed to the dark muddy liquid. This time we used the charcoal filter, and after a long wait, greatly to the astonishment of our attendants, it yielded a few glasses of clear water. Later we boldly renounced this wearisome method and drank the water as it came and suffered no harm thereby.

The name of the place is given in English maps as Ashim el esch; but Dr. Junker, in his plan of

Three Years in the Libyan Desert

the north-east part of the Libyan Desert which appeared in Petermann's "Mitteilungen," 1880, gives it as pronounced to-day by the Auladali, Dschebel Haschm-el-Aisch. The etymology is not quite clear. Our Beduins declared that "Haschm" was Beduin for nose, and "ische" for evening, thus "nose of the evening," because of the long shape of the hills stretching westward.

The summit of Haschm-el-Aisch is a gently rising stony plateau that in the north and north-east falls steeply down to the flat shore of the Mediterranean. Three Sheikhs' tombs greet the traveller from afar, and when he ascends the rocks he sees with astonishment that their stone crown conceals ancient hewn material. The sudden descent of the plateau, which represents nothing more nor less than the acropolis of an ancient town, the sight of endless plains terminating in the sea, was delightful after a long march through the flat steppes that form the entry to the desert. With the help of two of our men the ground was pre-liminarily sounded, and Monsignor Kaufmann determined to remain there a few days, as the district apparently contained important ruins. Three caves were discovered. We let ourselves down a deep chasm in turn, and two of our men, who accompanied us for protection and aid, easily climbed down perpendicularly by means of the hewn out hand and feet holes. The "spirits" prevented entrance into a cistern, since they kept a by no means pleasant snake ready to receive you at the bottom. Naturally, such subterranean ruins were first tested for fear of gases, etc., and for that purpose, after many years' interval, my cousin's "catacomb lamp," a metal vessel with a handle and movable top in which was a hole for a thick wax spiral, was used. It was let down alight by a rope in order to see if the air was pure.

On the ground of the eminence we could distinctly trace the foundation lines of different buildings, of which one in the shape of a semi-cross was perhaps a basilica. There were also indications that the hill was once strongly fortified and protected by walls. My cousin was convinced that the summit of Haschm-el-Aisch, which commanded the whole district, was undoubtedly a citadel of a Byzantine foundation, resting on a Roman or perhaps a more ancient basis. As he now writes to me, this "key to Mareotis and postern-gate of Marmarika" is evidently identical with one of the fortified places of Ptolemy.

From the "bridge of the evening's nose" we saw a large tent standing alone in the northern plain. Its white colour made us think it a Beduin one. After we had returned home, the master of the tent came, mounted on a white camel, to greet us. He

Three Years in the Libyan Desert

was a sergeant of the coastguard, a tall negro. Who can depict our astonishment when the stylish-looking fellow, in a yellow khaki uniform, armed with revolver, carbine, and the enormous kurbasch,[1] gracefully dismounted, touched his yellow fez, and saluted us in three civilized languages : " Good afternoon, sir," " Bonjour, messieurs," " Meine Herren, guten Tag "?[2] He threw a careless " Neharak saïde " at the Beduins. He ordered them as if it was a matter of course to look after his steed, the beautifully caparisoned white camel. Then he sat down on the chair we offered him, did not despise whisky and cigarettes, and related his life's story, and to this day I am uncertain if he was wholly or partly lying.

His name was Amadeus Haydn, his birthplace Rio, in Brazil, his grandfather the Emperor Don Pedro ! He knew Dresden and Vienna, kept a diary of the events of his life and other matters, among which the archæological notes were specially valuable to us. We would gladly have purchased his drawings, but the *petit-fils* of Don Pedro would not consent. To the question why, considering his origin and his knowledge, he had not made a greater success in life, he said he preferred a life of freedom, and when he had asked for and swallowed a fresh

[1] Horsewhip used on the Nile.
[2] Good day.

ELVÂNI WITH A GOAT SUCKLING A GAZELLE.

To face p. 40.

glass of whisky, he added in a whisper that perhaps the "damned" whisky was somewhat responsible. The black grandson of an emperor took his leave in the evening, having been presented with cigarettes and a box of sardines, and invited us to return his visit. Sheikh Muftah accompanied him down to the plain in order to pay him special honour while wild jackals bayed the moon.

We were forced to encamp at Haschm-el-Aisch somewhat longer than we liked. We had to get rid of our Italian servant, who fitted in nowhere, and so, although personally a pleasant, nice fellow, was really a burden to the expedition. A discovery about the endless treatises that he wrote each evening by candlelight determined us and explained his elegiac moods : they were love-letters! He parted from us unwillingly, and on his account I went back post-haste to Alexandria to explain matters to Schiess Pasha, and took the opportunity to supplement our provisions.

I returned the visit of the emperor's grandson by myself, with our Sheikh, on an excursion to the ruins of El-Almaida, on the coast. His spacious military tent, in which he dwelt with three other negroes, naturally Africans, in order to prevent the smuggling of haschisch, was clean and tidy, and the most precious thing that Amadeus Haydn offered me was crystal-clear water, which was regularly furnished to the military posts from Bir Hamam in zinc chests brought on camel-back. The swift ride through the plain to El-Almaida, through the wonderful morning air, was a beneficial change.

On our return at sunset, Sheikh Muftah discovered a white figure on the slopes of Haschm-el-Aisch, which we were quickly approaching, lying among the rocks with gun in readiness. We clearly saw the barrel glitter, and considered it wise to reach our camp, where a signal-fire was burning, by a detour, and as quickly as possible. Arrived there I quickly solved the mystery. My cousin was absent, so that only he could have been the enemy whom we escaped with such anxiety. But Monsignor Kaufmann had also been in great trouble. Alone in the field of ruins he had seen two armed riders approaching at a gallop, and in the twilight did not recognize them; he took us for enemies and lay in ambush ready for anything.

Early in the morning of June 19th the camp at Haschm-el-Aisch was broken up, and at 5 a.m. the caravan was already on the march in the borderland of Mariut and Marmarika. The day before the water-skins had been freshly filled at Bir Hamam. We went in a south-westerly direction through the low undergrowth of the sandy plain. The continual whistling of the Sheik or the hoarse " Ha, ha, ha" kept the well-fed animals at an even pace one behind the other. The moon rode high in front of the caravan, and if we looked round we saw the blood-red disk of the sun. The plateau of Haschm-el-Aisch flattened out noticeably, and the first gazelles were seen, four shy, pretty creatures, leaping merrily. And so the ships of the desert glided into the sandy plain of El-Halfa, a district of special interest for the naturalist, because, according to tradition, it was where the great prehistoric arm of the Nile had its mouth. In order that we might be able to reconnoitre the ground thoroughly, Sheikh Muftah planned to halt at the next Arab tent we came across. Towards noon the temperature rose to 113°, and we were glad to find the tent of a friendly Sheikh and to encamp there. Our dinner menu was Quaker oats and tinned salmon, and that of the Beduins their horrible flat cakes of bread baked with onions in the ashes. In the evening a fine black and white sheep was sacrificed, which the El-Halfa Beduins sold us for twelve shillings, and which was so greatly appreciated that Sheikh Muftah said his prayers twice over that night, a thing that always happened whenever there was roast mutton or roast gazelle.

A dinner of mutton in the desert is most romantic. It is the custom for the seller to share it as guest, and also any wanderer by the way.

Three Years in the Libyan Desert

It would be the greatest breach of patriarchal custom not to allow the stranger who passes by at mealtime or while food is being prepared to share it. Sheikh Muftah reckoned with this imperative necessity, as with his own and his Beduins' appetite. During the killing three Arabs came riding up, and so he quickly took the pan off the fire, hid the meat in a sack, and made his Arab coffee, in which the guests, Beduins from the west, shared. To Muftah's terror, and as a punishment for his cunning, the lean, bearded fellows hung about for hours, for they had evidently smelt fresh meat. At last they departed just as we returned from our reconnoitring.

We left the plain of El-Halfa after midnight under a sky of black rain-clouds which looked ready to burst, and we had a lively altercation with the Sheikh, whose "mafisch schitte"[1] seemed impossible to believe. And yet he was right. By candlelight we ate pieces of mutton roasted in the ashes and drank broth with it, while the cracking of the bones betrayed that the others were making quick work of the remainder, which all in order. For in the desert boiled or roast meat keeps good at most a day. Near the camels, already saddled, dogs might be seen as further boarders who had scented the banquet from afar.

[1] "No rain."

Thirty Days in the Libyan Desert

Our course now lay south into the desert itself. We crossed the route of the western Arabs, marked by occasional alame. They are signposts in the shape of slender heaps of stones. But the route showed still more clearly bleached skeletons, which tell the fate of one's immediate precursors in dangerous regions. It almost seemed as if the character of our escort changed on entering the actual desert. Before, in the early hours of the morning they used to march along shivering, the silence broken only by the monotonous "yap, yap, yap" or the encouraging "ha, ha, ha, ha." The children of the sun shivered in their white woollen burnous saturated with the night dew. As soon as the region without vegetation was entered everything was different; there, outside the pale of civilization, they felt themselves the true sons of the earth. When the sun rose there was a general shout of jubilation, in which we gladly joined. Muftah and Eluâni, who had formerly been sparing of powder, rode to the attack on their heavily laden camels, jumped off, fired under the necks of our own animals, who did not move a hair, and sang breezy verses which we had not heard before. It seemed as if the curtain of a great romantic stage was rising in front of us. Every fresh mist which rolled off showed sharper contours, the desert grew larger, and as

45

the sun got the upper hand became interminable. Only the aneroid told us we were always ascending, the last dark traces of the landscape we had left faded away, and at the same time Dschebel el-Boheb rose on the horizon out of the stony desert, and later, about 8 a.m., we saw in the far distance the ravine Gared el-Laban, with its short, steeply-falling chain of hills. After 9 a.m. we rode across them to the right of Gared el-Laban. At 11 a.m. we passed the remains of a little petrified forest, the thickest trunks of which had a diameter of 9 or 10 inches. At the same time we saw a herd of gazelles, and determined to camp in the neighbourhood. The heat was very great and about 2 p.m. reached 122° Fahr., and the fatigue of a ten hours' march justified that decision without the pleasant prospect of roast meat for dinner.

After a brief search Sheikh Muftah found a cauldron-shaped depression with a little vegetation in the sandy ground and low dunes around, an admirable and safe camping-ground. Although Muftah is one of the best gazelle-hunters of Mariut, neither he nor Eluâni, an equally excellent shot, had any luck in a chase of two hours. The ground was too flat, and the supple deer of the desert could sight the enemy a mile off. At 4 p.m. the thermometer was still at 115° Fahr., and it was only at six in the evening that a light refreshing breeze began to blow. We then loaded and saddled the animals for the first night-ride.

The next night the stars were, in the truest sense of the word, our guides. And to our question how he could be sure of finding the right way in the wild, monotonous desert, Sheikh Muftah answered by confidently pointing to the sky; he meant chiefly the pole-star. In order to procure water (what we had in the skins already began to taste very nasty) a forced march was undertaken to the nearest well, far to the south at Wadi Moghara; its distance from El-Halfa was reckoned three long days' journey. As the skins had not been filled again since the evening before the departure from Haschm-el-Aisch, very little was now left of the original six gallons of water. If the hourly evaporation during the hot part of the day is reckoned, six thirsty throats had to be satisfied with it; had any accident occurred, such as an unforeseen delay or a necessary detour, things might have turned out badly, and the constantly changing character of the sandy dunes made it only too easy to lose the way. We did not, however, think of the possible breakage of one of the water gheerbahs.

Muftah was conscious of his responsibility, and, regardless of the fatigue of the undertaking, he decided that, with a brief rest at midnight, we should go on without a break till the wells were reached—a forced ride of twenty-two hours, not reckoning the pauses.

The romantic side of the ride was unfortunately greatly lessened by the fatigue. Dates and dried plums, eaten in the saddle, formed our food. It was carried in the famous Berlin water-bags, which hung from our saddle pommels and admirably fulfilled their new duties.

The camels, roped in a long row, stepped out more quickly. We camped for a couple of hours near Gared el-Laban without unsaddling. Each lay down beside his beast wrapped in rugs, and at 2.30 a.m., still dead-tired, we were again marching southwards. I found myself in a condition of utter indifference. My cousin was in a far more parlous state, for he was continually falling asleep on his camel, and ran the risk of falling off and being killed. Therefore we both had the greater and more unstinted admiration for the only person who fitted into the situation, Sheikh Muftah. He danced along on foot by our side, his weapons slung on him, and invented the funniest jokes in order to keep us awake. And he kept up that behaviour until the plentiful and cool morning dew refreshed us. During the night we had crossed with great care a many-chasmed line of hills, which at six in the morning we saw shining

FRONT VIEW OF KASR EL-GETTAJEH WITH EXCAVATED MARBLES IN
THE FOREGROUND.

To face p. 48.

far behind us in splendid clearness, and looking like a chain of mountains. Then traces of petrified forests appeared again, and for half an hour we went through the numerous fragments of trunks of trees.

We then rode down over the Dschebel ed-Dara, situated in the direction of the oasis Siwa, and full of geological interest. There begins the fantastic ravine which we—as it forms the best and most romantic descent from the high table-land to the Libyan Desert, and as it had no name—baptized Bab-Frankenfurt : gate or pass of Frankenfurt. We dismounted here in order to take measurements and photographs, and, seated on the stony trunks of trees, wrote our observations in our diaries. After so long a march through the desert, Bab-Frankenfurt presented a fine picture. From the top of the pass loomed the distant chain of Gared Saadêh. Beneath us, about 300 feet below, stretched the endless desert, broken by a long, green, flat piece of land, with the blue basin of a salt lake, the long shape of which made the whole look like a river valley. The precipitous eastern wall of the pass, in which waves of sand lost themselves among the petrified trunks of trees, rose above us.

We rode down the pass, and at the further edge of the wadi saw the six white tents of a military station. About ten o'clock, amid incessant shots of welcome, we reached a group of four Beduin tents, where the women greeted us with the shrill sarlûl. It was high time that we pitched our tents, for a sandstorm was well on the way. We fixed the camp a few hundred paces from the Beduin tents. Already from the top of the pass Muftah had realized what was toward.

Scarcely were the tents fixed and the most necessary preparations completed, when the storm broke into the wadi and its waves beat against the cliffs of the plateau. It was fortunate that we had chosen in Alexandria low military tents. The more comfortable high ones would have been carried away by the first gust of wind. But even so the situation was serious, and, as we were dreadfully tired, really dangerous. The glasses of condensed milk which we carried to our mouths received their complement of "zimt"; the fine dust penetrated into the guns and revolvers as boldly as into boxes, chests, and rugs. Everything, above all the apparatus, had to be quickly hidden ; our escort crowded into the tent, and from within held the cloth fast, since the stakes, deeply rammed into the sandy ground as they were, seemed to give. And with it all there was a burning heat with a proportionately low thermometer. A sound of breathing on the ground excited our curiosity, and looking out of the tent we noted the clever tactics of the camels. They lay with their long necks close against the sand, their heads turned, as a protection, to the north side of our tent. Their eyes were shut, and they lay as if dead.

The hot wind lasted the whole day. We only ventured to excavate ourselves about five in the evening. A large caravan from the south had come up in the storm and was now steering for Moghara.

Before our Beduins thought of themselves they looked after the camels, who had had no water for five days. They drank while we took our guns to pieces and thoroughly cleaned them. The fine sand had even penetrated the mechanism, and our Kodak, hygrometer, and other instruments refused to work. A soldier came down from the military station to greet the arrivals. He did not know the German flag. What he told us of his station was something of a tragedy. The Beduins were hostile to the post, which was thirteen men strong; it had been placed in this exposed position in the desert only on account of temporary and political grounds. Our visitor had been nine times under fire, and as a proof showed us scars in his leg and arm. It resulted that the garrison was repeatedly without provisions and that soldiers perished in marching through the desert. We were implored to compose

a memorandum and to lay their grievances before
the Pasha. But without our intervention the
abandonment of the post had already been planned
at Alexandria, and the next year the soldiers were
recalled.

We gave the representative of Egyptian civilization the little that we thought we could spare.
Muftah was dispatched to procure a sheep for
supper. Rest was not to be thought of. Sick
Sudan negroes from the caravan sought the Hakîm,
the physician, whose rôle fell to me. All who had
legs came out of the neighbouring tents, especially
the wholly or semi-naked children, and assailed
us with questions. The older persons received a
portion of coffee and tobacco, and nothing caused
these big children more astonishment than Meyer's
two little Arabic conversation dictionaries, which
we so often had to consult. They thought that by
their means we could answer anything and everything, and that such power could reside in so tiny
a kitâb [1] appeared to them magic. They would
have greatly liked to try our guns, but that was
firmly refused. At 7.30 p.m., at a temperature
of 82° Fahr., we began our supper of mutton.
As usual, Muftah had said his prayers twice
over !

The fatigues of the last days took their revenge

[1] Book.

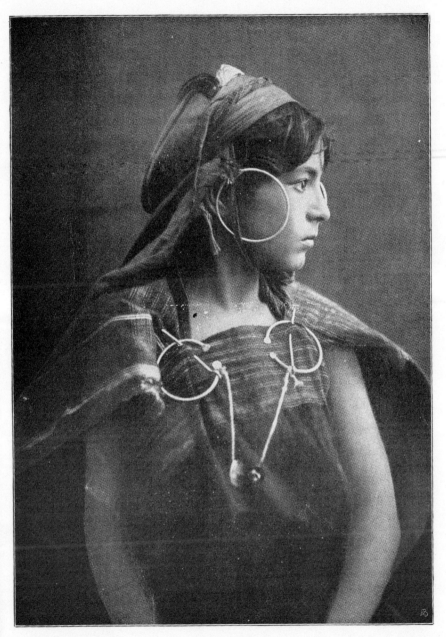

BEDUIN GIRL.

To face p. 52.

in that the nights did not bring us refreshing sleep. In addition, we were invaded by swarms of blood-thirsty mosquitoes from the salt lake. We had mosquito-nets with us, it is true, but they served only for the hands and head, the low tents not permitting a more extended use of the protection.

On the morning of June 23rd I woke with a bad headache and a feeling of sickness. A dose of quinine did good service, and without that most important remedy for travellers in the desert the malaria protozoa would have had an easy victim. My cousin that morning made an expedition alone on one of the camels through the wadi.

Before the mid-day meal we waded together down to the salt lake. The ground consisted of undulating dunes about 3 feet in height, among which grew tamarisks and some fodder for the camels. A red, edible fruit of the size of the beads of a rosary, "aineb-ed-dib," grew on single tall thorn bushes, which the Beduins call "rárdak" (ghardag), identical with Ascherson's *Nitraria retusa*. Fairly near the camp we found a group of springs. When the Beduins dug up the ground in that place, a thing they always do with their hands, after getting through a layer of sand seldom more than 6 feet deep, they struck a muddy liquid that after some time cleared off to a bright yellow; it was drinkable and had a slightly brackish taste. In that way Abd el-Al and Abu Sêf dug out a very large spring, and when we passed stood naked in the muddy water. At such places the gheerbahs were easily filled by means of a pail, and pails or cooking utensils served also for the camels to drink out of, a process which claims endless time and patience.

It took a short hour to reach the lake from the camp. The dunes fell suddenly down to the green rushy valley, in which the silvery surface of the salt lake glittered in the sun. Over the dry, black crust of mud my cousin, Eluâni, and I reached the clear water. Eluâni ventured into the sea of rushes on the right in order to dislodge "hammâm," by which term he understood a covey of ducks. He did not fail to shoot some. While Eluâni was so occupied we entered the water and had an excellent bath.

Returning home after hunting and bathing, we found our tent full of Sudanese soldiers. The little garrison had come down in order to gain intercessors at Alexandria, and one of the Askari had even brought the most beautiful gift that can be made in the desert, crystal-clear water. The chief spoke English and showed a childish glee when we offered him tobacco and a little whisky. The poor fellow had been a whole year at his post and longed for the fleshpots of Egypt. According to his statement, at certain times of the year the wadi is occupied by as many as a hundred Beduin tents, and once or twice a month he received orders from his superior, a German officer in the Egyptian service.

The visit of the soldiers *en masse* had an unpleasant result in so far that from that moment no Arab came near the tent. Sheikh Muftah, who had implored us not to show too friendly a hospitality to the Askari, looked very serious. About evening, by way of precaution, the position of the camp was changed and a double guard posted at night. That day the maximum temperature in the shade was only 111° Fahr. The rapid rise of the hygrometer was striking, showing the great increase of damp from 30° at two o'clock to 70° at eight o'clock. From the new camp we had a unique view of Ras el-Bakar, the cow-mountain, looking in the evening light like a lofty range of mountains which ascended in the south to the caravan route that led to the oasis of Bacharije. We reclined in our folding-chairs and breathed the refreshing night wind. The camels cowered underneath a rárdak 9 feet high with its big thorns. The beasts were given this time scheïr [1] mixed with chopped straw as extra nourishing food. Sheikh Muftah said his evening prayer twice over, for the third

[1] Grain.

sheep since our departure had been compelled to die.

In the night of June 24th the camels and our water-skins took in fresh water, and soon after 2 a.m. our caravan left the lonely desert valley. We marched over the stony desert through the ravine Dschebel Somâra, which rises east of Moghara up to the Libyan tableland that we had left by Bab-Frankenfurt. Instead of choosing the frequented caravan route to the Wadi Faregh and the Natrûn valley, we preferred to go straight over the desert plateau to the well of Emselich, and thence to march the whole length of Wadi Natrûn. This route also offered interesting erosions, and remains of a petrified forest. The most remarkable feature to my mind were the enormous gravel dunes, 10 yards in height, some of which we climbed in order to collect specimens, not unlike the Rhine pebbles, of the little stones, mostly round as a bullet and of a transparent yellow, about one-third of an inch in diameter. In the course of the day we crossed a low range of hills which had no name, and at noon we pitched our tents east of Dschebel el-Farr, in sight of Dschebel el-Laban, after a *fata Morgana* of two sinuous lakes had deceived us. We took them quite certainly for salt lakes of the Natrûn valley, while Sheikh Muftah with

KASR EL-GETTAJEH. PILLAR AND PRAYER NICHE IN
THE INTERIOR.

To face p. 56.

his "Only air, no water" gave the correct explanation.

In the evening there appeared at the camp, as a welcome guest in the midst of the barren desert —a wagtail. As it turned out, such birds were to be seen every evening. The jackals howled at night, but no one was inclined to go out hunting. The next day, after a short march, we came in sight of four conical-shaped mountains which looked like volcanoes; two were separate, the others were twins. The Beduins called the remarkable group El-Lischa. We shivered in the morning dew, although at 4.30 a.m. the thermometer stood at 72° Fahr. The sun rose on the horizon while the half-moon shone overhead and the wagtail accompanied us.

We crossed Dschebel Scharraff, which Junker's map places too close to the edge of Wadi Natrûn. It consists partly of immense slabs of mica, then sand again, and here and there basalt comes to light. The whole district between Gared el-Laban and our goal, Bir Emselich, has important geological interest. The sand of the desert is mingled with stones of the desert and fields of mica, flats with slight vegetation pass into absolute stone pavement, single slabs of which are sometimes of enormous size, and sometimes so evenly joined that they look like the work of human hands. The hills, not mere sandy dunes, are mostly conical, with deep crater-like clefts between them.

Bir Emselich was reached the following day. The waterless well is situated on a large stony hill, the Dschebel of a similar name. A square entrance leads down a depth of 6 yards and gives access to a not very spacious reservoir. The caravan marched from Bir Emselich at first in a northerly, then in an easterly direction. After a few hours over sand and stones, signs of vegetation began to show that we were approaching the edge of the Natrûn valley at its northern end. The character of the wadi is here that of the hattje; gazelles appeared in greater numbers, and a herd of feeding camels.

The crossing of the Libyan Desert from Moghara to Haschm-el-Aisch took three days. On June 27th we again found ourselves on the site of an ancient town, the last remaining token of which is a little building for divine worship, Kasr el-Gettajeh. Abu Sêf, the "father of the sword," and Eluâni helped the whole day in measuring and digging up the ruins. A pillar some 8 feet high, lying among the ruins, was set free, and numerous architectural pieces of beautiful white marble were found. The only inscriptions found at the Kasr were later Arabic, and a few wall-writings of European travellers like Pacho, who first visited the place, and also Dr. Gotschlick, the name of a well-known physician of Alexandria whose acquaintance we had made at Schiess Pasha's, as well as the name David and an illegible name.

The little Kasr measures some 7 yards long, and 5 broad, and 4 high, and in modern times served as a mosque. The shoulders of a cupola were to be recognized and also the prayer niche.

Our stay at Kasr el-Gettajeh was not to end without a surprise, which Abu Sêf had evidently long prepared. A spoilt child, as we remarked before, he had for some days suffered from home-sickness. Under pretext of gazelle hunting he asked, after he had industriously helped us all day, for some powder, with which he and a camel vanished. He had heard from a shepherd that there were friendly Arab tents in the neighbourhood and obeyed the call home. The affair caused us great embarrassment, especially as the number of the camels was now reduced to four. Whether Sheikh Muftah was in the secret has never been discovered. The fact is that the Mamûr Markaz declared later that he had given the "father of the sword" a good thrashing. In order to prevent further attempts at flight, especially on the part of Abd el-Al, who suffered from sleeplessness and indigestion, Monsignor Kaufmann told the Sheikh that Abu Sêf by his act had forfeited all claims to backschish, and he should not think of paying the amount due to the man who had escaped with the camel. This worked wonders and helped to discipline the remaining attendants.

CHAPTER IV

THE OASIS OF THE NATRÛN LAKES, OR THE "BALANCE OF THE HEART"—IN THE MONKS' CITADEL OF THE NITRIAN DESERT

The salt valley and the prehistoric Libyan Nile—We find bones of old African fauna—Heathen and Christian sanctuaries of Wadi Natrûn—Four strongholds in the sea of sand—Remains of the "hundred monasteries"—A journey through the Natrûn valley—Sheikh Muftah loses the way—The first tents of the Schuâbi—Arrival at Bir Hooker—Visit to Dêr Baramûs—The monks take us for enemies—Cordial reception in the monkish citadel—At the shrine of the "princes"—Wanderings through churches and dungeons—Amba John of Abyssinia—The monastery of the Syrians—Mangled library treasures—Dêr Amba Bischâi—The salines—Ride to Dêr Makâr—The tomb of the patriarch of the monks and the grotto of the forty-nine Sheiks.

THE salt valley, Wadi en Natrûn, the romance of which is only fully realized by those who traverse for a long distance the depression surrounded by ravines and deserts under the burning Libyan sun, once bore the name Wadi el-Habîb, "Valley of Love." And the name seemed to be justified when on the morning of June 28th, after a fatiguing ride

61

over stony wastes, we recognized in the distant undergrowth the black tents of the Schuâbi, and gradually approached the first well. Soft breezes were blowing, and we breathed amid luxurious vegetation. The nervous irritation caused by the everlasting hurry, investigations and travelling, increased by the lack of all comforts, gave way to a pleasant enervation. Even young Abd el-Al, who rarely emerged from his mixture of absolute kismêt and relative Beduin pride, woke into life, and his pleasant voice sounded delightfully on the edge of the wadi when, swinging his rifle, he walkėd in front of the caravan, and in monotonous rhythm sang his endless ritornelle : " Thy love resembles the lighthouse, which shines out to the distance ; like the spring which the eye sees in the desert and which brings rain ; like an overflowing river from which no swimmer escapes ; like the fire which consumes all things ! The springs of love are long since destroyed, no water flows therein ! "

The Natrûn valley not only belongs to the great historical places of the Libyan Desert, but is from a geological point of view the most interesting, and in conjunction with the south-west bifurcating Wadi Faregh, the most important part of prehistoric Egypt. Although it is easy of access, and is provided with admirable places for making investigations of every kind, only small expeditions of narrow

The Oasis of the Natrûn Lakes

and limited aims have so far skimmed rather than sounded ground so rich in problems. I may name the latest investigations on the part of Germany, the geographical and geological observations of Professor Stromer of Reichenbach, the results of which may be found in the treatises of the Sencken-berg Physical Research Society at Frankfort-on-Main. The interest of most of the visitors is concentrated on the old monasteries and the build-ings of the Salt Company. Therefore serviceable maps are wanting as soon as the boundaries of the salt lakes are passed. The entrance to the Natrûn valley is situated close to the metropolis of the Caliphs, near the pyramids of Abu Roâsch. After a day's journey to the west over serîr and stony wastes, the valleys of Faregh and en-Natrûn bifurcate, at first almost invisibly and then in a more accentuated way, through higher, even steep ridges, which at the slopes of the plateau by the monastery of Macarius assume the character of a rocky landscape. The north-westerly Natrûn valley winds and soon expands to several miles in breadth; the oasis basins surrounded by the desert present, in correspondence with the direction of the valley, a series of lakes, according to the season, at times ten in number. At Haschm-el-Aisch and near Kasr el-Gettajeh, the points already visited by us, the sides of the valley are almost lost again in the remaining eminences of the desert, and the wadi, becoming narrower, makes for the Mediterranean. It merges into the coast at Wadi Halfa, the starting-point of our journey to Moghara. As a whole the salt valley should be compared with a river valley which once formed a third, western arm of the Nile, proceeding from the delta at Cairo, and flowing into the Mediterranean between the old provinces of Mareotis and Marmarika. The remembrance of this prehistoric Nile is still alive in the desert. It is not only that the water of its wells brings the Beduins into direct connection with the "Bacher en-Nil." South of the wadi there is a depression in the desert which has borne for ages the designation of the "waterless river" ("Bacher bela mâ"). In the Roman period a river existed in the neighbourhood of the Natrûn district which is called "Lycus Fluvius" in the original authorities. Even if that river was only a canal which served to irrigate the wadi and part of the Auladali Desert, the problem of the "Bacher bela mâ," the prehistoric Nile, still remains to be solved. We happened in the wadi to come on the definite course of the waterless river, in which lay groups of petrified trees.

Blanckenhorn, who has written the history of the prehistoric Libyan Nile and has thoroughly studied it and the geology of the district,

PAGAN MINIATURE STELE
WITH THE GOD HORUS
(FROM THE CITY OF
MENAS).

DÊR ES-SURJÂNI, WITH THE MIRACULOUS TREE OF ST. EPHRAIM, THE SYRIAN.

To face p. 64.

The Oasis of the Natrûn Lakes

considers the remains of the petrified forests to be alluvial wood of the ancient Nile. When later on, in 1906, I went to Siwa with the Khedive, our caravan passed numerous remains of petrified marine creatures, colonies of sea-urchins, oyster and coral banks, objects which attracted the attention of the ancient geographer, Eratosthenes. They prove that in prehistoric times the whole of the north of the Libyan Desert was a sea-bottom. According to Blanckenhorn, the districts in which the Natrûn valley, the city of Menas and Alexandria are situated were inland seas in the central pliocene age, and the inundation district of the Nile of to-day only developed from the so-called rainy season. The examination of the remains of marine and river bones from the north-west part of Libya afforded a wider and unexpected result. Blanckenhorn's work in that direction sweeps away the old hypothesis that the mammals now found in Africa only lately dispossessed the primitive animals of Africa, that Madagascar alone has preserved the original animal world as a detached African district, and that antelopes, elephants, rhinoceroses, and horses wandered in the pliocene age from Europe to Africa! All that is now exploded and untenable, for the bones found in the district of the prehistoric Nile and its maritime mouth incontrovertibly show that Africa is the original home of its contemporary fauna.

The oasis of the Natrûn Lakes owes its fame to the salt extracted therefrom and to its sanctuaries. The ancient Egyptians called it "Sochetheman," the Romans "the salt field" and "Nitriæ mons." The monasteries and hermitages of the Christian epoch had their forerunners in the sanctuaries of the heathens. Where now there is desert and a continual struggle with nature on account of the scanty vegetation there was in the classic times of Egypt fertile land, with fruits of all kinds, olives, vines, and grain. An inscription in the principal temple at Edfu records the deities honoured in the oasis of the salt region, names the Horus town Schorp, the "regions of the goddess Courage," "the town of the valley," and other settlements, no stone of which now exists among the sand-dunes. The Horus town, with its temple and magnificent statue of the god, was situated on the mysterious mountain of Unnofer, by which the ancient Egyptians meant the hilly land of the desert.

But the brilliant epoch in the history of the wadi was in the time of the early Christians. Under pressure of persecution, especially at the time of the persecution of the Christians under the Emperor Decius (249–251), many fled from

The Oasis of the Natrûn Lakes

the valley of the Nile into the desert, and there in concealment led a holy life. Two men who are of the greatest importance for the history of monachism were such fugitives—Amonius and Macarius. St. Amonius is what Antony the Hermit was for the Theban desert, the patriarch of the monkish life of the future in the desert of the Natrûn valley. Wealthy from birth, he left his wife with her consent in order to establish the first monastery in the Nitrian Desert, the monks of which lived in isolated cells, and only assembled together for worship and edification on the Lord's Day and its eve. At the same time, in 330, St. Macarius repaired to the desert, in which he lived and taught for sixty years; at the end of the fourth century the communities founded by these pioneers of monachism numbered 5,000 souls.

Of the "hundred monasteries" which arose in the course of centuries from those beginnings, four still exist, namely, the "Laura of the Romans," Dêr Baramûs; the Syrian convent, Dêr es-Surjani; the Dêr Amba Bischâi and the Macarius convent. We saw ruins of others, of the Maria convent of the Abyssinians, and that of the Armenians. A mediæval Arab writer from Baalbek named Makrizi counted nine monasteries, among them one of St. Elias, of St. John

67

Kolobos, of St. Nub. If the number is exaggerated which gave the valley its name "of the hundred convents," so may be the Coptic account that 60,000 monks with palm-branches went out to meet General Amr ibn el'-As in order to make a favourable impression of the power of the monasteries. At any rate, and here all the reports agree, the monkish settlements were of great extent, and it is deeply to be regretted that the swords of the Mohammedans destroyed almost all the remains of their ancient splendour.

The night before our arrival in the actual wadi we very nearly had the misfortune to lose our Sheikh. He had gone alone on a gazelle hunt, and had been belated in the serîr. Our low tent and scanty fire (for we lacked fuel, and it consisted only of camel-dung collected during the march and dried in the sun), in spite of the sacrifice of much paper, were only visible in the twilight some thousand paces away. The simplest and the most usual means in such cases, to discharge the guns vertically, which combined the advantage of a shower of fire upwards with a sound audible at a distance, failed. Muftah, who was well provided with ammunition, would certainly have answered the first shot. So we were not a little alarmed when at nightfall the Sheikh had not returned. We took counsel about what should be done. That he had lost his way caused less anxiety than the fear that he had been surprised in the district of the Schuâbi. Eluâni, who knew everything and continually proved it, found a way out. He asked for "warrak rebir," by which he meant newspaper, a large quantity of which was taken with us and used daily for table-napkins, tablecloths, and wrapping paper. He then led his camel as far into the desert as he could without the possibility of losing himself, left me to hold the animal, jumped upon it, and fired a shot in the air, and as no reply came, followed with a second. We waited and waited in absolute stillness and darkness, but in vain. Now the newspaper came into action. Eluâni fastened a large bunch firmly to the mouth of his gun, set light to it, and swung the torch high in the air, slowly and in wide half-circles. Again anxiety, listening, waiting : but Muftah Dabûn gave back no sign. Eluâni was nothing daunted. While we feared that such demonstrations might perhaps cause danger to our own camp, he remained aloft on his living pedestal, fired his gun every five minutes, and brandished his newspaper torch. And after the fifteenth shot, out of the farthest distance one came in reply. Muftah had heard us, and, thanks to further fruitful signals, he returned to the camp in the course of an hour, but without booty.

After a six-hours' ride we encamped at the above-mentioned first tents of the Schuâbi. Near a bir which was nothing more than a hole dug out and full of water, like that of Moghara, grew some scanty fodder for the camels. The water was almost undrinkable. My cousin, very tired, was lying in the tent, which scarcely offered protection from the wind, which set the fine sand in motion. I visited the black tents, an event for the " harim," the part of the " bet " occupied by the women and children. In order only to make closer acquaintance with the stranger, sick children were brought him, until at last they brought a perfectly healthy naked little boy and a little girl. For nine shillings I procured for my cousin, who had already in the wadi shown signs of dysentery, a fine sheep, and earned as much praise as if I had brought an ancient inscription.

While we were sitting in front of the tent, from which Dschebel Hadîd could be seen stretching from east to west, a Beduin woman brought her boy, laid him without any ado on my knees, and said, " Effendi, heal him!" He had for some days been suffering from vomiting, but his temperature was normal. Our medicine chest was helpful, and the child was made happy with an empty shining tin. In the evening great

The Oasis of the Natrûn Lakes

joy reigned among the Schuâbis, for the child's vomiting ceased, and the Sheikh of the community, Abu Rîch, accompanied by all his people, came to thank us. He brought us two precious gifts : dry wood and fresh goat's milk.

After a terrible night (for no one had thought of the nearness of the salt lakes and their predatory fauna, the mosquitoes, who tormented us cruelly), about 3 a.m. a raging sandstorm arose, which lasted for some hours, and made us take an early bath in the well, about 5 feet deep and the same in diameter, before our people were struck by a similar idea. Then my cousin and I spent several hours in reconnoitring the surrounding district. News of our presence preceded us, for when we were ready to set out about 11 o'clock, stranger Beduins appeared with their sick, led by Sheikh Abu Rîch, and among them the most remarkable cases. A young woman showed her withered right hand, just like that of a mummy, and it seemed that if touched it would break off. My cousin put ointment on the black, decayed remains, consoled the poor incurable creature, and, as was his custom with young people and children, he touched the half-veiled brow and made the sign of the cross over it. We were very sorry not to be physicians. We could do nothing for the mother whose infant was suffering from cataract.

Three Years in the Libyan Desert

At length, to the tune of gun salutes and with a fresh north-west breeze, we left the camp, accompanied by the Sheikh Abu Rîch, while the boys rummaged in the sand for the wonderful things we had left behind : empty tins and such-like, and even cigarette ends. Abd el-Al went in advance in order to carry our greeting to a few tents.

At length, on June 30th, we came upon an isolated mountain (En Hêd), which Monsignor Kaufmann took to be the Mons Pernudj of the Coptic sources ; a few hours before we had passed the Zauja of the unfriendly Senussi monks, near the tents of the snake " El-Hanesch," and the first of the salt lakes, and now the buildings of the "Compania," *i.e.*, the Salt Company at Bir Hooker, became visible. It was seven in the evening when we camped there on the high borders of the desert. The Beduins omitted the customary salutes. With the German flag we hoisted the Egyptian flag we had brought with us, a crescent moon and star on a red field, in order to please the Mudir, M. Pensilum, to whom we had cordial letters of introduction. We did not foresee how soon the flags would be at half-mast. In the evening I paid a visit to the Saline Company's offices, which were close at hand. The Mudir was the company's head and the chief official of the province.

Here I received sad news. M. Pensilum, an

SHRINE OF THE PRINCES (DÊR BARAMÛS).

To face p. 72.

HEIK MUFTAH DABÛN SLAUGHTERS A GAZELLE.

The Oasis of the Natrûn Lakes

official highly esteemed by the whole province, had died on the previous day of dysentery, and his body was already on the way to Alexandria. " I called on Thy name in the wilderness, and Thou heardest me not," as the Arab lament runs.

The next day, accompanied only by our Sheikh, Muftah Dabûn, while the rest remained behind to look after the commissariat and water for the camels, we began with a visit to Dêr Baramûs, the largest and most important of the Natrûn monasteries.

We passed the extensive modern buildings of the saline factory, and then the route led directly over the railway embankment of the little branch line, built of the hard salt crust and made firm with sacks of sand. The dazzling surface shone like fine ice-crystals ; blood-red pools of water contrasted curiously with the enormously tall sword-grass that flanked the banks. Passing the low barracks occupied by the Beduins engaged in the saline works and the beginnings of a mosque, the foundation-stone of which had been laid by the Khedive with great ceremony five years before, the building having since advanced no further, after a short ride we again reached the desert.

The breadth of the Natrûn valley at that point is a little over a thousand yards. The long and highly interesting valley, with its ten salt lakes, of which, notwithstanding the midsummer heat, few were dry, has a population of five hundred—mostly Arabs and Beduins, and only twelve Europeans. Besides the name of the Salt valley, it is also known as Mizân el-Colûb—*i.e.*, "Balance of the Heart"—or as Wadi Djeffer, because the camels are taken there to be cured of the djeffer disease, or as the plain of Schiît, Askit, etc. The part of the great Libyan Desert closely bordering on it bears the name of the Nitrian Desert.

After a ride of about three hours we reached Dêr Baramûs. Already in the distance we had seen the massive walls of the monks' citadel rising from the sand. A few hundred yards in front of the monastery we made a brief halt in order to load our guns, a proceeding which was to result in a curious misunderstanding. The guards of the monastery had long spied us through a loophole in the battlements, and the proceedings with the guns aroused suspicion. When about 12 o'clock the bell of the little iron gate built deep into the massive wall sounded, we heard much talking in Arabic behind it. I handed in our cards through a slit, and asked in Arabic that they should be given to the Hegoumenos. "Who are you?" was the demand, while a monk was sent for who spoke a little English. "A priest and a schoolmaster, who have come from far-off Germany, desire to pay their respects to your head and to see the

In the Monks' Citadel

famous monastery." " No stranger ever comes to us in summer," replied another, immediately adding, " You have an Arab with you. What does he want ? " After receiving a satisfactory reply, they agreed to tell their head of our arrival. Meanwhile, high above us in the wall, a sliding shutter fell down, and the English-speaking personage— as we learned later, a novice who had attended the English school in Cairo—made further inquiries. He brought forward two arguments against admitting us : first, the business with the loading of the guns, and, second, the unusual season of the year. At last we obtained the head's permission. The heavy gate swung open. We were received with scrutinizing looks from bearded faces and the usual Arab forms of greeting and blessing, which were punctuated with our apologies and many inquisitive questions. We surrendered our weapons to one of the monks, and followed him to the Mandârah (the reception-room) which was reached through a luxuriant palm garden. Notwithstanding the preliminaries dictated by prudence, and influenced by the fact that a few weeks before an Arab had shot at a monk, I must confess that the kind and friendly treatment we experienced in Dêr Baramûs made entire amends. I had imagined to myself that the monasteries of the monophysitic Copts were worse. Still, Dêr Baramûs is an exception. Of the thirty monks who inhabit the little town formed by a chaos of houses, cells, chapels, and corridors, some at least understand a little of another tongue besides Arabic ; the chief priest or abbot, Abma Gabriel, knows Coptic pretty well, and was not a little proud when his knowledge of Greek and Coptic manuscripts was proved to the monks. Coptic is the liturgical language of the Copts, but even the priests only understand it with the help of the Arabic translation written by its side. The ordinary speech of the monks throughout Wadi Natrûn and in other places has for centuries been Arabic. We were shown to seats of honour in the reception-room, and crouching down on them in Arabic fashion, we drank the customary sugar and water and the indispensable coffee, and exchanged greetings with Abma Gabriel, the young head of the monks' colony. I will pass over in silence the dinner that he provided for us, that comprised all the luxuries and the tastiest dishes of Arab cookery, and was eaten in Arab fashion—with the fingers instead of with knives and forks. The Abbot joined us, in spite of the fact that it was a fast day, and zealous novices waited at table and kept off the flies with flabella. As a general rule, the monks' food consists of bread, dates, onions, and lentils, the same as that of the Beduins. What the gardens do not supply is from time to time procured from the villages of the Nile valley.

During our survey of the monastery, which took four hours, Abma Gabriel's kindness showed itself in a special manner. The German priest and his companion were allowed to see things usually closed to travellers. The monks repeatedly said, "We Copts are as close to you in respect to liturgy and church customs as in origin." To the question why they did not, like so many of their brethren of the last decades, join Rome, they replied, "What would become of our possessions and of our father in Alexandria?" By the last they meant the Patriarch, who bears the title "the holy Pope and Patriarch of the town of Alexandria and all the countries of Egypt, of Jerusalem, Nubia, Abyssinia, Pentapolis, and all the lands in which St. Mark preached." He is mostly chosen from one of the Nitrian monasteries, and comes to the helm perhaps as a saint, but in entire ignorance of his duties.

Untiringly the novices dragged our utensils and photographic apparatus about. The remains of a once valuable library were accessible to us, and towards evening a bath was prepared for us, which, however, we refused, when we saw that it was the font that was brought into use. The monks declare that El-Baramûs is the wealthiest of the four Coptic monasteries of the Nitrian Desert which alone survive out of a great number. The history of its origin in wrapped in mystery and legend. The monks derive the name from Abu Musa. Abu Musa, the negro, was a bold robber, a Berber by descent, who, after the murder of a hundred men, became a Christian, and as a monk wrote a number of books. He belonged to those who kept the forty days' fast without taking any food. Others derive the name of this monkish stronghold from Ba, or Pa, Romeôs, and designate it as a monastery " of the Romans," of the saints Maximus and Dometius.

The three-storied outer wall, supported by lofty interior pillars, is 170 paces long, and almost as broad. An observation gallery with spy-holes runs below the battlements; at certain spots steps lead to a special parapet. Thence by devious ways, up staircases and over a drawbridge, we visited the Kasr, a strong tower with many chambers and dungeons. It shelters among others a chapel dedicated to the Archangel Michael. In the course of our visits we discovered that the other Nitrian monasteries liked to place chapels to Michael in lofty parts of the buildings. Very little remained of the mass of fragments of manuscripts which J. Butler saw in one of the adjoining chambers; what there was were mostly fragments of valueless late Coptic

In the Monks' Citadel

and Arabic works. The monks brought us here a green glazed terra-cotta standard lamp, the antiquity and value of which they greatly cried up, as if we had been thinking of making a purchase. In a third underground chamber a hard fruit, something like peas, was stored, to serve as rations in cases of dire necessity, such as famine and danger.

From the parapet of the mighty tower the eye roves over the endless sea of the desert. How often had we been at close quarters with its great beauties as with its many dangers, and yet it always offered fresh enigmas! We had traversed it in cool nights under a full moon, amid the hoarse cries of hungry wolves and cowardly hyenas and jackals ; under a tropical heat, bathed in blinding sunlight, men and beasts dragged themselves wearily over the never-ending plain in order to reach the next well. We were as well acquainted with the mysterious waves of the simoom as with the cool ripples of the deceptive oasis lakes surrounded with vegetation. And its history, the thousands and thousands of years' history of the desert, spoke its language to us from the wild cleft wadis of Somara, with their curious hilltops and petrified forests of giant trees, to the bleached bones of its noblest beast, which only too often pointed the road by which our latest predecessors had gone. And just here on the roofs of El-Baramûs did not a little piece of the history of the earth and of humanity pass before us when we looked down over the sandy plain? There below, in the direction of the wadi, in prehistoric times flowed an important arm of the Nile; yonder were the prehistoric caravan routes, later the pilgrim routes of the mighty Pharaonic people. Yonder for the first time appeared the strange ascetics, wrapped in the pallium of the poor and wise, who, a race of virtuous, self-denying Christians, built the walls on the battlements of which we were standing. But the desert had conquered those rulers too, just as it did not permit even the mightiest potentate of the modern age, the bold corsair who fought a battle in Wadi Natrûn, to tarry there. The desert is an image of eternity, and as such never changes for the philosopher.

The kindly monks aided our imagination by attentively pointing out hidden charms, and enriched our experience by relating strange stories. "Our earth is hard," said the good Hegoumenos, but the expression of his face was kind and gentle. The sun had deprived the man of all desire to philosophize. He was never tired of communicating the impressions which

THE ABBOT (LEFT HAND LOWER FIGURE) AND THE PRIESTS OF THE
COPTIC MONASTERY OF DÊR BARAMÛS.

To face p. 80.

the painful longing to return to his family produced in him. And Dêr Baramûs concealed a still stranger man, a solitary among the sociable persons of this community cut off from the world. A quietist in the stillness! A sage amid the unrest of the desert! A talented saint in the company of careless, thoughtless monks! An aspiring character and yet without ambition, a personality, a recluse, a noble man! Before the priests and brothers took us to the top of the Kasr we had been in the principal church. The Hegoumenos was not there. A bold novice, the same who managed to articulate a little English, gave the necessary information. We were waiting for the high priest in the transept, opposite the Haikal.[1] He entered clad in a fresh garment. "The Bishop is coming—he wishes to see you," he exclaimed in an impressive way. Meanwhile the monks assembled; a semicircle was formed, and the Hegoumenos with the strangers stepped forward. A deep silence. All eyes were turned to the door, on the threshold of which an impressive figure appeared. Clad in a brown, fluttering cloak, a black turban on his head, the Bishop seemed to incorporate one of the earnest, fascinating figures of the early Christians whom the African sun endowed with nobility, gentleness,

---

[1] The place of the high altar.

and energy and an unselfish love of humanity. A painter would have found in him an ideal model for his Christ. When he had withdrawn, the monks loaded him with praise. We learned from them that Amba John, a scion of a noble Alexandrian family, had been for many years Bishop in Abyssinia, and was here engaged in hagiological and ascetic studies. Perhaps we may see in him the future Patriarch of the Coptic Church.

The principal church, dedicated to El-Hadra, consists of nave and aisles, which in the Haikal become three altar apses. The usual folding doors divide those from the church itself, in which close to the entrance to the sanctuary stands the reliquary with the bodies of the saints Maximus and dometius. The two Romans, as these saints were called, were sons of the Greek Emperor Leontius. The story is well known how Maximus, who led a very holy life, was elected Pope of Rome, renounced the honour, and with his brother Dometius went to sea, and later dedicated themselves to a monkish life in the Libyan Desert. The Coptic Synaxar [1] relates their arrival, life, and death in Wadi Natrûn under the 17th Tubeh thus : " They came here to St. Macarius and told him they wished to dwell with him. As he saw that they were of noble descent, he thought that they would

[1] See p. 93.
82

not be able to endure the sojourn in the desert, and described to them the hard life led there. But they replied : 'If we cannot remain with you, we will wend our way elsewhere.' Then he instructed them in the ways of the sand-hills, showed them a valley, and gave them directions how to build themselves a grotto, and showed them from whom to procure their bread and to whom to sell their work. They spent there three years without consorting with any one ; they went to church in order to celebrate the Eucharist, but observed perfect silence the whole time. Father Abu Makar wondered that they kept aloof from him all this while, and he wished that the Lord would explain their action. He arose and went to them, and remained with them overnight. When he awoke at midnight, he saw how the two saints got up in order to pray. It was as if a fiery rope reached from their mouths to Heaven; devils surrounded them like greedy wolves, but the Angel of the Lord drove them off with a fiery sword. As soon as day dawned he clothed them in the holy garment and bade them farewell, asking that they would pray for him. They made him a reverent bow, but spake never a word. When they had ended their course, and the Lord desired that they should cast off the cares of this world and enter into eternal rest, the elder fell sick.

Three Years in the Libyan Desert

He sent to Abu Makar and asked him to come to him. When he came he found him in a fever ; he comforted him and calmed his heart. Then Father Abu Makar saw that the troop of saints, prophets, and apostles, St. John the Baptist and the Emperor Constantine, had come down and surrounded the saint until his soul departed with fame and honour. Then St. Abu Makar wept and said : ' Blessed be thou, O Maximus ! " Dometius did not cease to weep for his brother, and asked St. Abu Makar to beg Christ to unite him with Maximus, and three days after St. Maximus's death Dometius fell sick. St. Abu Makar was informed, and while he was on the way to him, he saw the troop of saints who had appeared to fetch the soul of his brother Maximus : they had now taken the soul of Dometius to themselves, and with songs of praise were ascending with it to Heaven. When he came to the grotto he found that Dometius was dead, and he buried him beside his brother. Maximus died on the 14th Tubeh, and Dometius on the 17th, and St. Abu Makar ordered the monastery to be called by their name, and so is it named to-day, and their memory endures for ever in Heaven and on the whole earth." So far the narration of the Synaxar.

Various pictures in tempera are to be seen above

and on the shrine of the saints. At the side is the entrance to the Haikal and a reading-desk. The square high altar in the large apse of the Holy of holies was uncovered, and the monks showed the so-called sacred wood, a right-angular wooden panel with crosses and inscriptions, set deeply in the mensa, and lent by the Patriarchs of Alexandria, corresponding to the cavity for the reception of relics of our altars. There was a cupola over each of the three apses. In different parts of the sanctuary we came upon fragments from Roman times, such as capitals of pillars and lintels of doors. The above-mentioned font was in the narthex. Abma Gabriel showed as a curiosity, in a cellar belonging to the church, the large wine amphora which contained the sacramental wine pressed out by the hands of the monks. A valuable treasure of the monastery was an amphora containing a wine that was fifty years old, some of which was offered us to taste. It reminded us of very old Malaga. In the same room was kept the holy chrism, concealed in a niche in the wall. Then we visited the highly characteristic refectory of the monastery, the bakehouse for the sacramental and other bread, and the smaller chapels of Mar Girgis and El Emir Tadrus.

There were interesting scenes when in the shade of the palm-grove we photographed groups of the

Three Years in the Libyan Desert

inhabitants of the monastery. The unrest and vanity of the younger men, combined with the extreme seriousness and care-laden aspect of the elder, lent the photographs an atmosphere of mingled joy and sadness. We were invited to photograph the hen-house of the monastery, and great astonishment was expressed when we found the subject, of great interest naturally to the inhabitants and a great rarity in the desert, unworthy of our camera. When our Sheikh urged our return, and we refused the invitation to stay the night on account of the exposed situation of our camp, the whole troop accompanied us outside the gate, calling down blessings on our heads. The night was far advanced when we reached the camp.

A few hours south-east of Baramûs, and nearer one of the salt lakes, the saline Rasunia, is the Maria Monastery, Dêr es-Surjâni, universally known through the finding of valuable Syrian and Abyssinian manuscripts. In 1842 Lord Curzon obtained about a thousand manuscripts for the British Museum, while already in 1715 Assemani, the distinguished keeper of the Vatican Library, succeeded in buying manuscripts and apographs in the various monasteries. Unfortunately the monks realized too late the immense loss which they owed to Lord Curzon and to

In the Monks' Citadel

Henry Tattam, the English Coptic scholar. Later, the Coptic Patriarchate forbade the sale of manuscripts under strict penalty, and had the valuable codices brought to Cairo. The name of the monastery reminds us of the Syrian colony of monks that settled here, the most flourishing time of which was in the period of reforming activity of Moses of Nisibis, in the first half of the tenth century. There in the middle of the wall grows the tree of St. Ephraim, a magnificent tamarind with a trunk over 3 feet in thickness, which grew from a staff that the great Syrian Father of the Church (d. 379) placed at the portal by mistake. The monks say their evening prayer at the foot of that tree.

The four Nitrian monasteries are very poor in artistic objects, but some remains in the Syrian Maria Monastery are of much interest to the student. Its old El-Hadra church is a basilica 90 feet long by 40 broad, with three aisles and cupolas. It was, perhaps, originally cruciform. The choir and sanctuary are divided from the rest of the church by a thick wall with a folding door. In the nave is a square basin of marble for the washing of feet. As in Dèr Baramûs, two bronze hoops hang from the ceiling by chains. They were the ancient chandeliers, of which, according to Kaufmann's " Archæology," two types have been preserved on Coptic ground, one with a deep rim and outstretching arms which held the glass oil-lamps, and a flat type with pierced rims and holes inset for the glass bowls. It seems they used similar chandeliers in the ancient basilica of St. Peter at Rome.

The tarsia work of the doors [1] which divide on one side the nave and choir, and on the other the choir and Haikal of the El - Hadra church, are of special interest. The first is in four parts, with six panels, of which the top rows represent Christ and Mary and St. Peter and St. Mark. The names are written in Greek, often with the Coptic article. The portrait of Christ reminded us of early Christian models from the fifth to the eighth century. The Lord appears in the nimbus of the cross, with spear over the serpent and the lion, according to the words of Scripture: " Super aspidens et basiliscum ambulabis et conculcabis leonem et draconem." A Syrian inscription on the lintel relates how Moses of Nisibis, in the year 1238 of the Seleucides period (926–27 A.D.), had the work of art executed. It runs: " To the honour and glory of

[1] The losses which the Nitrian monasteries have suffered through the thefts of foreigners can never be restored, and also from destruction by ignorant monks, who permitted pieces of the tarsia work to be broken off the doors and carried away as souvenirs.

VIEW IN THE PALM-COURTYARD OF THE MACARIUS MONASTERY IN WADI NATRÛN.

To face p. 83.

In the Monks' Citadel

the Holy Trinity this door was fashioned in the year (thousand) and 238 in the days of the blessed patriarchs Mâr Kosmas and Mâr Baseleios by the care and means of Moses of the town of Nisibis, president of the monastery, that God, in whose holy name he made it, may reward every one who has taken part in its pious prayer." The folding-door between the transept and the Haikal is in six divisions, and in six rows shows in seven panels crosses and ornaments; in the top rows are saints with the names inscribed in Greek; the front view gives Dioskoros (Patriarch 443–58), Mark, Emmanuel, Maria, Ignatius, Severus (512–18). The Syrian inscription, carved in rough letters deep in the lintel of the door, runs: "To the honour, glory, fame, and exaltation of the Holy Trinity, to whom all adoration is due, this altar of the Virgin Mother's church was erected by Moses . . . the president of the monastery in the days of the patriarchs Mâr Gabriel and Mâr Joannes in the year 1225 of the Greeks (913–14 A.D.) on the 5th of the month May, so that it be in beauty a sign for every believer who has an interest in this altar and holy convent, for the saving of their life and preservation, for the pardoning of their dead and the forgiveness of their sins." Professor Joseph Strzygovski, one of the members of the Committee for the Coptic

Three Years in the Libyan Desert

and Arabic Monuments of Egypt, first drew attention to these important inscriptions, and also to the value of the ornaments of the Haikal.

The paintings on a dark blue ground in the apses of the strikingly lofty Haikal and the aisles form a unique decoration. They represent scenes from the life of the Virgin : the Annunciation and Nativity, the Ascension and Death seem to belong to the post-Arabic period. Other older paintings may be recognized under them on the same subjects. Perhaps Abbot Moses of Nisibis commissioned the paintings as well as the tarsia, since the inscriptions indicate him as their composer.

For the rest, the plan of the Haikal, the altars, and the exterior appearance of the monastery, are similar to Dêr Baramûs. Dêr es-Surjâni possesses a second characteristic El-Hadra church. It is very much smaller, is almost square, and has no aisles. It contains nothing of special interest except some low-relief marbles, a reliquary, and a desk with ivory legs, unfortunately very much worn. The remains of paintings in the refectory deserve no particular attention. There is a fine view of the Nitrian valley and over the desert from the tower of the monastery, in which are a chapel dedicated to St. Michael and the once famous library.

In the environs of Dêr es-Surjâni there were a number of other monasteries which have now dis-

In the Monks' Citadel

appeared, or are only to be recognized in scanty
ruins, like the Convent of the Armenians and the
Elias Monastery of the Abyssinians. The last
settled later in the " Monastery of the Virgin " of
Bu Johannes, near which Amba Nub was situated,
and Dêr Amba Bischâi, the third of those still
existing. As we learn from the " vita" of
Macarius, men came not only from Egypt in order
to be monks and saints here, but from " Spain,
Libya, Pentapolis, Cappadocia, Byzantium, Italy,
Macedonia, Asia, Syria, Palestine, and Galatia."
A late Coptic manuscript in the library of the
Earl of Crawford mentions six flourishing Nitrian
monasteries ; besides those still existing, the Convents of Moses and John the Negro. Abu Musa,
from whom, as we said above, Baramûs derives its
name, appears like John to have been an Ethiopian
or Abyssinian, and to owe his surname to his
descent.

Amba Bischâi, in the immediate neighbourhood
of Dêr es-Surjâni, boasts of possessing the best
water of any of the Nitrian monasteries. It is
also by far the largest, having an area of more
than 150 square yards. The pump which brings
forth the precious liquid is in the third of the court-
yards, and furnishes enough water for a tropical
garden with many culinary vegetables, of which
the monks are very proud. Whoever has had

personal experience of the disagreeable water conditions of the Natrûn valley knows how to value such a well.

Notwithstanding this favourable condition, Amba Bischâi in comparison with the Macarius Monastery seems to me to be most behindhand. It is astonishing how Coptic monasteries, the inmates of which enjoy freedom from taxation and from military service, even in the Nile valley itself, slowly sink into the quagmire of their own stagnation. Besides the Nitrian convents, few have any importance ; we may mention those of St. Antony and St. Paul in the desert of Petræa, and the wealthy Muharak in Central Egypt—the last with about one hundred monks. The big fortress-like monasteries at Sohâg, the celebrated " white " and " red " convents which are connected under the name of Schenûte, shelter families instead of monks. So that the observance to-day is extremely lax. A set of the rules of the Order of St. Antony printed in Arabic at Cairo in 1899 appears to have had no influence.

The buildings of Amba Bischâi underwent so much restoration at the beginning of last century that it is less easy than in the others to trace out the old kernel. There is scarcely anything left of the old library. It was in the Kasr, and was rich in illuminated books. What remains is mostly con-

fined to liturgical works and copies of the trans-
mitted sacred books. They usually have a note
at the end, and with full right, "ad mentem" of
certain robbers of the monastery. We read at
the end of a Synaxar, *i.e.*, a collection of lives of
the saints as they were read aloud for the edification of the monks, the threat : "This book is an
eternal inheritance for everlasting preservation in
the church of the great and perfect St. Amba
Bischâi in his monastery, which is situated in the
desert Schihat, in el-Asket in Wadi Habib, 'the
balance of the heart.' No one has the right to
remove the same from the inheritance of the said
monastery out of any frivolous ground, and any one
who acts contrary to this and does remove it shares
the lot and fate of Diocletian the unbeliever, Herod
the apostate, Simeon the magician, and Judas the
traitor ; on the obedient to the contrary will there
fall for ever and aye the blessing and reward of
God ! Amen ! Amen ! Amen !"

The mother church of the monastery, dedicated
to the titular saint, the disciple of Abba Amoi, is an
Oriental domed basilica with all the peculiarities of
Coptic planning. The roof and aisles are domed ;
six further spaces have cupolas, a bay in front in
particularly delicate brickwork. The windows of
the aisles are now walled up. We find here, too,
the curious separation of the nave and transept

usually called choir, by massive walls and doors which again show carved work. The usual ostrich eggs hang from the ceiling of the choir, and a pretty bronze corona. In front is a door leading into the Virgin's chapel; it contains a reliquary with the bones of the titular saint. The south chapel, dedicated to Abu Iskarun, has a splendid cupola. In the Haikal the tribune deserves attention. The throne which formerly stood in the centre of the back wall is no longer there. Six steps incrusted with marble, the lowest of which goes the whole width of the Haikal, the three upper ones being semicircular, lead to the throne niche, in which remains of delicate *opus Alexandrinum* are to be seen. Little is left of the paintings which formerly adorned the various parts, especially the Holy of holies. The decoration of the dome of the Haikal is specially worthy of notice, where pretty arabesques in concentric frames run round the central cross, and also the fragment of a picture of St. George in the transept.

The desert provided the most important of the building materials for the church, as for all the sanctuaries in the wadi. It is the light-coloured, easily manipulated limestone. Only where bricks were absolutely necessary, as for the domes and other vaulting, was the aid of heavy transports from the Nile valley called in.

In the Monks' Citadel

We were struck at Amba Bischâi by the little care bestowed on the equipment for divine service. The holy vessels were poor and mean ; the liturgy has sunk to a purely ceremonial service without any real comprehension of the proceedings. Everything is concentrated round the Kummus, the priest who prays to God, and who, according to the views of many of the monks, possesses a mysterious power of magic. Cleanliness is sought in vain in the monastic churches of Wadi Natrûn, but, notwithstanding, the visitor finds much to attract him.

He feels himself in closer contact with a past age than anywhere else. The monks in their citadels and dungeons, their fear both of civilization and of the Arabs, their method of managing the monastery, and their liturgy, are exactly the same as they were five hundred years ago. The historian finds here abundant sources. We were pleased to find, outwardly at least, adherence to the old faith, for the sake of which hard fights had been fought by the monks of the wadi. With the exception of the heresy of Monophysitism and the papal prerogative of the Patriarch of Alexandria, the ancient Catholic doctrine is still living there. The seven sacraments are firmly adhered to, especially the personal presence of Christ in the Holy Eucharist. Baptism precedes circumcision, but not on religious grounds.

Anointment was used not only for diseases of the body, but also for those of the soul and disposition. The strict celibacy of the monks, and the special reverence paid to the priestly calling, contrasted with easy divorce. The four great fasts were very strictly kept. Worship of the Madonna, saints and images, and prayers for the dead find acceptance with the Copts.

But what lends the Coptic service, for all its stiff formalism, its intrinsic character, and what for thoughtful persons who assist at it reveals the kernel within the hard shell and charms them with a piece of primitive Christianity, is its wealth of primitive prayers and ceremonies. While our own liturgy is connected with Gregory the Great, the Copts use two—the liturgy of St. Basil and St. Cyril; the first on ordinary fast and holy days, the Gregorian on the high festivals, that of Cyril in Lent and on the December fasts. The "præparatio altaris" is common to all liturgies at the sacrifice of the Mass up to what Roman Catholics call the "prefatio." The second part of the Coptic Mass, the anaphora with prefatio, sanctus, consecration, fractio and communion, is common in the main, but different in the wording.

The monks of Amba Bischâi, and also those of the other monasteries, have their own traditions about the "waterless river," the Bacher bela mâ.

In the Monks' Citadel

Hermits had settled near the hill of the "eagle's stone" on the bank of the stream; they were constantly attacked by river pirates until, through the hermits' prayers, the water sank and then vanished for ever. A monk learned in the Bible pointed out a passage in the nineteenth chapter of Isaiah, in which he declared the "spirit of Egypt" to be identical with the fructifying Nile. "And the spirit of Egypt shall be made void in the midst of it; and I will destroy the counsel thereof: and they shall seek unto the idols and to the charmers, and to them that have familiar spirits and to the wizards. . . . And the waters shall fail from the sea, and the river shall be wasted and become dry. And the rivers shall stink; the streams of Egypt shall be minished and dried up : the reeds and flags shall wither away. The meadows by the Nile, by the brink of the Nile, and all that is sown by the Nile, shall become dry, be driven away, and be no more."

On the return from Amba Bischâi we passed the saline works, where the extraction of salt was being carried on. Many salt mounds of two to three cubic yards were thrown up, and the pyramids of fresh crystallized salt looked of a blood-red colour. On account of the intense heat the men could only work from 4 a.m. to 10 a.m., and so the nights when the moon was full were extensively used as the time for extraction. There was a peculiar charm in looking at the black figures hard at work. At the edge of the salt lake was a railway carriage, which the Mudir's representative put at our disposal, ready for the return journey. We went at a very slow pace over the black natrûn earth, through grass and reeds as tall as a man. We stopped at one place in order to see a water-hole in which, only a few yards distant from the saline works, fresh water had collected, that was high or low according to the state of the Nile. In boring in that region fresh water was always come upon first, and deep below it salt water. We soon reached the factory again, where the " capo " of the six soldiers at the disposal of the Mudir once more saluted us. The " capo " is at the same time Mayor of Bir Hooker.

The salt works, with its chimney more than 170 feet high, a signal-post for the whole of the salt-lake region, were established in 1890 by an Englishman named Hooker, after whom the well, Bir Hooker, and the little colony of officials and workmen are called. He leased the salt privilege from the Khedivial Government. In 1896 the management passed into Swiss hands, and four years later an English joint-stock company took up the business, and it now provides salt for the whole of Egypt. The work of extraction goes on from June to

In the Monks' Citadel

August, and yields 60,000 tons of the best salt, which forms a thick crust similar to ice on the lake, and has to be taken off. The transport is effected by means of three small lines of railway and a larger express line, 45 miles in length. The factory produces every day 30 tons of soda, 200 tons of packed-up salt, and from 3,000 to 4,000 packets of table-salt, the last packed by eight Beduin boys. Both dark and light nitre and gypsum are also produced. Statistics show that in spite of machinery and the railway there is no essential increase in the amount of production. In the time of Wanslebius, as in the middle of the seventeenth century, the "saltpetre lakes" produced annually about 90,000 cwt. of salt, valued at £2,400. It was the one important source of revenue for the nobles, and was carried on camel-back to Terraneh, to be thence dispatched to Cairo. Among the possessions of the modern factory, in which machinery of German origin is used, is a carriage of historical interest. It is the same that was used by the Empress Eugénie amid Oriental pomp at the opening of the Suez Canal. Hooker had bought the carriage from the Khedivial stables in order to have some means of transporting distinguished visitors to the wadi, and many a pasha had occupied it. With the advent of the railway and under the Swiss administration

the carriage served as an ambulance-wagon, and
to-day it is exhibited as a valuable curiosity.

We started in the light of the red dawn for the
desert monastery of Macarius. The camels went
forward with slow and hesitating steps, and it
required many an exclamation of "zap, zap,"
breathed rather than spoken by the Sheikh, to urge
them on. Bir Hooker lay far behind us when we
rode along the slopes of the range of hills situated
to the south of the wadi. Down in the valley,
some 80 yards below the desert, a curious
vehicle was seen moving at the edge of the saline
lakes—a railway locomotive drawn by two buffaloes.
Want of coal or ignorance of the mechanism of
steam engines often caused such a curious combina-
tion. Our clothes were too much saturated with
the night dew, which even penetrated the tent
cloth, for us thoroughly to enjoy the comic episode.
The discomfort was most trying, and only vanished
when, about 7 a.m., the sun began to have great
force, and soon after a gazelle was seen passing in
the distance at the edge of the Dschebel. The
sight caused us to change the day's programme, for
we had not eaten fresh meat for a long time, and so
our stomachs gave the casting vote, since even at
Bir Hooker and its neighbourhood neither sheep
nor fowls were to be bought for their weight in
gold. The herds all pastured a day's journey away,

In the Monks' Citadel

and midsummer was an unfavourable time. The gazelle, which turned out later to be a fine buck, must not escape us. We dismounted and, covered by the camels, carefully followed the Sheikh till close to the edge of a depression. The clever animals were not alarmed by the sight of camels, while the sight of a man, even at a distance, made them gallop; it was customary to creep up to them in this manner, especially when the wind was favourable. So we were able to view the creature at close quarters. It was surprised in the depression, into which it had descended after watching our camels for a long time. An imprudent movement on our part unfortunately caused Muftah not to shoot at the right moment, and the slender animal fled at the noise farther into the hilly ground. Then we divided ourselves. The Sheikh was to try to secure the valuable meat, and we slowly descended the Macarius Desert in a southerly direction. After several hours two shots were heard; it was quite noon before the Sheikh reached us. He had only shot at the gazelle, and it was not till the next day that he succeeded in killing it, a welcome booty, in spite of the thirty years testified to by the antlers.

At last, very late, we reached our goal in the barren desert, the monastery of Macarius, the whitewashed walls of which were scarcely to be distinguished from the desert itself. The aneroid thermometer could go no higher, and the pocket thermometer showed close on 140° Fahr. We had only experienced greater heat in the south of Moghara. Exhausted, we got off our camels in order to seek shelter from the burning sun in the shade of the monastery gate. We were so tired and weary that it was only after a long pause that it occurred to us to pull the bell and announce the arrival of the strangers. The reception was less ceremonious than in other monasteries ; the monks seemed to have no suspicion, although we carried arms. As we discovered later, their whole mind and thought were centred on receiving the customary presents. Dr. Junker, in the description of his journey through Wadi Djeffer, censured the want of tact of these monks. How courteous and well bred in contrast was the conduct of the inhabitants of Baramûs! The five-and-twenty monks of Dêr Macarius paid scant honour to the great saint whose name the monastery bore. They seemed to foster vices and iniquities which St. Macarius strove to overcome and to stamp out. Yet it should not be forgotten that the inhabitants of individual monasteries change from time to time.

The story of the first founding of the settlement is told by the monks as follows :—

Born in the year 300, in Upper Egypt, the great

saint early withdrew from the world. Repentance for a past cowardly theft determined him to lead a godly life in strict asceticism, with continuous prayer, in a solitary place. His conduct attracted the attention of the people living near him. He was accused of hypocrisy and dissimulation, and was feared as a wolf in sheep's clothing. A maiden seduced him, but later, under terrible torture of body and of conscience, she confessed the saint's innocence. Then the eyes of the people were opened. They admired the will-power and self-sacrificing spirit of Macarius, who bestowed a part of his gains on the unfortunate woman. In order to escape the honours men paid him, he fled away and hastened into the Nitrian Desert, where he spent the last sixty years of his life. The reputation of his virtues attracted many disciples to him there, who carried his worship into all the provinces of Egypt. To them he recommended silence, prayer, devotion, humility, and mortification. Four churches were founded in the hermit colony under his leadership. His disciples could not say enough of his gentleness and patience. They also attributed to the saint the gifts of prophecy and miracle-working.

St. Macarius was repeatedly forced to combat the heresies which unbelievers came to the hermits to spread. Hieracites and Arians saw in him a skilful advocate of the doctrine of the holy fathers of Nicæa. The monks show the place of his first settlement in the wadi, near the Baramûs monastery; while here, where he was buried, a sanctuary arose with monks' dwellings. Dêr Macarius in its present form, with numerous ruins of other monasteries in close proximity, is the most exposed monks' settlement in the Nitrian Desert. I might also describe it as the poorest, but I gravely doubt if the monks are conscious of their poverty. The whole place bears signs of terrible decay. The garden brings a bit of tropical landscape into the desert. Only the most necessary care is given it, however, chiefly in regard to the vegetables. A view of it from the windows of the Mandârah was extremely picturesque. The architecture of the monastery is of different periods. The gloomy principal church, with the exception of the decoration of the Haikal and the before-mentioned reliquary with the bodies of three St. Macariuses, possessed nothing that we had not seen in finer and better condition in other monasteries. Whole panels of the carved wood doors are broken away. The names of foreign visitors adorn the nave, and, indeed, the monks themselves ask their guests to eternize themselves in that way. A very beautiful fragment of sculpture hidden in the sand appears to be part of an altar cabinet or an early Christian

SALT EXTRACTION IN WADI NATRÛN.

To face p. 104.

In the Monks' Citadel

ambos. A two-storied campanile stood out in dazzling white against the warm green of the palms.

The "Church of the Sheikhs"—esch-schiûch, *i.e.*, of the saints—lies over against the tower, and is another sanctuary, so-called from the martyrs buried there. The choir is enclosed by three pillars connected by wooden cabinets, and is worthy of mention. An inaccessible subterranean room is designated as the grave of the martyred monks. The story of the forty-nine " sheikhs," as told in the sacred books of the Copts, is sufficiently remarkable to be related here as a further example of monastic tradition resting on a historical basis. The cause of their martyrdom was that Theodosius, son of the Emperor Arcadius, in whose time this happened, had no son. He therefore sent messengers to the elders of "Schihat" (*i.e.*, the Nitrian Desert), asking them to pray to God that He would send him a son. Among the elders was one named Isidore, who wrote to the Emperor and informed him : "God does not desire offspring from you, so that after your death the heretics may not enter into a league with him." When the Emperor received this communication he thanked God and was silent. Meanwhile some ill-natured persons, among them his sister Pulcheria, advised him to marry another wife in order to have a son by her who should inherit the

Empire. He replied to them : "I shall do nothing against the will of the elders in the Egyptian Desert, because their reputation has spread over the greatest part of the world." He then sent an ambassador to obtain permission from the elders. The ambassador had a son, who asked his father's permission to accompany him, and he took him with him in order to receive the blessing of the elders. When they came to the elders and had read out to them the Emperor's letter (Amba Isidore had meanwhile gone to his last rest), they took the ambassador and led him to the body of the saint, and said to him : " This letter has come from the Emperor, and we do not know what to reply." Then the old man stood up and said : " Did I not tell you and the Emperor that God will not give him a son, who would pollute himself by false doctrines ; if he married ten women he would not beget a son." And then the old man lay down again. The monks now drew up an answer in writing for the ambassador, and as soon as he had departed the Beduins came. A very old man named Amba Jonas arose and said to the brethren: "Behold, there come the Beduins; their sole purpose is to kill us. Who desires martyrdom, remain with me ; who is afraid, go up into the tower." Some of them took to flight, but forty-eight remained with the old man, and the

In the Monks' Citadel

Beduins came and slaughtered them. The son of the ambassador, who was already on his way, turned round and saw the angels, how they set crowns on the heads of the old men who had died as martyrs. The name of the youth was Dionysius. Then he said to his father : " Yonder I see a troop of spirits, who set crowns on the heads of the old men; now will I go in order to gain a crown like theirs." And his father answered: " I will go with you, my dear son." They turned round, and placed themselves in the way of the Beduins, were killed by them, and gained martyrdom. After the Beduins had withdrawn, the monks came down from the tower, carried off the corpses, and put them in a cave. They prayed before them, sang psalms every night, and implored their blessing. Then people came from El-Bathanum, and stole the body of Amba Jonas and took it to El-Bathanum. It remained there some time, until the elders brought it back again to its place. Other people from Fayûm fetched away the body of the young man, and when they had reached Moeris the angel of the Lord took him, and brought him back to the place in which his father's body reposed. The monks had several other times separated the body of the young man from that of his father, and when they came the next morning found him again at his father's side, until one of the old men had a dream, as if somebody said to him : " God be praised ; as long as we lived in our bodies we were not divided, and also with Christ we are not divided ; why will you separate us from each other ? " From that day forward no attempt was again made to separate them, and when the place in the desert was destroyed, and people were anxious for relics, these were taken from their place, and brought to the side of the church of St. Macarius. A grotto was built for them, and in the time of the Patriarch Theodosius a church was erected to them.

The third church of the Macarius Monastery lies to the south, and is dedicated to the martyr Ischynon of Alexandria. The sanctuary is in the east ; two domes roof the choir. Other sanctuaries are found in the Kasr, which is protected by a wooden drawbridge, namely, a chapel of the Virgin (El-Hadra), in the choir of which a heap of torn fragments of Arabic and Coptic manuscripts represent the library of Dér Makâr. My cousin sought for something by way of souvenir, but found little that went back beyond the seventeenth century. The monks looked on smiling.

Behind the principal church of the monastery we were shown the " Macarius well." It is a sagje,

In the Monks' Citadel

i.e., a draw-weil worked by an ox, and furnishes good drinking-water. The waterwheel was fairly large, and instead of a pail, clay vessels brought up the clear water, a real gift of God, from a depth of more than 10 yards. Dirt and filth were not lacking in the monastery, and the rooms and cells of the community made a bad impression. The occasionally fresh whitewashed walls are reminiscent of covered graves, and there is little in the place to attract the stranger. If the monks of the wadi occupy no high place in civilization and culture, those of the Macarius Desert have the sad privilege of representing at its worst the "nobility of the Egyptian people," as they were considered in Schenûte's times. The knowledge of the low condition of these monks seems to have reached distant Arabs. Our Sheikh, who was a native of Mareotis, before our visit to the monastery had characterized it by the little flattering epithet "battâl," *i.e.*, bad. But since we accepted their hospitality, I will refrain from showing how right he was. We were filled with an acute feeling of sorrow. What had become of this historic, once flourishing, and now desolate place? The long series of venerable figures who had once dwelt in holiness in this place, and whose names are celebrated not only in the Synaxars of the Copts and the East, but in the writings of the Mother Church, truly deserve a better memorial.

Close to the monastery of Macarius traces of hyenas and wolves lead to ruins which the Arabs describe as remains of the " Kasr benât," Castle of the Virgin. We were told it was a "convent." They are not the only ruins in the neighbourhood. A dozen or so of lesser ruins may be found in a circumference of a few hours' ride in the Macarius Desert, fallen to pieces and buried in sand. We may learn from the report of a French missionary, Père Sicard, how quickly the waves of the Libyan sand ocean do their work, and swallow up even monumental remains. He relates how in 1701, in that neighbourhood, about three or four hours from Dêr Macarius, he saw "fifty monasteries, easily distinguished one from the other, but desolate and almost in ruins." My cousin judged that excavations in that part of the desert would be wholly unfruitful.

The return from the Macarius Monastery is marked in my diary with a little cross. It was extremely trying. The burning heat made us twice attempt to rest in the shade afforded by the camels. But each time we had to give up the idea, for the heat of the sand penetrated our thin burnous, and was so unendurable that we preferred to ride on. Bir Hooker was reached

In the Monks' Citadel

in the night. When the big camp-fire was at last visible, and we saw the white figures of inquisitive Arabs crouching near, we knew that our discomfort and fatigue were over.

CHAPTER V

THROUGH THE LAND OF THE AULADALI—THE
DISCOVERY OF THE TEMPLE OF MENAS, THE
"PRIDE OF ALL LIBYA"

Departure from Wadi Natrûn—Muftah's "weakness"—Through
the land of the Children of Ali—Kom Marghab—*Fata
Morgana*—The Pasha deluded by the mirage—Story of
the enigmatical Sidi Melûnte—Arrival at the ruins of
Karm Abu Mina—Dangerous illness of the leader of the
expedition—Eureka : the holy city is found !—The vineyard of Father Menas—History of Menas—Departure and
return of the caravan—Strange farewell banquet in the
casino at Mex.

ABU SÊF'S flight was long forgotten, and we had
become accustomed to the discomfort caused by
the abstraction of a camel. Our stay in the
wadi resulted in an extraordinary amount of
change and disturbance. We were at fault in
sparing our Beduins too much, while only Sheikh
Muftah, who was never tired, accompanied us to
single monasteries with one or two camels. Eluâni
and Abd el-Al remained behind with the other
animals, so that the whole time the camp, high

BEDUIN AND CHILD AMONG THE MARBLES OF THE HOLY CITY.

To face p. 112.

above the horizon of the desert, was visible to Bir Hooker and the company. When we set off at noon on July 3rd for the Auladali Desert, Abd el-Al and Eluâni showed signs of something like homesickness. At least they would have preferred a direct and speedy ride home, and it required constant threats of the Mamûr and of withholding the backschish agreed on in order to keep the otherwise excellent fellows in check. And as regards ourselves certain ominous signs became apparent, although we made light of all obstacles. They began with an increasing nervous irritability which produced disputes every moment, and slowly passed into the early stages of dysentery, one of the most serious illnesses that threaten the European in this and similar climates. The quick and sudden death of the Mudir, at whose villa we were expected as guests, and where we had only to pay a visit of condolence, showed that the insidious enemy was in the immediate neighbourhood. Then came a third : our provisions, which had got low, could not be supplemented from the canteen of the company. The canteen—rarely required by Europeans in summer—contained at that time only tins of preserved provisions, condensed milk, and such things, for which we long had had the greatest distaste. Only a case of soda-water, a few eggs, and several hens of the poorest sort were at last delivered to us, and gratefully received. The water question became more and more acute. In the monasteries the water was good and free from all objection, but that was no longer the case with Bir Hooker, the big cemented well of the station and its environs. At other seasons it might be possible to procure wholesome and excellent water from the Beduins; but we were evidently unfortunate, and I suffered severely from diarrhœa, while my cousin was more affected by the want of suitable food. At times the medicines provided by Schiess Pasha for such occasions were beneficial, and also the glass tubes filled with caffeine pastilles of a Rhenish factory.

The first day's ride was stopped after a few hours, for Sheikh Muftah, who on the journey to the Macarius Monastery had only succeeded in killing a wounded gazelle, had better luck. While Eluâni was preparing a good soup, and Abd el-Al was toasting little pieces of the meat at the open fire, people brought the last farewells of the acting Mudir. He sent some minerals as a gift, among them fine specimens of salt, natrûn, and gypsum. Sick persons from distant tents were also brought to us, and the few pots of milk with which they presented us were a welcome honorarium for the little assistance and advice we could give them. To the great joy of the men, who saw that it was done on purpose, my cousin offered some of the women who had come with them Arabian coffee. It was known that women must not eat or drink in the presence of strangers, least of all take the men's drink, coffee. When the camp was broken up the next morning, the numerous Schuâbi Beduins who had appeared on the scene paid us spontaneous homage. Everything was ready packed, we were aloft, swaying on the heavily laden camels, when there came up a few pitifully sick persons, among them a child covered with skin eruption. The ointment was stowed away in one of the chests, but as my cousin did not hesitate to have them unloaded in order to give the much needed help, loud testimonies of gratitude and of praise of Allah were offered.

That day the caravan passed the north-west high ridge of the wadi, everywhere collecting information about "Antikât." We camped early, and successfully conquered the dangerous exhaustion with the remains of the gazelle soup and some strong red wine with eggs. Eluâni was the hero of that day, for after a brief chase he brought home a fine gazelle. We had hitherto been very sparing of our ammunition and could now be more generous. So in the afternoon we had a shooting match for the Beduins. An empty bottle stuck upside down in the sand at a long distance, with a lemon on top of it, served as a mark for the Sheikh and Eluâni, while a big tin biscuit-box, which we, too, occasionally hit, did the same for Abd el-Al. The shooters lay on their stomachs, and the whistling of the bullets, which jumped over the sand raising slight eddies, sounded far into the desert. On this relatively happy day, Sheikh Muftah, our bold and indefatigable guide, for the first time showed signs of human weakness. In miserable situations, when a glass of whisky could work wonders in reviving and promoting energy, and was really to be regarded as simple medicine, Muftah always refused it with signs of the greatest horror. Further, when he learnt the contents of the different chests, he would never permit that which contained the liquid strictly forbidden by Allah and the law to be placed on his camel. In the evening by the camp-fire the pious Moslem turned to my cousin with the words : " Kaufmann Effendi, I have pains in my back and shoulders ! " He was told that he should go to sleep, then it would all pass over, and be as before. There was a brief pause, and Muftah said : " The adwîge [1] with which you rubbed the sick boy in the desert would help me, so sure as Allah lives." My cousin then told Muftah to sit near our folding chairs and ordered Eluâni to rub his back

[1] Plural of " dawa," medicine.

A MENAS AMPULLA (FOURTH CENTURY).

Portrait of the patron of the Libyan Desert between camels, with
a Greek inscription.

To face p. 116.

with whisky and to massage the painful places. We signed to Eluâni, who took in the situation, not to spare his strength, and the Sheikh must have had something to endure. But he held out, and so it availed nothing. When it had lasted long enough, Muftah, turning to my cousin, said : " Effendi, the pain is not on the skin, it is inside! I will rub myself, and frequently, for several days." We gave him the remainder of the whisky together with the bottle, and without Eluâni's information, who secretly watched the Sheikh in the evening, it was clear that his quite inconsequent liveliness was due to the " inside treatment," which the son of the desert had carried out as thoroughly as possible.

The following days again made great demands on our strength, since everywhere we came upon and surveyed ruins. The temperature was more striking than ever : in the night there was a great fall of the minimum thermometer to 33° Fahr. ; one day at 1.30 p.m. there was a maximum of 115° in the shade and something over 140° in the sun, while in the morning at sunrise it was already 84°. This considerable heat had no effect on the temperature of the body, and the dryness of the air helped us over all difficulties. Without the dryness the heat would naturally have been intolerable, for it corresponds with that in the engine-room of a battleship during the passage of the Red Sea, when a change of stokers every two hours is necessary. The Bed-uins protect themselves from the heat in a fashion very incomprehensible to the northerner. While we were inclined in the heat to take off our khaki coats and to travel in bathing-drawers and white Tunisian burnous, the sons of the desert, as soon as the sun began to shine in good earnest, wrapped themselves up in thick woollen rugs; their heads vanished in a turban of from eight to ten thick folds, so that only the nose and the sharp prying eyes were visible. Later on, during the excavations, experience taught us the necessity of this strange way of keeping off the sun, and I now wonder that neither my cousin nor I suffered from sunstroke.

We were marching in sight of the slopes of the mountain El-Nêd, at the edge of Wadi Natrûn, in order to visit the ruins of Medina Kiffari, already surveyed by Dr. Junker, the African traveller. On his maps, published in " Petermanns geographischen Mitteilungen " in 1880, the ruins are marked as very much to the north-east of the Kasr el-Gettajeh, and Junker took about a day's journey between the two places. Strangely enough, neither Sheikh Muftah nor Eluâni, who was skilled in gazelle hunting in nearly every corner of the Auladali Desert, knew the "ancient city" even by name. No one in the tents we occasionally passed had any knowledge of it; indeed, everybody declared that

Through the Land of the Auladali

Kiffari was not Beduin, and it was evident that the place bore another name. The draughtsmen of Junker's map, who drew according to the notes in the explorer's diary, were obviously at fault, for a careful and minute search of the district gave only a few disconnected ruins of an older time. But in the course of those researches we heard of the existence of a large field of ruins north-east of the spot designated as Medina Kiffari, ostensibly the largest in Mariut. We decided to seek it later on, and at the moment proceeded on an easterly route straight across the Auladali Desert, in the hope of striking on the traces of an old caravan route which tradition said once led from Alexandria to the Nitrian monasteries. The temple of Menas, if not situated on that route, must lie in the neighbourhood, and thus it was of importance to locate one or other of the ancient wells. This traversing of the desert was, however, fruitless. We came upon no tent, and what was worse, no well from which we could replenish our gheerbahs with fresh water, for what they contained had acquired a disagreeable taste. The way led through a part of the desert sporadically without vegetation or with scanty undergrowth. Early in the morning of July 6th we saw a few Beduin tents, the dwellings of poor people, who entertained us with a dish of milk. I have for the second time a note in my diary " Ill and wretched," and we determined to keep up as long as was necessary to discover the large complicated ruins, but to return unsuccessful rather than to court certain death.

At length, at the Kom Marghab, we came upon an encampment of twenty-three tents, the sharply defined rows of which clung to the yellow chain of hills like a little black village. The strangers were offered Nile water, with which the zemzemien, *i.e.*, the round bottles that hung from the pommel of the saddle, could be filled. Those Beduins live in the district of the delta and fetch their water every few days from one of the numerous canals of the delta which extend their fertilizing arms into the desert region. We twice saw the spectacle of the *fata morgana* from half way up the ridge. In the distance was a long glittering strip of lake which we took to be Lake Mareotis. In the course of a few hours it vanished. The remarkable appearance of the srâf, also called moije scheitân, that is, devil's water, at times deceived the camels. An entertaining story was current in Beduin circles, and the Sheikh of the Kom Marghab mentioned the names of the persons concerned. A pasha who years ago had travelled in that district beheld the wonder from the same Kom. As the man was speculating in the region of the neighbouring province of Behêret in reclaiming the steppe land, and

A BEDUIN IN THE CENTRE OF THE RUINS OF THE CITY OF MENAS AT THE TIME OF THE DISCOVERY.

To face p. 120.

saw the water at much closer quarters than we did, he inquired concerning the Sheikh of that district and desired that he would give him all rights to the place, for which he was willing to pay a sum to be arranged, and would permit the encampment to remain there in perpetuity. A meeting was fixed to take place at Damanhûr for the purpose of drawing up an agreement, and the cunning Auladali Sheikh accepted by way of earnest, in the best sense of the word, a big handful of guineas—that is, English gold sovereigns. When later the Pasha was told how he had been deceived by the devil's water, he did not take the matter badly ; he remained as before a special friend of the Auladali.

I myself had an apparition that day which I regarded as a sick man's vision, and which I at first believed when Eluâni hurried up at my cry and led me away, saying in terror that no man dared look at it. I saw a giant shadow of a camel-rider over a hill of stones which somewhat resembled an ancient building. The figure stood upright, not inverted, and its dimensions were similar to those of the spectre of the Brocken.

At the Kom Marghab there was again heard, at least in the conversation of our people, the name of a mysterious personage behind whose significance we could not penetrate. From time to time during the long march the Beduins related long stories.

Eluâni at least was indefatigable, and in the evenings by the camp-fire he continued them, surrounded
by an eager listening circle of stranger Beduins.
We understood very little of these tales, and
could never see the connection. But it was perfectly clear, from the ever-recurring name Sidi
Melûnte, that they concerned him.

The endless repetition of such stories about a
man who could only be some very important Sheikh
excited our extremest curiosity. When Muftah
was first asked who was this Sidi Melûnte of whom
everybody was talking, the conversation stopped,
and nothing more was heard that day. As they
would not explain, there seemed no doubt that the
mysterious Sheikh was a suspicious character,
perhaps the leader of a great Beduin disturbance or
a political conspirator. Sidi Melûnte continued to
appear in the tales, and at length Muftah and
Eluâni, yielding to our energetic demands, confessed
that he was a great Auladali Sheikh, but that he was
dead. They evidently told us that to get rid of the
matter. Sidi Melûnte continued to play his part,
and from the little we could gather of the legend, it
seemed that his person was wrapped in a veil of
myths, similar to the legends of the Elf Lêlet in the
" Arabian Nights." Repeated questions had only the
result of making the men grin amiably, just as if we
were making a joke which must always be laughed

at. We determined to find out later something more definite about this mysterious personage, and to inform the Mamûr Markaz or the municipality of Alexandria. But fortunately the matter was explained, and, indeed, at Kom Marghab. A serious interview with Eluâni, who at length realized that we were not to be trifled with, resulted in the confession that Sidi Melûnte had no existence at all, much less was he buried even as a legendary hero. Muftah's and Eluâni's tales were in fact legends and fairy-tales, well known in the Arab world, by the famous Abu Zet el-Hilâl, and Sidi Melûnte turned out to be a recurring, unimportant ordinary Beduin interjection, just as any story-teller might say after a long pause " That's the story," or as underbred people have the bad habit of saying Mr. So-and-so without meaning anybody in particular. But we were still suspicious, and did not believe even this explanation, and it was only later that it was confirmed. The discovery of the conspirator Sidi Melûnte would have been so very interesting.

We left Kom Marghab on the night of July 7th, in order to continue our exploration of the Auladali Desert, this time from east to west. A very fatiguing ride over the steppe, half desert, half hattje, led to the ruins to which the Beduins give the name of Karm Abûm.

The small supply of water in the zemzemien was

long exhausted, and the liquid in the skins could only be drunk without nausea by mixing with it a generous quantity of red wine. We were suffering badly from diarrhœa. Sheikh Muftah well realized the danger of the situation, and was more amiable than ever, a fact that only irritated us, for neither would confess his condition for fear of rendering the expedition futile. During the night we froze at 38° Fahr. Towards morning it got warmer (at 6 a.m., 68°; at 8 a.m., 84°), and the damp sank in the same time from 85° to 46°. Even now I still marvel at Muftah's ability to find his way, a thing he could do even in the thickest fog. Seated on the supple camels, that almost trotted, imagining that they were going home, we gently descended the depression that resembled a wadi. For over an hour it was filled with mist, in which we enjoyed the spectacle of a "mist-bow" with a fairly clear colour spectrum. Was it a good omen? At the moment no one thought of any possibility, and in my cousin's diary I find close to the passage about the bow some sentences which refer to the encampment made when the fog lifted, in order to rest and eat, and especially to seek among the sporadic tents for milk, eggs, a fowl, and water. He writes: "Our gheerbahs were empty, all but one, and that was already begun. But we could not possibly drink that water. It was equally nasty, used to make coffee or for washing purposes. It is a pity that a chemical analysis is not possible! Until we can procure drinkable water we have to manage with a little brandy or whisky. The latter did much service, for yesterday evening Eluâni fell from his heavily-laden camel, and we all thought he must have broken his neck, poor fellow! I rubbed him with whisky, and his first word when he recovered was the 'ghost' that he and Ewald had seen at Kom Marghab, and that had seemed to me so remarkable, because the giant camel-rider was not seen on the clouds, as is usual with such apparitions, but over the hill : *Deo laudes qui malum avertit.* Eluâni is now absent with Abd el-Al in order to fetch something for the exhausted explorers to drink. The Sheikh has fastened the German flag to the stock of his Arab gun, since there are no poles. They were used for fuel. The Sheikh is preparing Arabian coffee. I cannot even look at the tinned provisions any more."

The scarcity of water to which Monsignor Kaufmann here alludes in all its bearings made us feel anything but cheerful, even when two fowls were brought in and our hunger better appeased. In the height of summer the wells of the Auladali Desert, if not dried up, are merely mud-holes, and the water of the few cisterns has a salty taste. Even though suffering physical ills ourselves, we had to heal others, and the sight of diseased folk, of a child with ulcers on its breast, a man with a gaping wound in his leg, the edges of which were sewed together by means of a tent nail and thin string, made us forget our own sufferings for a moment. Fortunately we had plenty of carbolic and iodoform.

We were filled with scant hope when in the late afternoon (July 7th) the little troop approached the region which neighbouring Beduins call Karm Abûm and Bumna. Sheikh Muftah would under no circumstances camp there, for it was infested with robbers and enemies. But my cousin was utterly exhausted and required a day's rest, and he did not lose his energy until he had succeeded in insisting on the camp being pitched at the Karm, near the ruins and stones of an ancient city. Then as soon as the Beduins had put up the tent he lay down on a folding chair, apathetic, and his pulse slow. He asked me to make him brandy compresses, while Muftah sought for milk, but in vain, and Eluâni and Abd el-Al hastened to the well Eisêle, the one to bring back water as quickly as possible, the other to water the camels. My cousin remained in that state all night and had no sleep. Only the brandy compresses gave him any relief, and there was one moment when I thought he was dying. As he had the same fear, he would not let me hurry off to Alexandria for a doctor. He became much worse when Muftah brought some milk from a tent, unfortunately only gheerbah milk, *i.e.*, preserved in goat-skins, the horrible, indescribable taste of which caused vomiting.

When things were at their worst, Eluâni came hurrying up from the northern Karm with two gheerbahs of water. The well of Eisêle from which he came is one of the best in Mariut, but unfortunately, before the arrival of our people a herd of nearly a hundred camels had been there for three or four days, and the water he brought us was muddy and somewhat brackish. But it was not absolutely stale, and lacked the nasty taste of the gheerbah that induces nausea, and which resembles the smell of small unventilated cabins in ocean-going ships when Poseidon forces us to pay him tribute.

In spite of his weakness, my cousin retained the interests of the archæologist and the tiny hope connected with this region of ruins, and he urged a survey. The camp was set up on a flat, yellow Kom, close to the spot on which later the excavation buildings were erected. The sea of ruins mentioned above could not be seen from it, and the reader may picture my amazement when, in my first walk over the series of Koms, I suddenly saw that chaos of limestone blocks, all confused and without order, no one stone lying on the other. It was a dangerous climb, for, as a caution against the Harami, whom I later came to know as brave men, but who were then embroiled in a quarrel with our Sheikh's family, I was heavily armed, and my gun hindered me at every step. So I climbed about in order to find the ruins of a building or some relic to relieve the suspense and arouse curiosity. But I found nothing. The hand of man and the desert had in the course of many centuries accomplished the work of destruction, the sight of which was both terrible and grand. Close by was a series of barren hills, the " Koms," the surface of which was covered with fragments. On our long ride through the desert we had often been able to fix the age and epoch of the upper layers of ground from such fragments of pottery and vessels, and the eye quickly became accustomed to pick out from the hundreds of pieces those which showed some little decoration or traces of workmanship.

And now I had the good fortune to find on one of these Koms a fragment with the remains of a design, and then others with clear signs of a stamped impression. A little piece of a rim with a camel's head decided the question. I had seen in the Cairo Museum and at Schiess Pasha's examples of the so-called Menas ampulla, where the saint appears as patron of the Libyan Desert between two kneeling camels. There was little doubt that

BEDUIN TENT IN THE ANCIENT GARDEN LAND OF THE CITY OF MENAS.

COOKERY IN A FIELD OF ASPHODEL.

To face p. 128.

The Temple of Menas

my find was a fragment of one of them, and my joy
was so great that I executed a real wild Indian
dance, quickly packed up, and, without fear of subterranean chambers or Muftah's enemies, ran head
over heels to the camp in order to bring the news.

"Karl, it is the Menas temple," I shouted, and I
am sure my news helped to save my friend's life.
In any case he recovered his strength, and when,
shortly after my return, Sheikh Schuchân dragged
or rather carried up to us his second wife, with the
help of one of his sons, and the consumptive young
woman collapsed in front of us, Kaufmann himself
fetched a third folding chair out of the tent for the
sick woman. It was Schuchân who in default of
everything else had sent us the gheerbah milk. His
tent was not far off, and later he became our friend.
We saw at once that nothing could be done for his
wife ; we gave her some alleviation, and ordered her
to lie out in the sun, instead of remaining, as she
had for weeks, wrapped in rugs in the tent. We
gave Schuchân to understand that danger was near.
"I thank you," replied the handsome bearded man ;
"everything is in God's hands." Five months
later, when we returned to Sheikh Schuchân to
begin the excavations, his wife had been sleeping
for two months in the soft bed of the desert, the
mightiest of all cemeteries.

On the same day Schuchân's son brought us an

"Antika," his personal gift, because we had presented his mother with our extra chair, some ground coffee, and a good deal of sugar. What the boy placed on my cousin's knees was nothing less than a fine intact pilgrim's bottle, with the portrait of St. Menas, the camel as symbol of the desert, and a Greek inscription : " Eulogia ton hagion Mena," " a memorial in praise of St. Menas." The clay vessel looked so fresh and clean that it might have been finished only that moment. It must have lain in a sheltered place under the ground, and so my cousin inquired about the spot where it had been found, and rewarded the boy with a handful of lumps of sugar. " That's for my mother," he said. For, to the great advantage of his beautiful teeth, his Beduin ignorance prevented his recognizing the use boys generally make of sugar. " You can have any quantity of them [early Christian antiquities] here close at hand."

The little antiquity acted as medicine to Monsignor Kaufmann. We must immediately go to the spot. He accompanied us, and what had hitherto been only conjecture became almost certainty. After a little digging, which Schuchân's son accomplished by means of our spade and his brown hands, we came upon a perpendicular hole, rounded at the top, out of which were taken one after the other little jugs, ampullæ, and a few lamps, all of light yellow terra-cotta, and as well preserved as if they had been left there the day before, instead of more than a thousand years ago. The finding of a complete potter's furnace, for such it was, resulted in further confirmation. Although in no condition to do so, my cousin wished to survey the field of ancient ruins. He felt certain that they were of an early Christian character. In the centre was a pile of freestone which Sheik Muftah took for an ancient palace of the Caliphs; the position of the ruined blocks showed an enormous apsis. "We must dig here; this ought certainly to be the apsis of the Menas Temple." Kaufmann's talent for divination did not deceive him. Where others would only have seen a confusion of free-stone blocks, we actually came upon the end of the great basilica of the Emperor Arcadius, an ex-tension of the tomb of the patron of the Libyan Desert. The only doubt my cousin still had was due to the unexpected size and extent of the field of ruins, which pointed to a whole city.

We were not the first explorers who had come to Bumna or Karm Abûm. But no one had foreseen the immense importance which the ruins were to have for history. The intrepid young J. R. Pacho, whosedescendants still live in Alex-andria, was the first to give any information about Bumna in his "Relation d'un voyage dans la Marmarique," which appeared in Paris in 1827. We held Pacho in great esteem; it was he who had laid the foundation of research in Cyrenaïca, and his tragic and early death will always be remembered. In 1825 he passed Bumna, which he designated as "bourg romain," coming from Abusir, on the way to Kasr el-Gettajeh, where I sorrowfully read his name on the walls of the castle. Also W. Junker, the African traveller, who was an excellent guide for us in many ways, while crossing the Auladali Desert in 1875, saw perhaps the ruins of Bumna. At least I am inclined to that view. The Medina Kiffari of his map, which we sought in vain in reference to the site of the old city, can only be Karm Abu Mina. It is especially to be remarked that he describes granite blocks on that spot, where the ruins are certainly of limestone. A mere passer-by might easily make such a mistake. When in 1907 I was preparing the edition of my "Beduin Songs," the third in the trio was my predecessor in the literal sense, Professor Hartmann of Berlin. The distinguished Berlin Orientalist had, a few years before us, travelled in the neighbourhood of Bumna when on a little journey in the desert to collect linguistic and poetical materials.

Information concerning the etymology of the

The Temple of Menas

Arabic name "Bumna" was first given us by the tribes of Beduins settled there, so far as Beduins can be said to have a settled habitation. A wealthy and distinguished race, that of Abum Dêr, so named by the ancient ancestor " father of the monastery," have from time immemorial set up their tents for some months of every year near the Karm. This gave us the key to the meaning of Bumna and Abu Mina; Karm Abu Mina only means the "Vineyard of Father Menas."

Thus the city of Menas lives in the Hilalije cycle of Arabic legends as the "vineyard of Father Menas," that is, in some of the tales ascribed to Abu Zet el-Hilâl. We did not know that at the time, but we were familiar with a more important Arabic source which filled the chief place in the scientific material my cousin had collected for the expedition. I mean the description of the sanctuary of Menas at the time of its decline, published by the French archæologist Quatremère, in 1810, which is still extant in a Paris manuscript, the work of an Arab traveller. The curious tale of the traveller, who lived about the year 1000, might have been taken for the product of Oriental imagination until the excavations confirmed its statements. In the translation which Kaufmann gives in the first folio of his great Menas work, it runs as follows : " I left Terenouli—a Coptic episcopal city in the south-west part of the Nile delta [the present village Terraneh is meant]— and followed the road to Barca, and so reached Mina, which is composed of the forsaken cities in the midst of the sand desert, the buildings of which are still standing. The Arabs hide themselves in them in order to waylay travellers. Splendid well-built palaces, encircled by strong walls, are to be seen. They are generally surrounded by vaulted colonnades, some of which serve the monks for dwellings. There are a few springs of fresh water, but they are rare. Thence you come to the Church of St. Menas, an immense building adorned with statues and paintings of great beauty, where lamps burn continually day and night. At the end of the building is a large marble tomb with two marble camels, and above them a man who places a foot on each of the camels, and one of his hands is closed, the other open. This statue [in Arabic the sense of the word statue is the same as sculpture], which is also of marble, is said to represent St. Menas. In the same church are portraits of John, Zachariah, and Jesus on the inner side of a large marble column at the right of the entrance. In front of the figures is a door which is kept closed. The statue of the Virgin Mary is also to be seen covered with two curtains, and statues of all the prophets. On the exterior of the building there are figures which represent all kinds of animals and men of all callings. Among others may be distinguished a slave-dealer with a purse in his hand. In the centre of the church is an erection in the form of a cupola, under which are eight figures, if I am rightly informed, representing angels. By the side of the church is a mosque, the mihrab of which is on the south, where the Mussulmans come to pray. All the ground round the building is planted with fruit trees, chiefly almond-trees and carob-trees, from the soft sweet fruit of which syrup is prepared. Many vineyards are also to be seen, the grapes and wine of which are transported to Egypt."

If this description is taken in conjunction with the aspect of the ruins when we first saw them, it demonstrates in an astonishing manner with what thoroughness the desert swallowed up and destroyed the proud palaces of the ancient city and their surroundings of luxuriant nature and lofty palms. What remained of the "pride of all Libya," as Sophronius styled the temple of Menas? And where no longer one stone stood on the other, was it possible that some monument was preserved in the bosom of the earth that might give future races an idea of its ancient splendour?

It is here advisable to say a word about the

Three Years in the Libyan Desert

Egyptian national saint and patron of the desert, and to describe him in a more definite manner than he appears under the veil of legend. Who was Menas, to whom early Christianity dedicated one of its finest sanctuaries, to whose tomb in the oasis troops of pilgrims · travelled, to whose temple Athanasius and Constantine, two of the greatest figures of early Christianity, stood sponsors? The Ethiopian texts newly discovered by Kaufmann give the first complete information. Besides the romantic story of the martyrdom of Menas they offer numerous facts of historical importance.

St. Menas, whose memory is celebrated by the Roman Catholic and Greek Churches on November 11th, and by the Eastern Church on the 15th of the Coptic month of Hatur, was an Egyptian officer in the Roman service. His mother was named Euphemia, and his father was colonel, and as such was promoted to be Prefect of Phrygia, in Asia Minor. The young Menas, whose parents had given him a good Christian education, was not attracted by the military profession, but his father's successor in the prefecture, who loved the young man, was forced to compel him to become a soldier. So against his will Menas entered the regiment of the Rutiliaces, and all went well until the persecution by Diocletian of the Christians of Asia Minor, which was carried on with great severity,

BEDUIN HOUSE BUILT OF FREESTONE FROM THE BASILICA OF SIDI JÁDEM, DISCOVERED
BY THE EXPEDITION.

To face p. 136.

The Temple of Menas

especially against the Christians in the provincial
divisions of the army. The decree came to
Kotyaion — now Kutahia, where in 1833
Mohammed Ali of Egypt concluded a peace
with Turkey, and where in 1850-1 the revolu-
tionary Kossuth was imprisoned—the garrison in
which Menas was then stationed. As he was
thoroughly disgusted with military service, he fled
into the outskirts of the desert, and lived there like
a fellah, a life of self-denial and hard work. There
he had a vision which stimulated him to martyrdom
and prophesied the importance of his future
sanctuary. "Thy martyrdom will be greater than
the martyrs of a crowd of blood witnesses, thy
name will be honoured, and troops of people from
every quarter of the earth will come and take
refuge in thy sanctuary, which will be erected in the
land of Egypt, and thy power will manifest itself
and wonderful things, signs, and cures will come
about through thy holy body."

As a result of that vision in the desert, our officer
defied the authorities and, indeed, in unusual circumstances. It was the day of the riders' festival
in the stadium of Kotyaion. The country-folk of
Phrygia were assembled, as well as the inhabitants
of the town, with the heads of the community;
all the military had taken their places, surrounding Pyrrhus, the governor. The games were

about to begin, when a young officer stepped into the arena and in a loud and clear voice declared himself to the armed troops as an adherent of the proscribed religion. The man was recognized to be Menas. But the governor was forced to carry out the decrees of Rome. Menas was imprisoned. They wished him well for the sake of his family, and because he was popular as an officer. In vain, at every fresh hearing, he acknowledged Christ, and every fresh attempt to urge him to obey the Imperial edict was useless. Then the governor had to take the matter seriously. He began with threats, but as they availed nothing he had to proceed to business. All the horrors of the Imperial Roman inquisition were gone through; neither the grim torture of whipping with thongs of ox-hide nor the tearing of the flesh with iron scorpions could break the courage of the believer, and at last his head fell by the sword. Thus died Menas in 296 A.D. As during the processes of torture the martyr had indicated a wish to be buried in his native land of Egypt, they went so far as to have his body burned. When the executioners had departed (the scene was the place of execution before the gates of the town) friendly Christians snatched the body of the martyr from the flames and preserved it in a wooden coffin.

The Temple of Menas

Now it happened that after a time a portion of the Phrygian troops were ordered to Cyrenaïca, and the command was given to a Christian officer named Athanasius. He desired to fulfil secretly the wish of the saint and also thereby to ensure a higher protection for his army, and for these reasons took the corpse with him on his campaign. At the Lake of Mareotis, the first stopping-place between Alexandria and Cyrenaïca, a great battle was fought, which he won, and when Athanasius came to return he wished to take back with him his war talisman, Menas's body. But the camel refused to carry the wooden chest any longer, and so the saint was buried in that spot.

The place of burial soon became known. A lame boy saw a shining light over it and was healed there. A shepherd whose sick beasts rolled first on the ground and then in the water announced everywhere that his flock had suddenly been healed. "And all the people who suffered from various diseases came to the grave and were made whole." The leper princess from Byzantium, barren women, people suffering from elephantiasis and other diseases, lunatics, all found health and salvation at the fountain of youth in the city of Menas.

A church was soon built over the grave in the days of Athanasius, Patriarch of Alexandria, "with the help of God-fearing King Taos," *i.e.,* Constantine the Great. The whole of Egypt with its bishops and priests took joyful part in the consecration of the sanctuary of Menas. As the church quickly became too small, it was extended by the building of the enormous basilica of the Emperor Arcadius. The Emperor Zeno built a city and erected a palace for himself near the temple, and set up a large garrison there as a protection against the Beduins. He regulated the transport of the sick to the sanctuary, of which it is said at the end of the Ethiopian texts : " The fame of its miracles reached to the boundaries of all lands."

On the afternoon of July 10th, 1905, the fashionable world which was assembled in the casino of Mex, the sea-bathing suburb of Alexandria, and filled the terraces of the large restaurant by the sea, where a band was playing, saw a strange sight. Two camels were seen approaching from Bab el-Arab, the Beduin Gate, and they carried among a quantity of baggage not less than four riders. The spectators soon realized that the animals were greatly fatigued and were moving with uncertain steps, a fact that caused the riders, two Europeans and two Beduins, to dismount as soon as possible. Neither of the two camels would cross the railway lines, and both were terrified when a couple of carriages of the Alexandrian tramway rushed along fairly near the line, bringing fresh visitors to the seashore. For the sake of Abd el-Al we had given up the journey by the Khedivial railway from Amriah to Alexandria. The young Beduin was so anxious to see " Iskanderije," to walk the streets of a real medine (town) and to admire the unveiled white women and girls of whom he had heard so many tales in the Arab tents. Now his camel gave him a sign not to enter the forbidden paradise where everybody fed on meat and sugar and tea. We ordered him to fasten the camels to a stationary buffer of an empty never used track by the side of the railway.

Sheikh Sidi Muftah, who, although already paid off, had joined us out of friendship, saw the impossibility of bringing the camels of the desert nearer to the ways of civilization or into the street traffic of Alexandria, where only the sleek, almost hairless fellah camels feel themselves safe and immaculate among the elegant coupés and automobiles. The Beduins, however, were abundantly compensated when we invited them to a last meal together in the casino of Mex.

While the sight of the sea rejoiced us after our long travel in the desert, our hearts beat higher when we caught sight of the casino in all its prosaic and appropriate extent. Here was bread, which we had not had for weeks ; here was clear, transparent water and the fleshpots of Egypt. We did not shout "Thalassa, thalassa!" but from the depths of the soul "Something to eat!" Something nicer than bismuth, morphine, and quinine, though without the last we should never have got through. But I do not mean that the last nimbus of the romance and magnificence that was ever present in our journey through the desert had fled and faded. Only an hour before we had found enchantment in the ride over the narrow dam of the Lake of Mariut, and my cousin, ill as he still was, shared the enthusiasm and the silent astonishment of Abd el-Al when from the heights of Abd el-Kader the young Beduin saw for the first time the distant view of the medine of Alexandria, surrounded by sea and lake, with its slender minarets and the lighthouse, which he thought were "awanûd" (columns) so delicately built that they threatened every moment to fall down.

The experiment in the casino of Mex went off favourably for our astonished sons of the desert. Not that the sight of nomad Beduins was new to all visitors. Dozens of them are to be seen daily in the bazaars and in certain native and Greek cafés of Alexandria. But it was an event when we entered the casino with them. As one of them had to remain with the camels, Sheikh Muftah took the first turn. The restaurant was nearly empty) the people were in the open air on the shore or watching the bathers), but it quickly became the goal of discreet and indiscreet curiosity. We sat down at one of the tables on either side of the Sheikh, who did not feel specially comfortable in the chair of Western civilization. Fortunately he had become familiar with the general way of sitting down, for in the desert we had often put him in our third chair in order to have some fun, for after ten minutes he secretly drew up his legs and crouched on the chair as he would have done on the sandy ground. The casino chairs did not allow of that. Muftah took in the state of affairs with great dignity. Inquisitive passers-by annoyed us more than they did him, and as, at that hour, there were only cold dishes, the meal went smoothly. Of course he used his fingers, after a trial of the fork made him mistrustful of the sharp points of that instrument. Only iced soda-water was drunk, and the popping of the cork when the bottles were opened was greeted with great delight. " Rasâs," he cried each time, "a bullet!" The waiters vied with each other to serve us, and I am very doubtful whether they took greater interest in the Beduins or the unwashed, sunburnt, and dusty Europeans. One of them asked if we were Turkish officers and came from Barca. Monsignor Kaufmann replied: "We are Germans, and have been a month in the desert." When we left there we were approached by the first reporter. The farewells of Muftah and Abd el-Al were touching. The latter would not cease kissing our hands, and the Sheikh, tears standing in his hawk's eyes, said, embracing us repeatedly in turns: "You are my sons; I am your father!"

We looked back for some time at the fine fellows through the clouds of dust made by our carriage.

EXCAVATION OFFICES (KASR A'BUMNA), WITH THE RUINS OF A CHAPEL IN THE FOREGROUND.

To face p. 14.

CHAPTER VI

HOW THE BEDUINS EXCAVATED THE EGYPTIAN "LOURDES" IN A CAMPAIGN LASTING TWO YEARS—A WALK THROUGH THE MARBLE CITY

In front of Mamûr Markaz's house—Engaging a Sheikh—To Karm Abu Mina for the second time—A rebellion among the Auladali—The strangers are treasure-seekers—They intend to build a Christian city—My housebuilding—Beduins as workmen—A walk through the ruins of the Marble City—Our assistants—Diplomatic intervention—The "German officers" signal to German battleships.

FOUR days after the discovery, on July 11th, 1905, a telegram in the *Frankfurter Zeitung* spread the news of the finding of "an early Christian city in the Libyan Desert, with every sign of its being the long-sought sanctuary of Menas." Some days spent in travelling in the delightful Fayûm district, where Monsignor Kaufmann again became absorbed in ruins and antiquity-dealers, soon restored his health, and took us out of the way of reporters. Schiess Pasha advised us not to give any information about the magnificent find until we had obtained permission to excavate from the Egyptian Government. For my cousin was determined, notwithstanding that our scanty means would hardly allow of more than a normal journey home, to excavate the sanctuary of Menas. Brugsch Pasha, the able Vice-Director of the Cairo Museum, and Maspero, the Director in Chief, the celebrated Egyptologist, and Director-General of the "Service des Antiquités," promised to support the official request, and the Ministry fixed November as the time by which the permission would certainly be secured. But one little thing was lacking—money.

Only a man of great energy and determined to carry out a plan and to fulfil a great aim could accomplish what Monsignor Kaufmann did in the course of the following years. He had to contend with many difficulties : want of money, hostility, and jealousy ; he had to lead an ascetic life on the edge of the great desert, all of which was the harder to overcome because constant intellectual exertion and attention were bound up with the other worries. I considered the circumstance that I was able to accompany him into the wilderness as the greatest good fortune of my life. For was I not to visit a high school which would lead me into the midst of the ancient world and the enchantment of Africa, for which as a schoolboy I had been an enthusiast? If, all the same, I had and still have no other aspirations than to be and remain a modest country schoolmaster, a desire founded essentially on the joy and satisfaction that calling gives me, the satisfaction is doubled because as a young man I had the advantage of these valuable experiences.

We returned home for the summer, partly to procure money, partly to make preparations for a great excavation campaign. But we landed again on Egyptian ground on October 18th, this time at Port Said. I must here mention a curiosity of civilization that so many travellers in the English sphere of interest bitterly complain of, and which almost spoiled our voyage. Obliged by circumstances to travel via Brindisi, we chose one of the so-called "greyhounds," that is, one of the quick steamers of the type of the *Isis* and *Osiris* of the Peninsular and Oriental Company. Stiff English etiquette prevails on those boats, and many people consequently avoid them. All went well on the first day until the evening, when the last dinner-bell rang. Having washed our hands and tidied our hair, we innocently entered the dining-saloon, and I do not know who at the moment was the most astonished, the elegant company of ladies and gentlemen in correct evening-dress, who ostensibly took stock of the two Germans, or we ourselves in our comfortable travelling suits,

Three Years in the Libyan Desert

For not even the short black sack worn by my priestly cousin counted with these people as a wedding garment, and unfortunately they are being more and more imitated by the German upper middle classes when on their travels. We made two attempts to fight the fashion and the foolish convention, foolish on account of the inconsistency which permitted any sort of costume at luncheon, and compelled travellers who knew as little of each other as passengers in the restaurant car of an express train to parade in the evening in dress-coat and white tie. On the third day we gave up the struggle and dined in our cabin, our better clothes having been packed in luggage sent on in advance. At any rate no measures were taken, as was the case with the Cairo professor, to prevent us from dining in the saloon. The third day the *Isis* entered the troubled waters of the Canopean Nile, the sand-dunes of the Egyptian coast came in sight, and we could see the immense lighthouse of the Suez Canal, which warns ships of the enormous moles of over 2,250 and 1,600 yards long stretching out their stone arms into the sea to protect the land against the mud of the Nile.

The Board of the "Direction Générale des Antiquités" would not meet until November, and we should have to wait until then for their consent to the excavations. Meanwhile Sir Gaston Maspero most kindly authorized my cousin to make provisional attempts at excavation, and so there was no reason why we should not put the work in train. Thanks to the kindness of Dr. Bode, Director of the Berlin Museum, we had money in our purse. We had met him—and he is one of the great men of art—at Vienna, on our journey across, at the house of the Ambassador, Freiherr von Tucher, and we were safe for the beginning of the work, the most difficult part of so great an enterprise.

It was during this beginning of things that no one thought of writing up the diary, or what archæologists officially call the "Journal." It was the only period when we neglected to do it. Endless visits to pay, negotiations with the Governor of Alexandria, who fortunately decreed that the ground of Karm Abu Mina was Government territory (we were prepared for extortion on the part of the Beduins) and much else left us no moment of leisure. On a hot afternoon in the beginning of November, armed with a letter from the Commandant Hopkinson Pasha, and after a donkey ride of many hours, we appeared once again at the dwelling of Mamûr Markaz of Mariut in Amriah. He had everything prepared for our entry into Bumna, and wished to accompany us himself to the Karm at the head of a cavalcade of soldiers. To his joy—

for the official had never been in that division of the district of Libya under his charge, and the authorities only appeared at the "Gebel," the region of the Beduins, in cases of special need—my cousin declared that he must refuse the convoy of Askari, for it was necessary not to alarm the Beduins, who without that would find difficulty in accounting for our reappearance.

Then came an important part of the programme, the engagement of our workpeople and the purchase of horses. After a brief reception the Mamûr had chairs brought out, and we sat down in front of the official residence. All sorts of Beduins and Arabs who had been summoned crouched around. The negotiations were carried on in English and Arabic. Mamûr Mahmud spoke to us in his best English and treated with the Arabs in Arabic, and we often heard a "jálla, kelb!" ("Get out, you dog!") or a similar expression, which those so entitled evidently received as a mark of esteem, returning a friendly and devout " Hâtr, Effendi, hâtr!" ("At your service, sir!"). The choice of a responsible Sheikh who would later be the head of our colony of workmen was a quicker process than might have been expected in the East. We had refused Sidi Muftah, the leader of the expedition of discovery, because his temperament seemed to us to unfit him for a settled post, and because we had become too intimate with him. Others whom we interviewed, and who respectfully kissed our hands and those of the Mamûr, pleased us still less or made exorbitant demands. Then there appeared a good-looking Beduin of about thirty-five years of age, with small, cunning eyes and a black moustache.

"Gentlemen, I have been in Berlin, I have been in Frankfort. Take me!"

The Mamûr had reserved this surprise, and he had calculated rightly. His candidate, Sheikh Sidi Sadaui, pleased us at first sight. The examination we put him through revealed that he was descended from the tribe of Gneschat and that his character was irreproachable. He had always pitched his tent in the close neighbourhood of the Mamurije, and had rendered service to the chief official shortly before by the capture of a murderer whose robberies had been the terror of Mariut for a decade and had extended to Barca. The man, Ibrahim Abu Challât, was soon after executed. Sadaui had a wife, was moderate in his demands—the customary formula, "My house is thy house," we of course knew was merely Oriental politeness—and we could grant his one request, that he might not leave behind his friend Abd el-Alim. We thought to inaugurate the work with the aid of these two men and to procure workmen from the families of Beduins who dwelt in the

immediate neighbourhood of Karm Abu Mina.
The Mamûr also promised to have Eluâni summoned, who had gone with his camel to the
province of Beheret, whom we were determined
to teach to be our cook and general servant.
We had to give up the idea of European aid,
and of a colony of Italian or Greek workmen, not
only on account of the greater expense and the
almost impossible provisioning, but also out of
regard to the Beduins, whom those men would
simply have chased away. Similarly the employ-
ment of fellahs, the Egyptian peasants from
the delta, would have resulted in murder and
killing and expulsion. The people themselves
confirmed this later.

The Mamûr now bade his soldiers bring up
the horses, partly samples, at the sight of which
my heart bounded; they were splendid animals
of noble race, for all knew the names of their
ancestors. The price asked by the Arabs varied
between £4 and £20. The Mamûr, who was on
our side and keen for our advantage, advised us
to take two of the cheaper animals, which would
greatly improve with good feeding. This appealed
the more to Monsignor Kaufmann because he
preferred a docile horse to one of race. So we
bought two steeds : Abiad, the "white," and
Achûs, the "grandfather," occasionally called "el

THE EXCAVATIONS OF THE CITY OF MENAS.

NORTH WALL OF THE CONSTANTINE
BASILICA.

PRINCIPAL GATE OF THE MENAS
MONASTERY (COINOBION).

SUBTERRANEAN CISTERN CORRIDOR.

CRYPT PORTICO.

RECEPTION AND DINING-ROOM (TABLINUM).

HALL OF PILLARS.

To face p. 152.

Excavating the Egyptian " Lourdes "

achmar," on account of its red colour, both complete
with saddle and bridle. The business ended, the
Mamûr put a nice room, intended for the English
inspecting officers, at the disposal of his guests.
In the evening the customary sheep was sacrificed
before the Mamurîje, while in return we had a
second charûf slaughtered for the numerous
Beduins who had come on our business. Sheikh
Sadaui, the future chief of our workmen, related
his experiences in Germany, sitting round the
big fire, which lighted up in fantastic fashion the
white crouching figures and the piled-up chests
which contained our equipment, provisions, etc.
As a young fellow he had with other Auladali
accompanied a German "doctor," a Stuttgart
impresario I imagine, on a tour through Germany.
But his impressions had nearly faded away. He
always came back to speak of the Alexanderplatz
in Berlin, and of an arabîje drawn by a dog, a
baker's little barrow, and over and over again
one asked the other, "Yes, Sheikh, was there
meat every day there?" "Not only meat as much
as I liked," was the answer, "but also white,
foreign bread." "The Germans are good," philo-
sophized a lusty old man, "praise be to Allah!"

When we approached the ruins of Karm Abu
Mina for the second time, the heavens looked
as if they intended to assure us that this visit

we should not suffer miserably from thirst. The clouds rolled themselves up in a threatening knot, and the sun peeped from under them, so that swift shadows passed over the yellow clayey, rather than sandy, desert. Schuchân's tent stood in its old place ; the bearded Beduin recognized the Effendi from afar and hastened to welcome us. We stopped near by, quickly dismounted, and entered his " bet," the airy house of the desert. " There lies Mirjam," he said, pointing to a lonely grave on the plain ; "now I am alone with my children." The big camel's-hair winter tent, about 20 square yards in size, was arranged for our use, the rush mats laid in the centre, two couches built up with rugs, while our people made themselves comfortable round about, so far as they were not busy with the horses and baggage and the preparation of the food. Schuchân, who as an adherent of the Senussi despised coffee, brewed a sweet " chai Senussi," and after tea we went to bed with a feeling of perfect security. The dark-skinned company crouched round the fire for a long time, and Schuchân, whose trend of thought I know, would have replied to all the information regarding the purpose of our return, " I thought so ; the two 'nemsaui' are mad!"

Early in the morning I still lay under the brown tent when my cousin returned from a survey of the excavation field. He had feared the possibility of an encampment of strange tents during our absence, and was now content. But we made a less pleasing discovery. One of the little Schuchâns had been playing with the Kodak, which had been hung up on the tent. Sand had thus penetrated into the machine. The photographic apparatus therefore refused to work. The arrival of the eight camels hired for the transport of the baggage was hailed with joy, for now we could have our own tent, under which the chests and boxes and the two camp-beds with wire-wove mattresses, and, last but not least, we ourselves, could be better sheltered. But we greatly deceived ourselves. On that November day the first winter storm of the desert came up, and so certainly from the south and so torrential in character that Monsignor Kaufmann determined to go back at once to Alexandria in order to fetch wood for a little "house," while Schuchân and Abd el-Alim remained behind to guard our things. But the ride to Amriah and the journey to Alexandria had to be put off for a whole day. The wind eloped with the European tent, and, shivering and dripping wet, we took shelter with Schuchân. Soon Sheikh Muftah Dabún, who had heard of the arrival of his Effendis, came to greet us and embraced us as if we were really his long-lost sons. This evidently aroused great jealousy in our new Sheikh Sadaui, and we were glad to depart, having first provided Abd el-Alim and Schuchân with sufficient powder and shot. Fate so willed, it turned out, that the task of housebuilding at Karm Abu Mina —that is, of the first wooden house—fell on me alone. My cousin found other duties in Alexandria, and had to go to Cairo, and I hoped on his return to welcome him with a log-house ready for habitation.

Thanks to Mohammed, the hotel factotum, I at length found a native carpenter in Alexandria after a dozen had declared they would not go to the Beduins in the Gebel. Beams and boards were dispatched to the address of the Mamûr, who was to forward them by camels, and my carpenter travelled with me. His luggage consisted of two big sacks, in one provisions, such as bread, onions, dates, and in the other all kinds of tools. I had myself bought nails, locks, and hinges. The carpenter, a capable young man, took farewell of his relatives as if he was never to return, and went with me by train to Bahig, the station on the Khedivial private line then in course of construction from which the city of Menas is now most quickly reached. When the train stopped at Bahig, and my man saw Bahig—that is, merely a poor little station-building on the wide steppe—I had much ado to get him to accompany me farther. Horses were procured, and in the evening we arrived at Bumna, where the wood awaited us. Early next morning there were fresh scenes. " I shall never return home alive," said the victim, throwing himself on the ground and calling on Allah for help. As after many hours had passed the carpenter made no attempt to begin work, Sadaui put an end to that state of affairs by simply holding his double-barrelled pistol to the man's head. The argument was effective. The three of us completed a box-like structure measuring about $4\frac{1}{2}$ cubic yards with two tiny windows and a real door.

A roof was lacking and many details when we found we were out of large nails. The carpenter had considerably underestimated the quantity that would be needed. I determined to procure help from the Mamûr at Amriah, and rode over with the Sheikh. After several hours' ride, when we were just near our destination, a storm of tropical violence burst over us. The elements seemed to be let loose; our horses started at each flash of lightning, and there hovered before me the uncertain form of the umbrella of civilization, which would, however, have been of little use to me. The earth shook, the road was unrecognizable ten paces off, even by the Sheikh, who was well acquainted with the neighbourhood, and there was no sign of the storm abating. The tempest continued to howl more wildly, but the rain was a little less violent, and then Sadaui said in his laconic manner : " Effendi, we have lost our way." We had to seek for Beduin tents, for the district was wholly unfamiliar. After riding about for a long time we met a young Beduin, who told us that we had been going in a northerly direction towards the sea instead of an easterly one, and as we were thus nearer our point of departure, we returned to Karm Abu Mina without nails. At night the Sheikh rode over alone and procured supplies.

The next day the carpenter showed evident signs of suffering from dysentery. He was so terrified that he would take no part in the construction of the simple roof, to measure 4½ square yards. It became a grotesque episode. Sadaui once again held him in check with the pistol on the roof, and the man still continued to throw himself on the ground and implore help of Allah. So it happened that I was as glad as the pretended victim of the desert when my carpenter could pack up and travel home under the escort of an armed man. His honorarium was modest enough ; four days, including travelling and board, brought him a whole pound ! Later on he often worked

Excavating the Egyptian "Lourdes"

for us, but was not to be persuaded to a second excursion to the Gebel.

By the middle of December the works on the site of the old city were in full swing. The Beduins began to come at first out of curiosity, and some allowed themselves to be hired in the hope of profiting by the treasure that was to be dug up. As was to be expected in the East, there were spies among them, and they every week gave information to the Khedive, who was then energetically carrying on the construction of his private railway into the desert, about the doings of the "Nusrani," the Christians. If we became suspicious of such a spy, a stern "inte challás!" ("You can go") sufficed to make him speedily shake the dust of the city of Menas from his feet. After six months I came to know the Khedive well, and personally informed him of all that was going on at Bumna, so that nothing more· was to be apprehended in regard to spies. At first we had fifty workmen, mostly Auladali of various Kabyles, also negroes, so far as they were freedmen of the Beduins. Our most faithful workmen, who stayed with us the whole two years, belonged to a negro family named Chêr, who pitched their ragged tent with us, and three men, Father Chêr and his two sons, Massaût and Hassan, actively engaged in the digging. People who undertook to work for us brought up all their goods and chattels with them—that is wife, children, tent—on donkeys or on a camel, and had to pitch their tents a hundred paces from the Kuschk (kiosk), as they called our log hut, so that we soon had at our back a little village of tents. That greatly lightened the work of the guards—that is, of the permanent night sentries— who could concentrate their attention on the extent of level ground in front of our house. A large, empty Beduin tent which I bought at the Souk, the weekly Arab market of Bahig, served for the bachelors and certain stranger workmen who had no home, or for some reason or other stopped with us in passing. From the first day Monsignor Kaufmann introduced a strict and energetic discipline as the only way to be successful with these veritable children. All who saw the excavations in progress were united in their admiration of the performances of the sons of the desert. Lazy persons and those who would not submit to the kanûn (the rules) were unmercifully dismissed at their second lapse, and had forthwith to strike their tents. Visits of relatives and friends were only permitted on the jom dschûma, the sacred Friday of the Mohammedans, our pay-day, but the Ghaffir had to be informed, and he, in his turn, told us. No stranger was allowed to remain in the camp overnight, and it was known all over

THE EXCAVATIONS OF THE CITY OF MENAS.

CATACOMB.

TOMB OF ST. MENAS.

STREET.

MARBLE STAIRCASE LEADING TO CRYPT.

STORE-CHAMBER.

TOMB-CHAMBER.

A WINE-PRESS IN THE HOLY CITY.

BASILICA OF THE HOLY BATH, WHERE THE SICK WERE HEALED.

To face p. 160.

Mariut that our sentries had orders to shoot all persons secretly approaching it at night without the password. We had promised Hopkinson Pasha never to go to the works unarmed, and at night, at least, to set a trusty guard.

Work began at sunrise. At the first appearance of dawn the Ghaffir woke the people in the Sheikh's tent, and very soon the little fire flickered up before each " bet," where the men brewed their Senussi tea and ate their flat cakes of dry bread. The older ones prostrated themselves, and their morning prayer to Allah rang out clearly. Only in the few winter months had they water at their disposal for ritual ablutions. From April to November the use of water, the giving out of which was under strict control, was forbidden under penalty of instant dismissal, for the quantity at our disposal was not always sufficient for cooking and drinking. When the sun rose a horn was sounded, and my cousin came out with his ominous black roll-book in order to call the roll, while the Sheikh gave out the tools, axes (fass) to the men and youths, picks (haschêri) to the women and boys, and baskets (zállak) to those employed in carrying away the rubbish. In marching to the works these lovers of the sun shivered and wrapped themselves in their thick burnous. In December and January the minimum night temperature was very low, sometimes a few degrees below freezing - point. The morning generally set in with cold dampness and thick mist, but about 8 a.m. the sun broke through. The maximum day temperature varied with a cloudy sky between 59° and 68° as a rule; with clear weather in winter the temperature was high, and 86° in the shade was quite usual in February. Of the intense summer heat an idea may be gathered from what has already been said in earlier chapters.

The people marched with a goose-step to the works. There we divided them into groups, according to their day's task. With time some of the more intelligent types showed themselves capable of independent work, and so we had smart foremen. For nearly two years we had a Druse of the name of Slimên (Suliman) esch Schâmi—that is, from the land of Scham (Syria)—whose speciality was underground digging. The man often did not see the sun for half a day, and in exciting episodes, such as the discovery of the tomb of Menas, could not be persuaded to come up for the dinner-hour, and ate his meal by the light of an oil-lamp or a stearine candle. Some astonished us by their colossal strength and took it very ill if we did not make use of it for any difficult transport. The Sheikh Sadaui was the overseer; he had an excellent *flair* for finds and directed the work to be done at places where something was likely to be immediately forthcoming ; one of the Effendi was always on the spot to conduct proceedings. For in their absence no object found might be touched or put aside.

In winter, work lasted from sunrise to sunset ; from March to November from 5 a.m. or 5.30 a.m. to 4.30 p.m. Reckoning the half-hour pause about 9 a.m. and the dinner-hour at noon, when the horn was again sounded, it gives an average day of not quite ten hours. Those who know what it means in the hot season to do hard physical work under a burning sun which between 11 a.m. and 4 p.m. is of a tropical heat will be able to estimate correctly the performance of the scantily nourished Beduins. No one except a native of the desert is disposed to hold out in such a place for more than a week, and even he must be treated reasonably and at certain times be spared. So my cousin allowed poor families who had worked for months and were tired out by the pressure, one or two weeks' holiday with full pay. Such was their gratitude that not only would they go through fire and water for their Effendi, but they became ever more useful and expert. At the dinner-hour only were they allowed to go to their tents, where the women-folk had prepared food. Breakfast was eaten at the works among the ruins of the ancient city.

Three Years in the Libyan Desert

When at the end of November we received the permit of the Ministry my cousin proceeded in grand style. The authorities gave up sending the customary surveyor who was appointed by the Government to assist at all excavations in Egypt, but who had little or nothing to say, and yet was a sufficiently heavy burden on the purse of the excavator. I wonder if a Turkish official would have held out longer in the Gebel than my Alexandrian carpenter?

Monsignor Kaufmann writes as follows about his first systematic proceeding in the great Menas work : "At the beginning of the systematic excavations about the end of November, 1905, three points aroused attention. First, the trough-like depression in the northern direction near the centre of the ruins ; it was almost circular in form, about forty yards in its smallest diameter. A Beduin named Schuchân, whose family had from time immemorial pitched their tents every winter in the Bumna district, thought he saw some years before our arrival a pale, bearded man looking out from among the ruins. He and his sons, who were afterwards among our workmen, threw stones at the apparition until it vanished. The circumstance that just at that spot a sculptured marble figure had been seen—for such would the 'Afrîte' have been—encouraged us to dig there. But the circular

Excavating the Egyptian " Lourdes "

trough which we might have supposed to be an ancient theatre turned out to be a water basin connected on one side with the Xenodochia and on the other with the sacred bath of the city of Menas, and in any case destined for the use of the pilgrims and monks of the sanctuary. Secondly, near the spot where we made this trial digging was the potter's oven, and it was easy to excavate it. It had given the expedition the first likelihood of finding the lost temple of Menas. Here, quite close to the later extensive excavations, buildings came to light, a whole series of furnaces, with canals for bringing water and a fine cistern, and rich booty in the shape of terra-cottas. Thirdly, the semicircular heap of ruins in the chaos of stones in the centre of the town offered a point of attack for the discovery of the holy city. But the work, since the Beduins we had hired must first have some training for the difficult though interesting task, and one which excited their curiosity in the highest degree, could not be begun until the end of December. After the first clearance, the removal of a deep layer of freestone ruins, attempts at excavation were made, proceeding from the supposed principal apsis and then longitudinally from east to west and across from south to north. Soon we came upon fragments of architecture, disks of columns, fragments of inscriptions, and some fine capitals, on some of which we deciphered crosses and the Christ monogram, a circumstance that undoubtedly showed that the great basilica in which Menas was buried must have been at that spot. The further course of the excavations, however, showed that it was the extension built by the Emperor Arcadius, while the celebrated burial-place was farther to the west, directly under a second and older basilica. Among other things we found fragments of mosaic, lamp-glasses, Menas ampullæ, and fifth-century coins under the rubbish heaps two or three yards high."

Beduin imagination enlivened each new find in a peculiar way. They dug whole mountains of splendid marbles out of the depths. The sharply outlined white acanthus capitals which the earth gave up were for them "chairs" for the nobles of the old palace of the Caliph, which they declared the ruins of the ancient Christian acropolis to be. They peopled the great halls of the basilica with royal pomp, and when slowly and carefully the spade penetrated the depths under the earth and came upon the once splendidly equipped tomb of Menas, the children of the desert were sure that the royal tomb filled with gold and treasure would now be exposed, and we had great difficulty to make them approach the precious object, protected, as they believed, by monsters and serpents! It was only when the symbol of the Cross, first concealed in monogram figures, then clear in fine chiselled relief, came out more frequently, that one or the other of them recognized that it was a question of the monuments of an early Christian church, and then their suppositions went beyond the bounds of the excavations into the prodigious. A Mecca pilgrim who was passing through, wondering at the sight of our activity, repeated the words of a Sura in the Koran in which a mysterious city is mentioned that lay in ruins, and that after a hundred years Allah awoke again to fresh life. " ' How,' asked the wanderer, ' shall God give life to this city, after she hath been dead?' And God caused him to die for an hundred years, and then raised him to life. And God said, ' How long hast thou waited?' He said, ' I have waited a day or part of a day.' He said, ' Nay, thou hast waited an hundred years. Look on thy food and thy drink : they are not corrupted ; and look on thine ass : we would make thee a sign unto men ; and look on the bones of thy ass, how we will raise them, then clothe them with flesh.' And when this was shown to him he said, ' I acknowledge that God hath power to do all things.' " I told the errant philosopher the Frankish counterpart of his story, the legend of the monk of Heisterbach.

The first great event of the excavations was the

discovery of the tomb of Menas. During one of
the long trial diggings we came upon a subterranean passage. At the beginning of January,
1906, during the morning pause, we were summoned to the " Bir." We were sitting on the
drum of a column and taking some refreshment.
I remember it all as vividly as if it were to-day :
almost simultaneously with the words of Slimên
that it was a well, loud shouting came from the
direction of the Kuschk, which was three minutes'
distance from the place of excavation. It was the
voice of Abd el-Grim, the Ghaffir, who was trying
to keep off stranger Beduins. My cousin and I
went across the hill that formed the central point
of the ancient city, and met two handsome Arabs
in spotless burnous, and armed in a way not usually
found in the desert. They carried Martini rifles,
and their cartridge-belts slung across the shoulder
certainly fulfilled the purpose of making the necessary impression. When they saw us, they greeted
us very politely, and one of them took some papers
from his red-leather bag and said, " I come from
the district of the great Gássabe (Marmarika), and
only want a letter read for me which I have carried
about for a long time, and must otherwise take to
Alexandria." The letter was in German, and from
a Viennese lady who, in affectionate terms, invited
the man to go to Vienna, described the route via

THE EXCAVATIONS OF THE CITY OF MENAS.

BAPTISTERY.

TOMB GALLERY OF THE PERIOD OF CONSTANTINE.

CONSIGNATORIUM, OR CONFIRMATION HALL.

BASILICA OF THE EMPEROR ARCADIUS.

To face p. 168.

Excavating the Egyptian " Lourdes "

Alexandria and Trieste, and, as is usual in such cases, concluded with more expressions of affection. The lady also promised to send money for the journey, and did so, for months after the man came again and stayed until one of us went to Alexandria, where a sum of £10 or £12 was awaiting him. The two strange men who appeared so suddenly at the Karm were haschisch smugglers ; one of them had carried on an excellent business at Vienna in selling cigarettes, and spoke a little German—the Viennese dialect, naturally—and was glad to find some one who could read his letter. We did not consent to write the reply for him—mistrust of all was our best safeguard—and so with many expressions of thanks the smugglers departed, after they had been permitted to rest for an hour in one of the tents.

The work went on again, and the ostensible " Bir " could be examined. It was clear at the first glance that there was a subterranean corridor of large dimensions, which was filled up right to the top of the barrel-vault. Before excavating, it was necessary to remove the masses of freestone several yards high above the ground ; only then would it be possible to penetrate the subterranean building. So in the following days our suspense continued to grow. A splendid crypto-porticus began to appear, and on January 19th the first sgraffito came to light with an adjuration of the Father Menas, ABBA MHNA. Then the porticus branched off at right angles, and led directly into the magnificent tomb of Menas, where fragments of mosaic, lamp-glasses, and fine marble-work filled the chamber with a mass 12 yards deep.

At this time the conversation in the tents of an evening was almost exclusively of the subterranean vault we had discovered, and we were so excited that we could scarcely sleep, and more than once paid a night visit to the tomb, for we lived in fear that unauthorized persons might enter it at night, to wit, our Beduins. For they were not to be persuaded from their conviction that it was a royal tomb which would be filled full with treasure. One morning we went over to the works, and Suliman was the first to descend into the vault, where he had begun to empty the adjacent catacomb. But almost immediately he came up again and, pale and stammering, said : "Effendi, there is an enormous snake down there!" As the Druse in his excitement had left his lantern in the vault, we lighted stearine candles and went in with Suliman and Sheikh Sadaui. The first narrow cleared space went through the heaps of rubbish into the catacomb, right and left of which the tomb chambers branched off. My cousin crawled on his belly, the candle in one hand, a nabût in the other for defence, in case the supposed king should actually appear. We followed, and by the light of the lantern which Suliman had left there we saw clearly on the otherwise smooth ground a long serpentine track, as if some one had dragged in the dust a rope a few inches thick. It vanished where the passage became narrower, and so there was no doubt that a snake was in question. The Beduins saw it in the course of the following days, spoke of its enormous size and fiery eyes, and were terrified when we laughed at it. They declared with Sheikh Sadaui that the animal was the ghost of the king, and guarded the treasure ; if we did not kill the snake the enchantment would never be removed. And as we did not bring the cunning sentinel of the tomb into our power, they believed so, and still continue to believe so. We made use of their fantastic imaginings in so far that we assented, and supported them with the observation that any one entering the sacred chamber without our permission or at night would come under the ban of the subterranean king and must die.

As the work progressed, similar things occurred in all parts of the ancient city, and especially whenever it was a question of subterranean places, such as tombs, cellars, and cisterns. According to the season, the people when working underground discarded all clothing.

Three Years in the Libyan Desert

During the proceedings for the discovery of the tomb of Menas, if we may so name the high-lying central sanctuaries of the city of Menas, and after the discovery of the tomb of Menas, the basilica of the tomb and the Arcadius basilica and the great baptistery were discovered. Other important finds we owed to a systematic study of the ground or to chance.

As soon as it was possible Monsignor Kaufmann and I, every day after work was ended and checked, and the finds were delivered up and an inventory made of them, took a ride to refresh ourselves. The air was then clear and cool, and on summer evenings a fresh breeze came from the distant Mediterranean. As it took us an hour to ride round the site of the ancient city, we were able to learn a great deal. On horseback we could sound the countless yellow mounds of rubbish of the ancient city which spread far into the steppe, and make sure of many buildings slumbering beneath the ground. We were thus led to the discovery of one of the basilicas situated in the south-east periphery of the city, which served for a little Beduin cemetery, and especially to that of the south-west cemetery, the excavation of which was postponed till later. It includes a portion of the steppe to the south of the principal temple, notified by numerous large depressions of from 4 to 8 yards in extent, in which vegetation was not lacking. They were nothing else than tomb-chambers that had fallen in. As such a system of burial was not to be expected in that territory, a fox of the desert was kind enough to draw our attention to it. A workman pursuing a " taleb " came, as he put it, on a burrow, and wanted to dig the delicious roast meat out. He was delighted to lay bare a staircase, delighted because such cases meant extra backschish. The place was of course sounded next day, and resulted in the discovery of the first tomb chambers of the south cemetery.

The discovery of the north cemetery and the large basilica connected with it also occurred in a curious way : one evening an ancient Beduin appeared with the offer to show us for a backschish the spot where many years ago, when pitching his tent, he had found a " dead man with a beautiful gold ring." We took him at his word, and the next day began the work crowned with the greatest success.

Rowland Snelling, the editor and manager of the most important English journal in the Nearer East, the *Egyptian Gazette*, coined the name the " Marble City of Mariut " for the sacred city of Karm Abu Mina, which he constantly visited. It has as much right to that name as to the other title, the Egyptian Lourdes. Marble was the precious

material which adorned all its splendid buildings :
the earth rendered up whole mountains of costly
island marble during the excavations ; and if the
beauty of the ruins and of what the devastations
of Islam had left was to be admired, it had to
be remembered how much that was precious had
found its way or been dragged into the limekilns.
The sacred tomb already mentioned formed the
central point of all the splendour which caused the
most celebrated ancient chronicler of primitive
Christianity, the monk Epiphanius of Aschumneïn,
to exclaim : "Nothing in the region of the Nile
is to be compared with the temple of Menas in
Mareotis." It dominates the whole of the city
of Menas with its buildings. In Monsignor
Kaufmann's guide to the excavations we read :
"Where the yellow mounds which lose themselves
in the desert rise up highest, there in the centre
of the city is the principal temple of Karm Abu
Mina. These heights give the best orientation for
the place. In the far west the low ridge of hills
of Abu Machlûf, which runs south into Wadi
Natrûn, stretches across the desert. On its slopes,
where we had constantly watched herds of gazelles,
lay the ruins of a well station of the ancient
caravan route and the remains of a country house.
Farther to the south ran the pilgrims' route to the
Nitrian Desert, the halting-places of which were

easy to follow. In the south-west we found the ruins of the ancient basilica of Sidi Jadem, and the old Median road of Schakâne. In the east the Beduin grave temple of Sidi el-Fakir looked down from the near eminence and showed the exact route which led from Alexandria over the lost Mareotic port Loxonetae and the city of Menas to Barca, and between Amriah and el-Hamam coincides with the modern caravan route. In the ramifications of the ridge of hills lay villas and farms of the Roman epoch. And lastly, in the north, the plateau at the edge of the desert hides the heights of Abusir and the sea."

Two marble staircases led down into the tomb of Menas—one from the Menas church itself, high-arched, and of thirty steps 2 yards broad, and the other from the Arcadius basilica. A crypto-porticus 5 yards higher and 16 yards longer to its geniculum, with a coffered vault, led the way to the tomb itself. In the uppermost thick pieces of the walls, Simi, *i.e.*, badges of Beduin tribes, are inscribed, a sign that during their decay the ruins must have served as places of refuge or hiding. The tomb of Menas itself lies deep under the floor of a Constantine basilica, and is in the shape of a large hollow chamber, its lower parts archi-tecturally decorated, with a semicircular opening at the top. From the upper church it is possible to look directly into the saint's grave, to which lamps and votive offerings of all sorts were brought. In the Greek and Ethiopian lists of the miracles that happened at this place, it is told how it was necessary to descend under the ground in order to carry the offerings to the saint. There Menas revived a man killed by a crocodile who had been dragged to the tomb; his voice sounded warning in tone, unmasking the transgressor, and finally, according to the legend, things happened that were not to be expected in so holy a place. The lower walls of the tomb were covered with the finest marble. On the south, over the grave itself, stood the celebrated large relief already described, of 4 square yards in size : Menas as a Roman warrior, praying, and at each side a camel at rest, as an image of the desert and of Egypt, as the patron of which he was honoured. There was also a little chapel with a cupola decorated with gold mosaics, the ruins of which showed everywhere traces of burning, and then again a catacomb with its graves.

All this was below the foundation of the oldest Menas church, the basilica consecrated in the time of Constantine by Athanasius the Great, and built of limestone. It has three aisles, with a triple choir-end, and is in its whole extent somewhat more than 22 yards broad by 38 long. The altar,

YOUNG SHEIKH. SIDI SADAUI, OF THE TRIBE OF THE GNESCHAT,
THE OVERSEER OF OUR BEDUIN WORKMEN.

IN FRONT OF THE MAMURÎJE : BEDUINS WAITING FOR THE DINNER
OF MUTTON.

To face p. 176.

the frame of which is still to be seen, stands exactly
in the east, immediately over the saint's grave, so
that we are reminded of the Confessio, the apostle's
grave in St. Peter's at Rome. Only the grave
of Menas is very much deeper down than the
last resting-place of the fisherman of Lake Gen-
nesareth. In the west aisle of the Constantine
Menas church a deep shaft just behind the catacomb leads down to the holy well, of which we
shall speak later.

The Constantine temple, having become too small,
must have been early enlarged by the addition of
an enormous building, the basilica of the Emperor
Arcadius, an immediate continuation of the original
church on the eastern side. There began, as described above, the principal burial-places, and the
magnificent building of the Arcadius basilica has
not wrongly been compared to St. Paul's Church
(outside the gates) at Rome. It belongs to the
same period. The roof is supported by fifty-six
lofty marble columns, the sockets of which are still
to be seen, while many of the pillar-drums lie
broken on the ground, where they are partly
hidden in the beautiful incrustation. According to
Kaufmann, there is nowhere to be found in such
perfection the type of an early Christian basilica
as at Karm Abu Mina. The Arcadius basilica has
three aisles and a projecting choir-end, in front of

which is a strikingly large transept. The fine building is nearly 60 yards long, over 26 yards, and in the transept 50 yards, wide. The canopied altar is not in the apsis, under which many tomb chambers extend, but in the middle of the transept. It is surrounded by the lattice-work of the choristers' platform (*scola cantorum*), and directly behind are semicircular misereres (seats for the priests), over which at a special cathedra the abbot of the Menas monks presided.

Among the excavated subsidiary buildings of the Arcadius basilica the large cellars, chambers, and vaults must be mentioned, but especially the fine hall for the pilgrims as they arrived—the south atrium. Many of the beautiful marble capitals and such finds which were made here now adorn the Art Gallery at Frankfort.

The Menas basilica received a second extension on the west in the form of a fine baptistery of its own. Its ruins were from 12 to 14 yards high, and the work there was carried on with constant danger to life. The monumental baptistery is a central building, square outside, octagonal within, reminding us of similar architectural work at Ravenna and in ancient Byzantium. "Among the ecclesiastical buildings in Egypt and Nubia, which number nearly one thousand, the temple of Menas alone had as part of it an independent baptistery." It measured

Excavating the Egyptian " Lourdes "

26 by 25 yards. In the floor of the middle cupola
a small flight of steps led down into the circular
marble piscina. The baptism was carried out, in
accordance with the custom of the early Christians,
by dipping under and standing in the water, and
confirmation immediately followed in a neighbouring
pillared room, the consignatorium.

Monsignor Kaufmann has shown, in the various
archæological publications concerning our expedition, how little the praise of the temple of Menas
was exaggerated ; how, except Jerusalem, no other
sanctuary of the early Christian East can compete
in romance and mystery with the pilgrim city of the
desert. He alludes to the filial churches which
grew out of this one everywhere in Egypt, Greece,
and the Roman Empire, and were held in solemn
honour, and shows the threads and connections
between the sanctuary and the then known
civilized countries, from the Blue Nile and Central
Africa to Gaul, Germany, and Russia. Finally, he
traces the history of the sanctuary of Menas, that
for almost seven hundred years was like an enchanted *fata Morgana* of white marble, the pride
of the Libyan landscape. Under the Emperors
Constantine, Theodosius I, and Arcadius, the
buildings in the city of Menas quickly increased.
The foundationary epoch of the fourth century was
followed by the building of the sacred city in the

fifth century under Emperor Zeno of Byzantium.
That period was the zenith of the pilgrimages of
the Menas worship, and lasted on into the sixth
century. In the seventh century the first signs
of retrogression became visible : the hordes of
Islam appeared on the banks of the Nile, and their
cruel rage exceeded everything that the Egyptian
early Christians had had to endure from the Roman
Emperors.

Many reminders of those times of decay and
oppression were to be met in a walk through the
ruins of the excavated city. Elaborately carved
and greatly destroyed crosses and monograms
showed the track of the marauder; later wall
supports at prominent points proved that the costly
building material had been carried away; and, in
fact, the Caliphs had not disdained to enrich themselves there. From the monumental remains
Monsignor Kaufmann was able to prove the
robbery of pillars by the Caliph El-Mutiwekil.
" Even now the repairs and supports may be seen
with which the protesting Patriarch (the Jacobite
Patriarch Joseph, 837–49) sought to repair the
damage." A few years after this robbery the Mussul-
man governor, Achmed ibn Dinar, used a murder
which had happened during the Menas festival in
the temple of the city of Menas as a means for
fresh depredations, this time on the treasure of the

temple. It seems to have given rise to the last destruction of the sanctuaries, which declined about the middle of the ninth century.

" If in regard to its traditionary sources and to those furnished by the excavations the great baptistery of the city of Menas is unique in its kind in the land of the Nile, it may be said of the convents that the early Christian world has not known their like. Together with the sanctuaries the buildings covered a space of more than 40,000 square yards." It is with those words that the second archæological report of the work of excavation announces the discovery of the Menas convents, the great monasteries in the immediate neighbourhood of the principal temple. The inhabitants of these buildings had charge of divine worship in the whole district, as well as in the national church, looked after the pilgrims and the sick who came to be healed, and cultivated the entire region, which was then an oasis rich in vines and palms. We excavated the great portico of the monastery, the cell corridors, the halls and refectories, storechambers, laundries, and steward's rooms of the most varied designations.

On the other hand, we were not able, unfortunately, to attack the pilgrim hospices or Xenodochia, which lie between the monasteries and a further characteristic sanctuary of the city of Menas, the bath of Menas.

The discovery of the bath of Menas and its basilica occurred at the end of the systematic excavation in the summer of 1907. It formed the brilliant conclusion of the great find, and perfectly rounded off the picture we had gained of the ancient pilgrim city. The foundation lines of extensive baths had been laid open earlier, but only now was the close connection of the baths with a further basilica established. By the side of a pilgrim's pool, with a surface of 150 square yards, and a large deep cistern built of freestone (all, of course, had long been without water), the baths of Menas were bounded by a region under which the imperial citadel of Zeno of Byzantium is to be sought. The basilica offers the fourth type of the early Christian churches discovered at Karm Abu Mina. It has three aisles, terminated at both ends in a semi-circle. The first baths are in the wall of the south aisle—semicircular baths with one step, with the waste hole inside, and square baths. From the south aisle a door led into other bathrooms, cells, waiting-rooms, rooms of all kinds, among which a ramified system of hypocausts and heating cellars was dug out. The pipes had supplied the Beduins of former centuries with material for bullets. In all the rooms we found water vessels and Menas ampullæ with invocations to the saint. But the most remarkable were two marble depressions in the principal aisle of the Menas basilica. They led up a step to dippers' stands, from which the pilgrims, as to-day at Lourdes, drew the healing water, whether for their sick on the spot or to take home with them. Archæological finds in nearly all civilized countries show how far the Menas water in the ampullæ travelled. The canals which fed the stands are still extant. They lead directly to the holy spring which I have mentioned in the west part of the Constantine tomb church, and near it came to light the Greek inscription of a pilgrim from Smyrna, in Asia Minor : " Take the beautiful water of Menas and pain gives way ! "

Monsignor Kaufmann's father, Herr Heinrich Kaufmann of Frankfort-on-Main, was the chief and most persevering helper, not only of the expedition in the desert but also of the excavations. Without the eager idealism of this man, who had grown old in a generous and lifelong sacrifice to work, the great problems would have been insoluble, and if two other men—men of the importance of a Bode and an Adickes—had not come to the assistance of the two excavators, all would have been ruined. I have already told how Dr. Bode became the sponsor of the excavations. The Oberbürgermeister of Frankfort, Dr. Franz Adickes, an art connoisseur, provided more, and Frankfort did not leave the desert in the lurch. It is only thanks to the subvention of his native town and its learned institutions that Monsignor Kaufmann was able to carry out his undertaking. But it was not always easy to raise money, and I could tell by my cousin's face when funds were scanty. And that was often the case. The outsider might have noticed this by the number of the workmen, which sometimes came to be very small, and then would rise to a hundred and more. Many a Beduin suffered as much by these variations as the two Effendis.

One of our people, long after our return, when a hundred cases full of marbles and things we had found had been dispatched to Frankfort, wrote a long letter asking, among other questions, what the Melek of Frankfort, King Adickes, was going to do with all the stones, which seemed to have a quite peculiar value for the Franks. Was he going to build a house with them?

We owed also to Dr. Bode's intervention prompt help in a diplomatic matter which almost brought the excavations into danger. After the works in the sacred city had been going on for some time, the Italian Government found it convenient to pro-

BEDUIN WORK-GIRL AND BOY WITH HIS BASKET.

To face p. 184.

Excavating the Egyptian "Lourdes"

test to the Foreign Office against our first project, the aim of which had been Cyrenaïca. They seemed to fear that the two German excavators would now attempt, from Egyptian territory, to penetrate into the Italian "reservation" in Turkish Barca, and had evidently no idea of our harmlessness. But other nations have in the course of the last ten years so much justified mistrust of them in the East that no one is any longer believed, and we were not surprised when serious-minded people suspected us as German officers, or if some of the Arabs, possessing to their disadvantage a veneer of civilization, denounced Monsignor Kaufmann because he was signalling with lights at night from the tower of the excavation buildings to a German man-of-war which was often to be seen at Abusir. The signalling did actually go on, but it was directed to the author of this book when he was expected back from a journey to Alexandria late in the evening, and furnished, on nights when the moon was young, good guidance for him and his Beduin escort.

CHAPTER VII

MARIUT AND MARMARIKA: THE LAND AND THE PEOPLE

The only real Arabs of Egypt—The Auladali and their branches
—A German Christian boy the ancestor of the Senagra—
Coast region, Gebel, oasis region—Caravan routes—The
Dherb el-Hagg—Oasis routes—The land in ancient times
—At the Gulf of Sollum—The Khedive's new railway—The
Lake of Mariut—A ride along the dam at Orkan—From Bab
el-Arab to Bahig, the station for the ruins of the city of
Menas—To the future terminus of the railway at Mirsa
Matru—The former capital of Marmarika.

THE Beduins with whom we preferred to have to
do during the excavations of the city of Menas,
and who formed the largest contingent of the
workmen, were Auladali, and belonged to the
great nomadic tribe which ruled the whole of
the north-east portion of the Libyan Desert from
Alexandria to Barca, and in the south from Moghara to the district of the Great Pyramids. Uled-
Ali means something like Children of Ali, their
ancestor, who once went westward from the southern
slopes of the Dschebel Achdar (Barca) in order

186

to obtain better hunting grounds, and whose tribe gradually took possession of the whole of the desert west of the delta of the Nile, and only stopped before the gates of Alexandria.

Rohlfs designates the Auladali as "the only real nomadic Arabs of the Egyptian Empire." They alone possess, according to him, all the attributes and characteristics of the true Arab of the real unmixed type. They alone are "as if they had come over from their peninsula," proud in bearing, muscular in body and perfect in form, with a physiognomy in which bold shining eyes, a nose large and not too hooked, a sharp chin and full lips play a part.

This real Beduin race differ as strikingly from the other types of Egyptian Beduins as their animals do. What a contrast between the noble, hairy camel of the Auladali, which for months together is content with the nourishment afforded by the scanty spring vegetation, and for the rest of the year makes no demands whatever except for drink every four or five days, and the hairless animal of Upper Egypt, the "bean-eater," which seems to belong to an entirely different species !

The Auladali themselves are divided into the real (Auladali Horr), holy (Auladali Marabtîn), and slaves (Auladali Abîde). The real are again subdivided into the red, the white, and the Snêne, and each of these divisions again consists of different Kabyles. The Marabtîn are not descended from the Patriarch Ali, but from a saint (Chêch), and hence are called holy. Among their thirteen Kabyles or clans the Schuâbi in Wadi Natrûn should be mentioned. In the third line are the Abîde, mostly slaves of the Marabtîn, who, so far as they live on Egyptian ground, now count as freedmen, but live, in fact, in conditions of voluntary dependence.

As at the migration of the Auladali from the hinterland of Barca skirmishes and disputes played a large part on account of "spheres of interest," the descendants of Ali and his wife Saïde regard the Tripoli Beduins as their sworn enemies, and especially their immediate neighbours in the Barca, the Harâbi, Brassa, and Aaugîr. But the Auladali are hostile to other tribes, even in distant parts, and quarrels easily arise when large caravans from such districts venture for any reason into the desert of Western Egypt. They break out against their neighbours mostly in predatory raids, so that detachments of troops are stationed on the Turkish frontier at Sollum and on the Egyptian at Bomba, the valuable booty often consisting of hundreds of camels.

I have described in greater detail in my book

Mariut and Marmarika

"Beduin Songs" how the chief tribes of the Auladali are divided into Kabyles and each Kabyle into single families called Aïd (Ailed) or Bet, *i.e.*, house, in the sense of tent. To give an example here, let us take the Kabyle of the Hawâra, who spread over almost the whole of the coast region west and east of Alexandria and there play a special rôle. They belong to the Auladali Marabtîn, and in case of war side with the Araûe (Hawâra Hasib el Araûe). Their tents are to be found along the Khedivial desert railway from Dechêle and Abd el-Kader to beyond Bahig, between Ramleh and Abukir, at Kafr el-Duar, and at the edge of the delta, and in Wadi Natrûn. Their chief families (Aïd) are called : Id, el-Hauwel, Abu'l Dea, el Leban, Ibrahim, el Moeni, Bu eschêge, Lebett, Bu chseiem, Abubaker, Schaber, Forscha, Eschesch, Akêer, Sûra, Bu sabu, Bu achmed, Sâlem, Adeïne, and as twentieth the Aïd Bu Aschêl. I shall speak later of the great patron of the Hawâra, Sidi 'Aun. Their badge—all Beduin tribes have a Simi—is ＼＼ㄑ. It is, for example, branded on the camel so that the parallel lines run on the left foot above the ankle, the first stroke of the following sign from the ear to the lower jaw, the other from the lower jaw to the nostril, and the small line from the nose to the upper lip. There are, of course, lower divisions of the Aïd, which mostly consist of a few tents, and change. In 1908 there were the following thirteen small families : Mohammed, Hamed, Gassem, Salem, Chalîl, Schibrîn, Emdana, Ehse, Mohammed II, Lâfi, Athman, Drîs, Esbêde.

It would only fatigue the reader if I went in detail into the other Kabyles and their divisions, but a tradition that is widely disseminated among a whole region of the Auladali must be mentioned, which relates to the Kabyle of the Senagra, a family of the Auladali abiad, the name of which is connected with a German foundling. It is told that a boy named Singer was the only creature saved alive from a shipwreck in the neighbourhood of Cyrenaïca. The Christian child adopted the manners and customs of the Beduins, married, and so became the ancestor of one of the most distinguished families.

In my estimation the whole tribe of the Auladali could have easily furnished six thousand armed horsemen, taking into account the entire Libyan coast plateau west of the delta of the Nile. Yet these Beduins, although for decades they have been forced to submit to the government of the Khedive, are exempt from taxation and military burdens. The English occupiers have frequently considered a plan of imposing military service on the Beduins, but they will only succeed in so doing

Mariut and Marmarika

when the Auladali Desert is no longer a desert but
fertile land, as it was for the greater part two
thousand years ago. Very significant of the
suspicion that holds in this respect was the attempt
at a census of the Beduins in connection with the
census of the Egyptians during the excavations in
1907. The news spread like lightning that by that
means it was sought to know the men capable of
bearing arms. One tent after another disappeared
in the night from our workmen's colony, and as we
heard and saw everywhere in the desert, they only
reappeared when the census officers and their
armed escort had departed. It was only in the coast
region that they could in some measure be counted,
for there, on account of the Khedivial railway, the
police exercised a certain control. We often discussed with English and Egyptian officers the
view that such attempts, which meet with difficulty
even among the fellahs, simply contribute to the
decrease of the nomad population that is in no
way so ripe for civilization as people are inclined
to believe. The spirit of independence is much too
deeply ingrained in the Auladali. Men who from
their boyhood only hear of the liberty, the deeds of
war and plunder of their fathers ; who would rather
see their loved ones die than seek a European
doctor, or deliver their enemy to the power of
European laws ; who for ages have had to defend

the barren ground of the desert against stranger tribes in the west and south, against white men and brown-skinned men in the Nile valley—such free-lances cannot be approached with the doubtful benefits and the shackles of our civilization without making them in the highest degree mistrustful, even hostile. They fall back step by step from such an approach, and with each step their ancient traditions gain in their eyes in depth and importance.

Only a few decades ago it depended on their favour whether a European or any one else dared venture beyond the environs of the town of Alexandria. The great salt lake lies between the ancient city of the Ptolemies and the desert. They had control over every one who came into the district of Mariut, and they exercised that control in a noble manner. Whoever did not attack their caravans, their possessions, their rights of convoy, was their guest. But they did not look with favour on a European traveller who undertook a big expedition. Almost all earlier explorers testify to that fact. Even Arab sources mention the dangers that threatened in those "ill-famed" districts. The Prussian General, Freiherr Heinrich von Minutoli, experienced in the Auladali Desert, which he entered with great hopes, chicanery and obstacles in abundance, and Heinrich Barth, the explorer of the northern coast of Africa, barely escaped with

BEDUIN CHILDREN ON THE STEPS OF THE EXCAVATION OFFICES.

To face p. 192.

his life in an attack during the descent of the Katabathmos (Agûbe).

The district inhabited by the Auladali Beduins
may be divided into three large zones. First, the
coast zone, including the line of the desert railway
now in course of construction. It is on an average
two or three miles broad, and alternates between
low hills and plain. Nummulite limestone rocks
are characteristic of the higher ground of the coast
region. Ancient stone bridges at Amriah and Bahig
show where the ancients procured the building
material for their settlements in the province of
Mareotis (Nomos mareoticus). Thus the fine
buildings of the city of Menas, when imported marble
was not employed, are of nummulite limestone.
The shore in the Mareotic district is flat throughout,
although limestone shows through the shifting sand
of the dunes. Almost unperceived the land melts
into the hattje, where a few palm gardens and wells
are situated, while the ridges of hills only show
vegetation in the spring. The southern part of the
coast zone is low land that is flooded like a lake in
winter. Dr. Wilhelm Junker was the first scientific
explorer of the coast district of Mariut in 1875.
Pacho, whom we have often named, had travelled
the neighbourhood earlier and described it in connection with Marmarika. For the latter the journeys
of Barth and Minutoli are the most important. In

the Marmarika district, and especially towards Turkish Barca, the rocks and ravines were higher and more romantic ; they sometimes contained ancient tomb chambers and there were traces of ancient fortifications on their summits. The whole of the coast zone is still pre-eminently the best settled, and the most fertile and most productive in Marmarika, while the Mariut portions begin a fresh development and leave a dreary impression on any one who traverses them on the Khedivial railway.

The second zone is the desert itself, and is called by the natives Dschebel, *i.e.*, mountains. It comprises the Libyan tableland to the girdle of oases. The oases themselves form the third characteristic zone that extends from the west to the east of Dscharabub by Siwa to Gerah, Gatara, and Moghara, and then over Wadi Faregh and the southern spurs of the Natrûn valley to the district of the Great Pyramids of Ghizeh. While the character of the third zone, the oasis region, is sufficiently known by what I have here written about Amonium, Moghara, and Wadi Natrûn, a word about the central zone, the Dschebel (Gebel), will be in order. Every one now knows that the desert in general is not an enormous plain full of sandy dunes. The Auladali Desert is composed of mountains and valleys, plains of sand and stones, boulders, and mud flats. The Auladali themselves make a careful distinction between the desert where there is vegetation, or steppes (hattje, retûbe), the desert of small stones with vegetation (serîr), with large stones (hamada), the sandy desert (raml), and the red earth (hamraje, daffa), the terrible bouldery desert without vegetation. The lower ground of the Libyan plateau consists of limestone, and the bold statement has been advanced that the sandy hills and dunes resting on it are deposits of the great Sahara, that always extended itself in that way. I think it is Professor Zittel's theory, and for my own part it seems not at all improbable. In the district of the city of Menas we constantly had sandstorms, which brought from miles away the fine dust of the desert, tiny quartz crystals, and sand-corn. After such a burning chamsîn that lasted for two days the whole of the excavations were covered with fine sand about $\frac{1}{100}$ inch in thickness, and in wells and depressions as much as 4 inches. The sand and stony desert is the most dangerous and most to be avoided, for nothing reflects heat like sand, and nothing is so powerful in its effect as moving sand crystals on exposed ground.

Remarkable rock forms and pillars provide the Beduins with landmarks, especially where the changing dunes in a short time easily alter the appearance of the landscape. Otherwise the Beduins help themselves by setting up an alâm, or sign-post, generally a construction of stones or a log set upright. In the clear air such signs, even if only a camel's skull, are visible at a very great distance. We erected on the Alexander route between Mirsa Matru and the Siwa oasis a big alâm in honour of the Khedive (alâm Effendine) near a hollowed-out stone, in which every one who had any superfluity of water left some, well covered over, for those who came after.

The caravan routes by means of which the desert is traversed are of the utmost importance. In the steppe region they are sometimes to be recognized from their road-like character, but we must not think of a single beaten path, but of a mass of paths which in places where the ground permits— in ravines, for instance—join together. The most important caravan route of the Auladali region is the Derb el-Hagg el Maghrabe, "the road of the west Mecca pilgrims." It was known in ancient times as a much-frequented caravan route which led from Egypt to the land of the lotus-eaters (Lotophagi). That people dwelt on the north coast of Libya in the neighbourhood of the Little Syrte, where to-day a kind of dish is prepared with the lotos, that grows there luxuriantly. The present pilgrim route was and is chosen by persons who make the pilgrimage from

Mariut and Marmarika

North Africa, Morocco, Algiers, Tunis and Tripoli by Egypt to the Hedschas. It runs nearly along the coast till its point of junction in Hamam. Thence go those which touch Masr (Cairo), southeast through the Natrûn valley, and others by the ruins of the city of Menas (now along the railway) to Alexandria. I have even met German workmen who in European dress chose these routes, fed in Beduin tents, and joined on to caravans. "They see there's nothing to be got from us," said a young German whom I met at the ruins of Abusir. That is quite the right view. He who travels in those districts without baggage and fuss has only need to fear if he disguises himself : I mean if he adopts Arab dress without having more than a superficial acquaintance with the Arab tongue, manners, and customs. Persons who thus represent themselves as Arabs, at least west of Mariut and away from the railway, risk life and limb.

That the Derb el-Hagg still has importance as an international oasis route, as the principal route between west and east, we were in a position to observe for nearly two years. Those who have money or can procure it from relatives prefer the cheap steerage accommodation of the coasting vessels. But for near communication and for trade the land route is almost exclusively used. So that

Three Years in the Libyan Desert

annually, with thousands of camels, great caravans of flocks of sheep are brought from Barca to Marmarika and Mariut, where the Auladali act as middlemen.

I have already alluded to the fact that communication between the oases of the north-east corner of the Libyan Desert lies wholly in the hands of the Auladali. The most important caravans ply between the oases Siwa, Bachrije, and sometimes to Farafra. The Senussi monks have in the course of the last ten years successfully extended the trade routes to the oasis of Dscharabub.

The principal route of the Siwa caravans is in no way the Sultan's route, which the viceregal expedition of 1906 took, and of which I shall speak in Chapter IX. They go rather from Amriah (Mariut) through the region of the city of Menas, over the pass baptized Bab-Frankenfurt to Wadi Moghara, and thence through Gara to the Siwa oasis. The reason why this route had for centuries carried on the date trade with the oasis was that the coast and district of Marmarika were shunned. The Auladali feared neither enemies nor robbers in the desert itself. I have shown in my book, "Siwa, the Oasis of the Sun-god," that there are a number of caravan routes to Amonium.

Moghara, then, is a thoroughfare of the route to the southern oases of Egypt, while the Natrûn valley is, as before, the junction for the routes running from Cairo and the Great Pyramids to the western desert. In olden times the little town of Terraneh, situated more to the north, took the place of Cairo. This ancient pilgrims' way is as forsaken now as that from the city of Menas through the Natrûn valley to Alexandria, a route trodden by thousands whose traces were successfully confirmed by our expedition.

Over the whole of the Mariut Desert are scattered ruins of old caravanserais and wells, some with traces of fortifications, and once doubtless provided with a garrison to protect them. In the second volume of his work on Menas, the leader of the expedition hopes to publish a map which will show these and other ancient ruins in the provinces of Mareotis and Marmarika. The ancient settlement of the region began, of course, from the shores of the Mediterranean. We counted more than a hundred settlements of Roman and Arab times, among them eight ruined towns within a wide coast zone in the province of Mareotis alone. The town of Marea, on the Lake of Mariut, which gave the name to the province, now surrounded by the lake, is not to be identified with the little heap of ruins attributed to it on the south bank, and was still standing far on into the Middle Ages, famous for its trade in fruit and grain. It possessed a mosque, a landing-pier, and a ruined Kasr, perhaps an Egyptian temple. H. Brugsch has proved that it was standing in the time of the Pharaohs. But the whole of the Auladali Desert seems to have been settled in ancient Egyptian times. Scarabæi and cylinders are found far in the desert, and especially in the Kom, at the edge of the desert. Larger buildings of Pharaonic times have seldom been preserved above ground. Near the city of Menas, at Gerbanieh, the granite columns of a temple were found, above which at Abusir (Taposiris Magna), situated on the sea, the walls of a lighthouse, "tower of the Arabs," are still standing, and a few yards away are the ruins of a temple 90 yards long. That the ancient Apis metropolis of Mariut still awaits discovery rests on information from the Beduins, who found a large stone cow, but covered it up again through fear and would not betray its hiding-place to us. In the Middle Ages the settlement of the whole district west of Alexandria had fallen into decay, and the ruins of towns that can be identified are Kobii, between Abusir and Alexandria on the sea, Halmyræ (Almaida), Alexandri Castra, that Monsignor Kaufmann connects with the ruins of Haschm-el-Aisch explored by the expedition,[1] and in the immediate neighbourhood, Menokaminos

[1] See Chapter III.

PINE CONE MOTIVE : MARBLE RELIEF
FROM THE CITY OF MENAS.

BEDUIN LOOM : WOMEN MAKING TENT CLOTH OF CAMEL'S HAIR (KARM ABU MINA).

To face p. 200.

Mariut and Marmarika

(El-Hamam). More easily traceable are the mounds of ruins of the town Parætonium or Amonia, in the ancient *nome* abutting on ancient Marmarika, which was the starting-point for the oracle of Jupiter-Amon and a much frequented port. Of the oases of the interior of Marmarika there were besides Siwa, El-Gara and Dscharabub, which now belong to the Egyptian region, the large oasis Audschile (Aug·la), in the Turkish portion of the Libyan Desert. This oasis was in the possession of the tribe of the Nasamones, who, according to Herodotus, had a special kind of hero-worship connected with incubation, had their wives in common, and among other peculiarities considered powdered locusts with milk a delicacy.

Near Parætonium, the present Mirsa Matru, is the Little Katabathmos, a mountain pass so called in contrast to the Great Katabathmos. It was a more important and more beautifully situated mountain pass, or more properly a descent from the rocky tableland to the district of the present Sollum, also in the frontier region of Cyrenaïca. There was a time when it was regarded not only as a boundary between two countries but as the way down from Africa to Asia. Both the Katabathmos now bear the name Akaba, the Beduin Agûbe. From the Gulf of Sollum the route leads to the

Three Years in the Libyan Desert

highroad of Agûbe el-Kebîr, to the port Mirsa Matru, and to that of Agûbe el-Zuraîr.

The ruling Khedive of Egypt has tried in the widest sense of the word to modernize the old caravan routes to the Lotophagi and the routes of the Hedscha pilgrims. One of his greatest, and as he thought the most fruitful of his projects, was the construction of a railway line through the Mariut Desert and into Marmarika, if possible, as far as the Turkish boundary. He imagined a North-Western Railway, the lightning express which would connect Alexandria with one of the ports to be built on the Gulf of Sollum, and shorten the sea route to Central Europe by nearly two days. Sollum would have been the ideal terminus for such a railway, especially in a commercial sense. I just touched that beautiful district of Northern Egypt in 1907, when with a small caravan I undertook a fruitless journey into the oasis Dscharabub. The large fine gulf named in the Catalan map of 1375 Porto Rio Soloma presents scenery that is unforgettable. In fine weather the island of Crete can be seen from the heights shimmering in the far distance. Ancient remains are not far to seek both in the gulf itself and in the surrounding district. The ancient landmarks of the Kasr Dschedîd are characteristic of the "new castle," a Roman fortress on the Turkish side above

Mariut and Marmarika

the slopes of the fertile Wadi Dafne, and of the Kasr el-Adschebia on the edge of the plateau of the Egyptian Agûbe. The scanty ruins of Kasr el-Adschebia mark a Roman castellum that controlled the great, still used north-west caravan route, to the oasis Dscharabub and Siwa and to the entrance to Cyrenaïca.

The strategic importance of the whole district of Sollum has not escaped the Turkish rulers, and it is certain that Egypt, which had to fight for its frontier on the eastern desert and in the district of Sinai, will have a similar contest in the west when the importance that the sphere of interest in the Gulf of Sollum has for the land of the Nile is better realized. In order to postpone that time, Lord Cromer opposed the carrying of the Khedivial railway to that point of the country. When I went to the shores of the Gulf of Sollum the Turks were busy improving their position by strengthening the frontier forts. The commander of the frontier troops had at his disposal some hundred men who were armed in the best fashion, but lacked their pay. Egypt was then on the point of placing its fortified boundary farther west at Sidi Barani, about 40 miles from the Turkish posts. I cannot say whether the coastguard administration, the officials of which always gave me a kind reception, had in the course of the last three years pushed their station farther east. In any case, Sidi Barani is, in respect to Sollum, a quite subordinate point, and has no possibilities for a good harbour. And in addition it would be very difficult in so distant a spot to prevent the plundering raids of the Barca Beduins, the Harabi, Agari and Brassa. For instance, towards the end of our excavations in the city of Menas 150 camels were taken from the Auladali, and although a strong corps of Sudanese recovered the booty from the robbers and Egypt took the law into its own hands, difficulties occurred from Cairo with the Pasha of Bengasi, and the Auladali never set eyes on their property again. And more, the blood-feud between the respective tribes plays an important part in these frontier disputes.

I have often mentioned the railway which Abbas Hilmi II has been constructing for several years at the cost of his Daïra Khassa through the western desert into the heart of the coast region of Marmarika. His next project—and so long as England rules in Egypt, his last—is the new flourishing Mirsa Matru. A fine station at Wardian, in sight of the new west harbour of Alexandria, forms the principal station of the vice-regal line, and was built from the plans of Gustav Kayser, the chief engineer. To Herr Kayser, who was always helpful and sympathetic in respect of

Mariut and Marmarika

our expedition, the Viceroy owes much in the most
difficult period of his undertaking. The mapping
out and surveying of the line is for the most part
his work. German material was everywhere employed, and the lately installed semaphore plant is
of German origin. I clearly saw that the Khedive
builds "on the cheap." He commanded native
soldiers to be employed in the desert, but in no
way earned their gratitude since, and it says much
for Egypt, they longed to be back in barracks.
From Wardian the line goes through the limestone
quarries of Mex and thence direct to the Lake of
Mareotis, to the Beheret Mariut. That lake, once
feared by the pilgrims to the temple of Menas on
account of the immense quantity of crocodiles, is
now more peaceful. It forms the frontier of the
western desert, and extends so far to the south
that the other shore is scarcely visible. In ancient
times beautiful villas adorned its banks, the shipping,
by reason of the Nile canals, was constant and
busy, and the most precious crops flourished on its
shores. I have spoken above of Marea, the town
of the lake which gave it and the surrounding
country its name, and is now covered by the waters
of the Mediterranean to the depth of $2\frac{1}{2}$ yards.
Many battles were fought on its banks, and one
of the most terrible events in the modern history
of Egypt is connected with the eastern half of

the lake basin, which in the Middle Ages was dry. When the English were besieging Alexandria in 1801, they pierced the chain of dunes from Abukir and let the sea rush in over the land, so that thousands of people were drowned, and one hundred and fifty towns and villages swallowed up by the waves. Mohammed Ali tried to save what was left; he built canals and dams, but even to-day more than 80,000 acres of cultivable land is covered by the sea.

The new line crosses the lake on a narrow dam, only a few yards wide, just sufficient to take the permanent way and the telegraph poles. On the south it is washed by the calm waters of the Beheret Mariut, on the north by the salt lake of Mex, and the firm salt crust which forms its shore is the ordinary road for the Beduins who go on foot. Thousands of flamingoes inhabit the Lake of Mariut, while death-like stillness prevails on the salt lake, which according to the season is either blood-red or shimmering white, with its snow and ice covering. I just spoke of the still waters of the great lake. But they can, as in ancient days, be wild and stormy. Monsignor and I once came to their banks in a heavy storm, and rode for our very lives. That was at the beginning of the excavations.

We had been at Amriah and wanted to return

Mariut and Marmarika

to Alexandria, but did not wish to wait for the only train of the Khedivial line, which did not start until the evening. We were warned at Amriah that a storm was coming up. But we hoped to get home dry, and were glad to procure two horses, which we promised to leave in a stable at Mex. When we were an hour from the lake the sluice gates of the storm burst open. We galloped right into it. We rode along the railway dam against the foe : the rain resembled waterfalls hitting our faces ; now and then there were flashes of lightning which made the horses rear, and they struggled with difficulty against the tempest. It was fortunate that we were wearing mackintoshes and could thus keep our revolvers dry. Even in such an uncomfortable plight we were amused at the way in which our pockets and our boots filled with water. Near the lake we had to leave the railway, the lines of which were possibly under water, and ride across the ridges of stony hills. We had often taken this route on donkeys and so were acquainted with the ground.

But, notwithstanding, having reached the top we missed the right way down, and sought to go along the shore of the salt lake to the dam. Usually the shore is half salt crust and half morass. I believe, as the gusts of rain made it impossible to see, the horses only found the right path by instinct. One false step might have been fatal, so we preferred to dismount and test ourselves the suspicious ground. At last, near a forsaken half-ruined custom-house, we reached the dam across the lake. Meanwhile it had grown darker, and the storm had attained its greatest fury. To wait until it had subsided was not to be thought of, since it would have meant hours, if not days. As the salt crust of the Lake of Mex gave way and was impassable, we led the horses up to the high dam and mounted. The waters of the Beheret Mariut broke loudly below us.

Our brave beasts quickly became accustomed to the situation, even under the impression of danger in walking between the lines over the sleepers. At first it was something like an egg dance on horseback, and we had moments of anguish and terror when a hoof went into the water, which we rather felt than heard. The roaring of the wind and beating of the waves sounded in our ears like wild music. At last we came into a heavy tramp and strained every muscle to compel the creatures to our will. We had reached the middle of this strange road when my cousin, who was in front, reined in his horse. I thought there must be persons coming towards us, and I pictured how difficult it would be to pass if they were horsemen. The wind and rain howled and clattered round us so that it seemed impossible to hear each other speak. At

Mariut and Marmarika

last I made out that my cousin wanted to know the time. "Did you hear anything?" he asked; "I am thinking of the evening train." Terror seized me. I sought in vain to read the big figures on the dial of my watch. It was too dark, and heavy drops covered it. Then we listened for a time on the west and occasionally heard a regular rolling. There was no time for lengthy discussion. Either we must climb down the steep slope to the salt crust with the horses, a proceeding fraught with direct danger to men and beasts, or we must risk a race and reach our goal before the train, which went slowly. The horses seemed to understand the decision. We rode one behind the other, at first in a slow step, then quicker and quicker. The excitement and the fatiguing ride made us perspire, and the water streaming from the sky was like a precious salve to our hot faces. If only neither horseman nor foot-passenger approached us from the other side! Listen! did not that sound like a whistle, a long-drawn-out distant call of the engine? But our courage increased with the growing danger. Horses and riders flew for their lives, and at last reached the place where the dam widens out: we were saved.

We stopped, standing close together, and congratulated ourselves. But no train was yet in sight. We must have been mistaken, and all we heard was the rolling of the surge induced by the storm. Then suddenly a faint light appeared on the Beheret Mariut ; it slowly increased and then doubled itself. A few minutes after, at a very moderate pace, the Khedivial train passed : the windows of the lighted carriages were dripping ; we thought we could distinguish people inside. But it is certain that none of them thought of the two horsemen who, veiled by the darkness of the storm, let the shadows pass by and stood dumb and silent at parade.

Before the construction of the dam, almost a mile long, which divides the Lake of Mariut and the salt lake (Mellaha), the district of Mareotis was reached, across the narrow tongue of Mex, and the gate of Mex is therefore still called Bab el-Arab (Arab Gate). The first station on the Khedivial railway after crossing the dam is a little Beduin village, Zauiet Abd el-Kader. It consists of a few whitewashed houses and some palm gardens, above which are a little cemetery and a mosque of the same name, that Abd el-Kader, a saint of the sect of the Mádani, erected there, since the "devil of Bumna" had, to the advantage of our expedition and the excavations, prevented him settling in the city of Menas. We shall speak of this fact in another place. The railway has only one line, and runs throughout at a distance of from 6 to 9

Mariut and Marmarika

miles from the coast, and in places parallel with the shore of the Gulf of Arabs. At Amriah it reaches the official seat of Mamûr Markaz, the Governor of modern Mariut. Here and at the next station, Kingi Mariut, a few houses and gardens of a European stamp may be noted, and also windmills on the heights, reminiscent of the long-forgotten days of Mohammed Ali.

Along the line lie fields of barley, and a few fruit gardens; in the south, desert and hattje alternate, and towards the sea the limestone quarries of Dschebel Baten make a pleasant excursion for the inhabitants of Alexandria. Ruins are not wanting in the district, although few of them are visible above ground. After a long ride through the desert, in which occasionally a Beduin or a herd of camels is to be seen, comes in the midst of a yellowish grey tract of land the little barrack railway station of Bahig, the point of departure for visitors to the city of Menas. In his "Guide to the Excavations and the Temple of Menas," [1] Monsignor Kaufmann has described the excursion to Karm Abu Mina in detail and given the necessary directions how best to travel and to extend the tour south to the monasteries of Wadi Natrûn. The Beduin village of Bahig is a mile and a half from the lonely station, towards the rise of the coast, where the ruins of

[1] Frankfort, 1909.

211

Three Years in the Libyan Desert

Abusir and a view of the Mediterranean form an attractive background.

Then, always in sight of the limestone ridge which hides the coast, the railway runs south-west and through the desert to Bir Hamam, the important caravan station, provided with good wells, and where at the present time interesting agricultural experiments are being made. From Hamam the line goes west close to the gulf, and then, still nearer the shore, in a north-west direction. Almaida is the next important station, directly on the coast after crossing the plain in a northerly direction from Haschm-el-Aisch, the heap of ruins examined by our expedition. A ruinous mediæval mosque with an Arabic inscription and a modern lighthouse in charge of an Arab are the monuments of Almaida. Thence, a few years ago, ran the automobile road constructed by the Khedive, which cost him nothing, since all that had to be done was to pull out the brushwood of the hattje and cast away the stones. It gave, however, the direction of the railway, which is now 168 miles long, and will soon reach Mirsa Matru, the capital of Marmarika.

I have seen the limestone ridges of Haschm-el-Aisch described as the key to this interesting district. A monument of the Græco-Roman period, the remains of the funerary temple of Kasr Schama el-Gherbie ("the Castle of the Evening"),

stands in the centre of the hattje, and the Auladali
shepherds like to encamp in the shade of the small
square walls, on which I found lines of the Beduin
" Diwan " scratched. The railway leaves that
building on the south, and after crossing longi-
tude 29 approaches Agûbe. We have spoken
above of the big and little Agûbe or Akaba, the
two Katabathmos of the ancients. The Auladali
call Agûbe Minor the district between Sidi Abd er-
Rahman and the Gulf of Kanaïs. The Agûbe is
for the most part pasture land—hattje. Its inhabitants are proud of their descent from the white
Auladali, and are bound to the soil, where they are
obliged to defend ancient titles of possession against
the advance of civilization. The picturesquely
situated station of Sidi Abd er-Rahman with its
dazzling pilgrimage mosque is one of the small
places under the influence of the Senussi. In
that mosque the Khedive, when he is inspecting
the district, often prays. These inspections of
the ruler are generally surprises. He comes as
suddenly as he goes, discovers the smallest defects,
and appears to leave little to his staff. How far
the care of the Viceroy goes—or at least went at
the time when Lord Cromer left him nothing to
govern—his officials have often complained to me.
A station-master once showed me an urgent request
for a report about a broken window-pane forwarded

from Germany, where the reigning Prince was spending his summer holiday!

Marmarika lacks wells or cisterns. The ancient cisterns still usable have for centuries served the Beduins for storing water. These cisterns generally have an accessible entrance on the surface of the ground, and the walls of the subterranean chamber are scratched over with badges of tribes (Simi) and Arabic proverbs.

Those who approach the district from the desert find a little paradise in the delightful wadis which are lost in the desert on the south, in the sporadic attempts at gardens in the plain, in the slopes of the Libyan tableland, and the Mediterranean with its shining white coast. In the region of the Agûbe the railway had no abnormal difficulties to overcome. In the environs of Sidi Abd er-Rahman, on the Gulf of Kanaïs, are some prosperous farm districts. The most notable is that of Bir Beta, about 12 miles south of the red mounds of debris of an ancient town. There fifteen wells afford good water and fertilize a large palm grove with its beautiful gardens. I saw the place at the season of the Egyptian spring, and with the nâna and schíje, mint and heather, sage and asters, wild violets and white clover, I was forcibly reminded of my native land of Germany. The green zone of the landscape is very striking at that spot, the white sand-hills of

Mariut and Marmarika

the coast lie west of the wells, near the high ridges of the land opposite, so that the Wadi Bir Beta winds between the heights; and an incomparably beautiful sight it is. The fine sand crystals of the coast hills shine like snow; on them grow tall green shrubs and bushes which make the hills look like forests. When the sun throws its dazzling light over the untouched smooth slopes, showing a sharp line of cultivation at the foot of the incline, the eye delights in the fertility of the tomato gardens which, surrounded by natural hedges, fill the small valley bottom. Unfortunately, ships come no more to Bir Beta. The inhabitants are obliged to take their exports to Bir Bakusch, an oasis 6 miles west of Bir Beta, where every three months in the harvest time a ship anchors each week. The Gulf of Bu Schaifa of Barth's map is a few minutes west of Bakusch. The rocky portions of its environs resemble those of Abusir in Mariut.

Here also the Khedive recognized the value of the land. His plan for improving the hinterland deserves attention. Former, and future, results of culture in that district are based on the important wells of Bir Geraule, situated on the road from Mirsa Matru which runs along the Karm Medar just beyond the tomb of the Sheikh Abu Hanesch and strikes the route of Bir Bakusch. At intervals in all these wadis there are Zauja of the Senussi

215

brotherhoods. Interest is further awakened by the
frequent presence of large tomb chambers in the
hills and slopes of the valleys, with from ten to
fifteen loculi for the reception of the dead; a
few belong to prehistoric times. The caves of
Abu Schasar in Kanaïs and those in the settlement
of Abd-errâsi Abu Reiïm near Mirsa Matru are the
largest. The entrance to the last is decorated with
a fragment of an antique frieze with denticulation.

About the centre between Ras el-Kanaïs and
Ras Alam Rûm are the gardens of the village Bir
Geraule, on the foundation of an ancient settlement.
The point is of importance, for a much frequented
caravan route leads from it to the oases of Gara
and Siwa, and in three days to the smaller oasis of
Gatara, made accessible by the Khedive. Browne,
the English traveller, who is, so to say, the re-
discoverer and finder of the temple of Jupiter,
started from here after taking ten days to reach Bir
Geraule from Alexandria. The well stations of
El Maddar and Bir Abu Batta lie to the south, and
Bir Abu Zister to the west, near Wadi Raml, that
forms the first stage of the Alexander and viceregal [1] route to Siwa. The track of the future
railway line is already indicated in the region of the
Mediterranean coast by the automobile road. The
rugged hills of the high plateau of the desert

[1] See Chapter IX.

GIRL OF THE TRIBE OF SAMELÛS.

To face p. 216.

approach nearer to the coast, which is partly flat, partly of cliffs. Behind Bir Geraule, at Mirsa Berek, the track crosses the broad tongue of land Ras Alam Rûm, which on the east surrounds Gulf Bu Schaifa, and then goes straight to the port of Mirsa Matru, the future commercial metropolis of Marmarika. Farther inland are the hills of debris of El-Baratûn or Parætonium.

Mirsa Matru, the fort of which is strongly garrisoned by coastguards, is a creation of Abbas Hilmi. When the Prussian General von Minutoli experienced there the unpleasantest days of his journey to Siwa, a hundred years ago, he found nothing except ruins and hostile Arabs. Now a Greek colony of more than a hundred persons is settled in sight of the splendidly sheltered road-stead; their chief industry is sponge-fishing. Other settlers from Syria and Armenia were not supported by the Egyptian Government, and were compelled after a brief trial to settle elsewhere; the greater number went to America. The sponges of the west coast of Egypt are distinguished for their beauty and fine quality. Numerous traders from the Turkish islands of the archipelago bring little squadrons of from eight to ten boats, with a crew of eight men, and, provided with an Egyptian licence, which costs £4 a year, share the sponge fishing. During the summer months a thousand Greeks on an average do business in the port and earn yearly, it is said, £20,000. The season lasts from May to October and extends over the whole coast as far as Sollum.

The sponge fishers are fine types of Greek islanders, and are extremely pious. At their own cost they maintain a church and priests in Mirsa Matru, the only Christian church in the whole of the west of Egypt, protected by the cannon of the fort, which commands the harbour and the town. Along the coast, and especially in the island of Ischaïla, a few days' journey to the west, are the graves of Greeks who perished through using ill-constructed diving dresses. The Government has at last forbidden the use of the diving helmet under heavy penalties, and so the men dive naked, provided with a rope and a marble stone, which takes them down a depth of 25 fathoms. At the first movement of the rope two men draw the diver up again. The necessity of obtaining a Government licence is in the interests of the sponge fishery, for it renders robbery impossible and thus the sponges flourish better.

The great question for the future of Mirsa Matru is again the water question. Drinking water is scanty ; the ancient cisterns are destroyed. At the request of the Khedive the Artesian Boring and Prospecting Company has made trials of artesian wells. When I last visited Mirsa Matru in 1907 a young German was at the head of the enterprise and was glad to see a compatriot. " If I hadn't my gramophone with me, I couldn't stand it here," he said, and, as I was on the way to Dscharabub with a small caravan, let me hear Wagner and classical music. About 3 miles south of the fort, and in other places, the rock was bored to a depth of from 100 to 200 yards. At 80 or 100 yards clay was struck, and later chalk, and it was hoped lower still to come upon a layer of grey Nubian sandstone. The company also prospected for petroleum. I heard later that the works were stopped as purposeless. It was a severe blow for the viceregal railway, and the continuation of the line to Sollum is beyond the range of probability.

The region of Agûbe Major begins west of Mirsa Matru and extends to the Gulf of Sollum. There the Senagra branch of the Auladali rule, and even to-day travelling there is only to be advised for those who have some knowledge of the country and are well armed. Sometimes the ruins of a Roman or an Arab settlement are to be seen. West of the above-mentioned island of Ischaïla are the ruins of an Arab Kasr, named, like the ruins at the entrance to Marmarika, Kasr Schama. They rest

Three Years in the Libyan Desert

on an ancient foundation. The Beduins west of Mirsa Matru still remember the attack made on Heinrich Barth, the German African explorer, in which he was wounded on his memorable march, and compelled to flee and return to Alexandria.

CHAPTER VIII

JOY AND SORROW WITH THE SONS OF THE STEPPES

Christmas Eve improvisation—Divine worship in the tomb of
Menas—Hail to the Kaiser!—Political unrest of the
Beduins—The two Effendi are to be spared in the general
massacre of the Christians—The Jôm dschûma—Fear of
the European doctor—Resurrection of the negro Chêr—
I win my horse Ibrahîm—The water caravan—A night
attack—Siwi, the chief of the three faithful comrades—
Visit of Europeans—Beduin pantomime: jealousy—The
iron donkey (Homâr hadîd).

THE "great day of the Christians" dawned—work
was stopped; an improvisation was to celebrate the
festival, at which Arabs from the near neighbourhood of Karm Abu Mina might appear. The
sun rose late, and came out from behind the tomb
of the Fessan Abd er-Rahman like a veiled ball
of purple red. Its first beams lighted up the
yellow ridges of the hills, and the numerous Koms
under which lie buried the joy and sorrow of
bygone races, the villas and huts of Christians,
who more than a thousand years ago lay a

whole night on the marble pavement of their great temple in joyful emotion, amid the singing of psalms to await the sublime mystery of Christmas. Then the early light showed the lines of black and grey tents, and swift as a cat Hassan climbed the tower in order to hoist the two flags, the German and the Egyptian. When the black, white, and red banner fluttered in the morning breeze, as if desirous that every thread should be bathed in gold, two hearts beat quicker and higher and thought of their beloved distant home.

No horn to-day drove the sleeping children of the desert from their primitive couches. Hassan, the black young son of "Happiness"—such was his father's name (Chêr), a slave carried off from Dar-Fur, now freed and a good workman—appeared for the day's celebration in a dazzling white linen shirt, his eyes beaming in his handsome face under the dark-red turban. He carried the mysterious box, the contents of which scarcely a Beduin has seen, and accompanied us to the basilica. Mansûr, whose father's name is "The Good," followed at a respectful distance, fully armed and keeping an eye on the camp. He looked after our safety during the night, and will not sleep to-day because it is the Id el-Kebir, the great festival of the Effendis. The marble of the

Joy and Sorrow

font glittered and shone in the beauty of the morning as we walked between the columns of the basilica of the Emperor Arcadius. The wooden gate which closed the entrance to the crypt opened creaking, and we descended the marble staircase to the tomb of the patron saint of the desert, the national saint of the early Christians in Egypt, the man in whose honour Alexandria once considered itself fortunate to be called the metropolis of St. Menas. Hassan had then to withdraw and keep guard at the entrance to the portico of the crypt. The box was placed on a marble pedestal and opened; the altar was soon set up. My cousin put on the priest's robes and the Christmas matins began. "Gloria in excelsis Deo," the message of joy and peace resounded from the walls of the tomb of Menas to the deep blue heavens which roof like a lofty canopy the opening of the confessio.

If only all the Christian heroes who once passed where we are kneeling could rise up from the darkness of the catacombs and tombs, from Athanasius the Great, from the Patriarch of Alexandria to the troops of pilgrims and the caravans of poor sick and needy persons for the transport of whom the Emperor of Ostrom had organized a special safety service! Even the heathens of a great epoch appeared in the tomb

Three Years in the Libyan Desert

in order to solicit the aid of the saint as judge ; Jews of Alexandria swore by him, and obtained immunity in his temple. How they all would see with horror and terror what had become of the splendid sanctuary after the storms of Islam had passed over it and destroyed the pride of Libya!

It was a justifiable exception on the high festival of Christianity to celebrate the liturgical sacrament amid the ruins and monuments of the early Christians rather than in the Kasr. The Beduins call the massive stone house built of the ruins that we erected from our own plans in the second year of our work the Kasr a' Bumna, or castle; it comprises a deep cellar, one large living-room, and the tower which played an important part as store-chamber and look-out.

Hassan understood how to use the spirit stove and made the tea for breakfast. He also now could cook eggs—the first time he cooked the egg-timer with them, and quite thoroughly, for half an hour—and as of his own accord he had opened a tin of corned beef in celebration of the occasion and offered it to us in his clean black hands, he earned a word of praise for his under-standing of our wishes. While we ate in Lucullus fashion at the folding table which had been pulled to the house door, and talked of Christmas-trees

THE EXCAVATORS IN A BEDUIN TENT.

To face p. 224.

Joy and Sorrow

and the snowy forests of the Taunus, a salvo of shots was suddenly heard behind the house, and then the whole troop rushed past, all in freshly washed burnous, most in yellow bullra (leather slippers), the low Beduin purple fez on their shorn heads. The second salvo was sent into the air in front of the steps, and Sheikh Sadaui in robes of ceremony stepped forward in front of all to offer congratulations. " May you indeed be happy all the years," he said, shaking and kissing our hands. During the whole day we were greeted with the beautiful formula " May the Lord prolong your life ! " And many a noble and beautiful word was spoken of Seidne Ese, the Lord Jesus, whom they honour as a great prophet.

Two days before Christmas I had bought a sack of rice, sugar, and dates at the Souk in Bahig, and kind friends had sent all sorts of things from Alexandria when we decided to spend Christmas in · the solitude of the desert. Women now appeared from each tent with their metal pots, in which to receive their rations, which were measured out according to the number of dwellers in the tents. As a rule the workpeople had of course to fend for themselves, only water being supplied, but to-day they were all guests of the Effendis. It gave us a welcome opportunity of making some return to our neighbours for their continued hos-

225   Q

Three Years in the Libyan Desert

pitality. Those neighbours came in troops, mostly on thoroughbred Arab horses; the women and children accompanied them on foot. As soon as they were in sight of the Kasr and the colony of tents, they set the horses at a gallop, and clouds of dust arose. A single rider galloped forward, stopped suddenly in front of the house, firing two shots. I had noticed a similar proceeding when I assisted at Beduin festivals, and was accustomed to the universal sign of approbation.

Our Christmas dinner consisted of two gazelles that we had shot, over the carving of which Sheikh Sadaui and Mansûr presided. But before the feast came the improvisation, a spectacle that could only occur in the open desert. All available horses were beautifully caparisoned: the stirrups were of engraved silver, the saddle-cloths of fine inlaid leather-work. The head ornaments alone of the horses of wealthy Arabs on such occasions represented a fortune. And the enthusiasm, the fire in each glance, every movement of the dignified Beduins in their flowing burnous, was a joy to behold as they stepped forward. The horsemen had loaded their guns and pushed up the ramrods again, the flintlocks in order, and then they swung themselves into the saddle. In a long row the field awaits the signal, and then they gallop over the ancient vineyards of the city of Menas and vanish

Joy and Sorrow

in the desert. The non-riders and the men who had been left behind assemble, and form a large circle, just as European children do in their games. We sat on our folding chairs in the open space, and then the actual improvisation began. The men and lads clapped their hands in time, and demonstrated in a monotonous rhythm by the typical formula – o o – –, joy, pleasure, and daring.

All eyes are directed to the distance, to the farthest Koms of the city of Menas, for there will the cavalcade first appear again. Joyful notes in a high treble are heard—a woman's figure draped in black climbed up the tent and discovered a cloud of dust. Women and girls rush out, and a hundred voices greet the horsemen with the chanting of the sarlûl of the Beduin women. The rhythm of the hand-clapping grows slower, attention is fixed on those who are approaching. Individual riders are seen galloping in front of the rest and winning the field. Terrified, we perceive they are standing in the saddle, bent almost to the horse's mane, swinging their guns in their free right hand. Sadaui, our bold young Sheikh, is the first. His pride would not let it be otherwise, even if he rode his horse to death. Now he flies forward, holding his gun aloft, balancing it on his bent head, and letting his hand fall. The fluttering figure flies over the plain, while the cavalcade gains on him from behind, and this display being successful, he again seizes his gun as he flies, swings it over head and shoulders and fires twice at short intervals at the very moment he rushes past. So far as they can, the rest imitate the Sheikh. Then the foam-flecked horses are reined in and paraded round for a time to recover breath. The performance was twice repeated in the course of the day.

A shooting match immediately followed, and Hassan spread out a large red rug, on which the small prizes destined for the winners (cigarettes, tobacco, sugar, tea) were arranged in neat parcels or in the preserved food tins so loved in Beduin households. The prizes nearly always fell to the old, even antediluvian type of gun. Owners of flintlocks did better than those who had modern guns.

Monsignor Kaufmann never liked me to take part in the shooting ; the Beduins ought never to see a white man make a miss. If it is remembered that people were there who, like Eluâni, could bring down a bird on the wing with one hand, it is easy to appreciate their inborn skill. During the shooting match a detachment of black Askari came riding up, commissioned by their officer to congratulate us on the Id of the Christians. They were entertained, and remained until evening. One of the soldiers took part in the competition with six cartridges from his carbine, repeatedly hit the mark, but gave a written receipt for the consumption of ammunition.

The other Christian festivals were spent more quietly, but the German Emperor's birthday was celebrated with great ceremony, and the Beduins came in troops to do honour to the friend of the Grand Seignior, the Sultan of the Franks and Almâns. In 1906 and 1907 the enthusiasm of the Beduins for the German Sultan overstepped all bounds. The events in Morocco had great influence; innocent Mecca pilgrims from Fez, Algiers, and Tunis were regarded as political envoys. Things were still worse in the Nile district, where the news of the unrest and discontent of the natives quickly forced its way into the interior of the desert and to the most distant oases. The large date caravans to El-Wa (Farafrah) and Siwa, as well as Hedscha travellers, were anxious for information and enlightenment. They were all fanatically enthusiastic for the rights of the Grand Seignior. The two Sultans, the Turk and the German, allied, would rule the world. An old Senussi priest in the Agûbe said that England's power once attacked would not reach farther than her ships' guns. The man knew exactly that England, France, and Russia together commanded more than a hundred millions of Moslems. "Why doesn't your 'Imperadûr' help the Caliph if he wishes to wave the green flag of the Prophet in Stamboul? Not only half Africa would obey the call of the Padisha, but also the Moslems of India, Persia, Transcaucasia, and Turkestan!"

Thence came, and still comes, the little-heeded unrest among the Senussi monks, the real lords of the whole of the Western Sahara. Lord Cromer's crushing iron rule, which suppressed every movement of Egyptian liberty, spread hatred of the "Inglîs" among the Auladali. At the time of the English death sentence on Denischwai, which was Cromer's Fashoda and the starting-point of the Nationalist movement, the unrest of the fellahs had long reached the Beduins. The talk of our workpeople around the tent fires turned on the right and wrong of the "Inglîs" at Bacher en-Nil, on the war that the Sultan would declare, on the question of friendship between the Sultan and the Imperadûr of the Germans. Our situation would have been a lost one if we had not been Germans, and my cousin used to breathe freely when the numerous English officers who came to visit the excavations were safely out of sight. The Beduins' guns were always cocked, and the days of plunder under Arabi Pasha revived. Wherever I went— and, accompanied only by one Beduin, I made a

Joy and Sorrow

number of excursions to discover how the land lay
—I found almost everywhere some one who had
taken part in the sack of Alexandria under Arabi
in 1882, and unasked related experiences of that
terrible time.

With a few hundred pounds all the tribes of the
Auladali could have been stirred up to a campaign
in the delta district. The brown-skinned fellows
imagined to themselves the delight of plundering
the houses of the Christians as in the time of
Arabi. And there was one period during our
excavations when matters looked serious for us,
for the hostility to the English assumed here and
there the character of a general hatred of the
foreigner.

In May, 1907, the Commandant of Alexandria
asked Monsignor Kaufmann to go and see him
on a matter of urgency. As shortly before we
had been shot at in the night, the matter was
most likely connected with that occurrence. The
greater was the surprise when the Commandant
drew my cousin's attention to certain intrigues in
Mariut. A sheikh, Ali Abu el-Nùr el-Gherbi, was
stirring up the Beduins and demanding the murder
of the Christians. Hopkinson Pasha, to whom my
good relations with the Beduins were known, asked
Monsignor Kaufmann to institute secret inquiries
through me and report to him.

Three Years in the Libyan Desert

On his return my cousin summoned our Sheikh and questioned him. He knew of the matter, but had feared to hurt us by speaking of it. Some Beduins had been present at an inflammatory speech of Ali Abu el-Nûr, and told how the man had asserted that the land of the Nile belonged to the Effendi, *i.e.*, the Khedive; that the English were the enemies of the Khedive, and the foreigners were intruders. The day would dawn when all Christians would be massacred. That the Beduins understood that this was to happen in the near future was shown by the declaration of our people: " If the Christians are murdered, you two will be excepted, for you are our friends and better than Mohammedans!" A day or two after some one brought a message that the fanatic was to speak at Bahig on Friday. I put on Beduin dress and, accompanied by Sheikh Sadaui and others, went to the market-place and heard the speech. Ali Abu el-Nûr made a good impression. He did not look wild, but more like a man full of kindness and benevolence. No inflammatory sentiments were uttered, either because the man had been warned or on account of the nearness of Alexandria. He spoke of the duties of prayer and ablution. Only at the end was the emphatic sentence perhaps suspicious: " This earth here, this land, belongs to Effendine; no one except Effendine is master here. The Khedive

A ROOM IN OUR HOME. MENAS AMPULLAE HANGING
FROM THE CEILING.

To face p. 232.

Joy and Sorrow

is our master." Few would have been aware of the meaning of such an allusion. But a categorical rumour went about that Ali was travelling in the Beduin districts at the expense of the Viceroy and had a free pass for all the Egyptian railways. But as our safety was rated higher than the favour of the Khedive, a truer report went about, and Ali had to disappear from the scene. To our great consolation his appeal to the Ministers and the Press, the *Times* among others writing of his inflammatory proceedings in Mariut, resulted in nothing.

In spite of the fact that each day brought hard, regular work, and that our personal needs and comforts had to be reduced to very modest dimensions, there was less monotony in our life during the two years of the excavations than might have been expected so far from civilization. This was due to intercourse with the people. They saw with what interest their personal circumstances were regarded. If any one was ill, aid in some form or other was obtainable at the excavation buildings. And the smallest gift was gratefully received by men whose wants were so few.

One day the tent of an industrious workman, Abd er-Rahman Snene by name, was burnt down. It was, so to speak, the only property which he had saved for himself and his family in more than a year's hard work, for earlier he had possessed literally nothing. On pay-day we gave him about ten shillings extra in order to procure cloth for a cheap summer tent. That kind of thing made the people friendly, and was doubly advantageous because the possibility of persecution and rebellion was always at hand. A single discontented man could make his whole Kabyle rise against the Effendi, and the dismissal of doubtful elements would easily give cause for discontent. Only absolute justice with decisive help in cases of need kept the people in check and proclaimed the good reputation of the " lords " of Bumna far into the desert. My cousin, the " old Effendi," exercised this strict justice, but if an intermediary was required, then it was the " young Effendi " to whom the matter was entrusted and who had to make things right with the " old."

Pay-day, the jôm dschûma, was fertile in disputes. The wages came to about 1s. 4d. per day each, and for this they had to feed themselves, not always an easy matter. On that day there was a Beduin market at Bahig railway station, a good opportunity for procuring dates and onions, corn, tobacco and tea, the chief articles of food of the " better " people. We always had to have small coins ready for the payments, since change was, of course, not to be expected. Every fortnight one of us fetched the coins from the National Bank of Egypt. With enough of them to pay over a hundred men, the reckoning and sorting took much time, the more as one or the other had generally had an advance. About evening on Friday the signal "fadoûs," which really means "meal-time," was sounded, and all the people assembled in front of the door of the house. In the doorway stood the large wooden table with the little piles of coins: the two Effendi sat behind it, I with the register. By our side stood a brawny fellow with his gun and a wild appearance, who represented law and order, and then in a long row, arranged by the Sheikh, the people came up as they were called by name. Each eye looked at the apparently calm face of the " old Effendi," and every one was glad when the payment was made without any criticism from him. For besides the sum to be paid, there was also written in the ominous cash-book the sins of each, and often a word of well-deserved praise. The people took their money without counting it, placed their hand on breast and brow in token of thanks, and sat down in parties in front of the tents in order to do all sorts of business together. Pay-day was an exciting one for our guards, for all sorts of relatives came to offer loans or ask for their repayment. As they were not permitted to approach until the end of the paying, they often lay concealed among the distant Koms for hours, and their presence was only betrayed by the shining of their gun-barrels or their inquisitive spying.

There was a negro who kept faithful to us of his own will, but who was held in low repute on account of his debts, which dated from years back and amounted to more than ten pounds. He constantly made us the request that when it came to his turn on pay-day it might be said, "There's no money for you to-day, be off!" Then his creditors could get nothing from him, and his numerous children could have bread, which the black mother baked in the hot ashes after grinding the corn between two stones.

But sometimes these occasions held surprises for us. A nice-looking young man of eighteen stepped forward and said, "Effendiat, I must thank you and wish you all the good in life. In the course of the year I have saved so much that I am able to marry." We pointed out to him that the small sum would scarcely be sufficient for the purchase of the bride and the expenses of the wedding, and that then he would have nothing, as before. He replied hesitatingly, "By Allah, I shall eat bread," which meant, "I shall not starve." Such candidates returned later with the woman of their choice and a tent of their own in order to begin again. Another man, a strong capable fellow with a splendid beard, who had been with us three weeks, asked to be allowed to go at

Joy and Sorrow

once : " I only wanted to get a new burnous, so that my brothers might envy me."

But there also came people who asked for work, with express declaration of their purpose. Very few wanted to earn money regularly, or to work for mere maintenance. Many relatively well-to-do men worked in order to earn the wherewithal to buy one of their wives a pair of bracelets or clothes, and such birds of passage generally obtained what they wanted in a few months. They lived in the bachelors' tent. More dangerous, but not easily put aside, were travellers from foreign countries. Pilgrims to Mecca, undertaking the arduous journey on foot from Tripoli or Morocco from lack of money, or on account of a special vow, or those returning from the Hedschas, when they learnt the presence of Christians, sometimes made an ostensible detour, and the inhabitants of neighbouring tents, to whom such guests were in no wise welcome, reported the amiable things said about us, of which "son of a bitch" was the least. But occasionally a more enlightened Hedscha pilgrim visited us, and then the evening talk was interesting. There were not lacking also solitary dervishes, oasites (from Siwa and Bachrije), and Beduins of stranger tribes, from the districts of western Marmarika. Among our most capable helpers were a few Druse Beduins from the slopes

237

of the Hauran in Syria, and a few fugitives from the Turkish territory of Barca. But I shall return to this.

Many a stranger, on whose face was written vagrant habits and worse, came merely to seek a cure for some sickness. Sores on the leg and arm, with big and little, were the chief troubles, due to lack of water and of cleanliness. We were very often consulted, too, for eye troubles. Egyptian ophthalmia is spreading terribly among the youth of the desert, and we used large quantities of boric acid and a certain collyrium. We ourselves experienced that the cold night dew on our uncovered heads, even under the shelter of the tent, brought on ophthalmia. After I was quite severely attacked and my cousin more lightly, we accustomed ourselves to sleep with our heads well covered up in Beduin fashion, not always a pleasant thing. While the men bore the handling of the " Hakîm," as was to be expected from their muscular, hardened figures, stoically, the women were more sensitive, just as they are in a dentist's waiting-room. Even sitting down on so unaccustomed an object as a chair formed an act that was accomplished with anguish and even tears. In time our guard Mansûr became sufficiently skilful for us to leave the treatment of patients needing assistance for several days in his hands.

Joy and Sorrow

He sprinkled boric acid, put collyrium into the eyes, just like a qualified assistant, and many did not even come to us when they needed no other help than the famous " German soup," the schaurbâ, the pectoral powder dissolved in water. Wounds of all sorts formed the ailments of the larger part of our patients. Severe wounds from fighting, bullet wounds, and such-like were not often brought to us in the early days of our sojourn ; the men might die or recover as Allah willed, and as it had happened in the desert for thousands of years, without the foreign Hakîm. They did, however, try many domestic remedies for open wounds ; for example, henna powder, ground coffee, and gunpowder. In cases of wounds occurring through shooting and family quarrels they feared to go to the Kasr to ask help of the Effendis, for the constant patrols and visits of officers to the Karm made the people suspicious. As friends of the English we should report them, or have them imprisoned ! In course of time that fear was seen to be unfounded, and gradually wounded persons were brought to us. The healing power of the "yellow powder" (iodoform) competed successfully with henna. Unfortunately many cases came to our notice which were either totally incurable or needed the help of a real doctor. Mothers came with their dying children, whom they brought from a long distance on a donkey or a camel. We breathed more freely when we had dismissed the poor creatures with a word of comfort, for we could not help them. Others might have been cured if they had consulted a doctor, but the Beduins preferred to let their loved ones die rather than seek expert help. Not even the offer of a free journey and free treatment, or the promise of accompanying them ourselves in those cases where they might have been saved, had the least effect. The most a son of the desert ever ventured was to call in the advice of a native healer. How such persons, fellahs or Beduins, treated and maltreated the patients I saw with horror, especially in cases of consumption, which are found in the desert more often than might be expected. The old medical saying, " Quod non sanat ferrum, ignis sanat" (what iron does not heal, fire heals) is branded to-day, as of old, in broad marks on the chest and back of Beduin sufferers from phthisis. The practice of cauterizing seems to have been transferred to human beings from the animal world, where sickness was nearly always treated with a hot iron, and, as we experienced with our horses and camels, successfully in certain cases.

Only in one instance was I able to persuade a Beduin to go to Alexandria for treatment. Our young Eluâni had doubly loaded his gun by mis-

Joy and Sorrow

take, and when shooting a large bird of passage loosened his thumb and injured his hand. I took him myself to the hospital of the German Deaconesses, where doctors and sisters vied in nursing the strange patient. It all seemed to him like a fairy tale—the amputation in a "dream," the beautiful soft bed, rare broth and food, and these Christians, benevolent "spirits," who instead of demanding money gave it; and when Eluâni later related at Bahig and at the Karm his experiences in Paradise there was always a word of praise for the Effendi. It did not occur to any one to imitate him, and yet Eluâni, the enlightened one, was descendant of a Beduin saint.

But a masterpiece was to seal the fame of the white Hakîm, a cure that resembled a resurrection in the eyes of the Beduins. Chêr, the often mentioned negro, one hot summer's day was employed away from the main body of the excavators in emptying a well chamber. Both his sons were working deep down in the earth; Massaût dug, and Hassan filled the cage, which Chêr let down on the rope. All at once Chêr uttered a cry and fell to the ground. His sons climbed up and carried their father into the tent. He was quite unconscious and still, and when mother and children called in other women, Chêr's body was cold, and his brow covered with cold perspiration. Everybody was terrorstruck, and the women set up the death-howl, so that not only the workpeople, but persons from the neighbouring tents came running up in affright. I ran to my cousin, who was working in the house, as fast as I could, and at the same time Hassan came with the news, "My father is dead." We all ran quickly to the tent, and Monsignor Kaufmann and I sent the men and women away. The old man was cold, but his heart beat, though very feebly and slowly, and, perhaps because of the noise made by the women, scarcely audibly. We did not know what it could be, and raising Chêr somewhat, my cousin gave him a tablespoonful of Hoffmann's drops.[1] All eyes were fixed on him and me, and the white medicine worked the miracle. Chêr opened his eyes and made a movement as if to be sick. But nothing happened, and he sank back on the ground softly groaning. As the pulse was strikingly better, my cousin said boldly, " Chêr will live." And the old man, who remained with us to the last day, grew visibly better, and in a week was at work again. It was explained to us in Alexandria that the illness was caused by a severe sunstroke in the desert. The result was that from far around, when people were dying, they sent to us for the miraculous white water, and

---

[1] Ether drops.

Joy and Sorrow

we were sorry to be unable to repeat the experiment.

Those whom we cured testified deep gratitude to the Hakîm wherever they met him. The following may be told by way of illustration. I might entitle the tale, "How I won my horse Ibrahîm." It was on New Year's Day. A light breeze from the confines of the desert brought the first scent of the spring flowers, which at that season cover the usually barren earth with a gay-coloured carpet. I was sitting in the tent with my cousin, poring over old plans, when suddenly we heard a shout to the north. It was an alarm signal for the sentries, who surrounded the ancient city in a wide circle. We hurried to the door, on which Eluâni leaned and pointed with his hand to the sentry tent at the north of the city. There we saw an Arab hurrying along on horseback, seemingly in the greatest excitement. For although the constant gesticulation of southern races did not necessarily indicate anything of importance, the talk of the stranger wrapped in his white burnous was continually punctuated by movements of the arms, and evidently announced great news. The sentry, who meanwhile had caught sight of us, abruptly broke off the conversation, grasped the bridle of the Arab's horse, and led the strange rider to us.

Three Years in the Libyan Desert

On coming closer I recognized my friend Abd el-Schuard, who dismounted, his eyes full of tears. " Effendi," stammered the son of the desert, who was generally master of every situation, "you must ride at once to the tent of Hassan Bu Ismain. Salme, his wife, is dying. We have all been there for some days. It is the eleventh day that Salme has had the illness."

Circumspection was necessary. Hassan Bu Ismain belonged to my most intimate friends. Salme had often hospitably prepared tea and food for me, when after a long expedition my way chanced to lead by her tent. With this sort of people, the treatment of illness is a ticklish business. If the cure is successful, then the joy of the Arab knows no bounds. If it is unsuccessful the doctor must be on his guard, for the sick person's family will always see in him the murderer who manifestly brought about the invalid's death, and he will certainly be pursued by the vendetta.

I consented to accompany Abd el-Schuard, and made it clear to him that I only did so for the sake of our friend Hassan Bu Ismain, a distinguished Arab Sheikh. But I pointed out how much Hassan's negligence was at fault in allowing his wife to be ill for eleven days before sending the messenger.

Joy and Sorrow

The horses were saddled. Eluâni took the travelling medicine-chest, and let one of our workwomen who was very clever in such cases sit behind him on the horse. Abd el-Schuard offered me Hassan Bu Ismain's horse, a magnificent four-year-old Arab steed. He rode my beast. The cavalcade, speeded by the good wishes of our people, was soon on its way, and after a three hours' ride we reached Hassan's tent. He came to meet us outside the encampment, and after the customary forms of greeting, bewailed his need in extravagant terms. In the men's tent, which it was impossible to avoid, although we could hear the sick woman's groans, sat about twenty members of the family, who each had to be greeted, and who expressed the hope that with God's blessing the cure would be successful. With an " If God wills," I left them, and entered Salme's chamber. I had first gently to explain to the women who were standing round Salme wailing and groaning that the invalid must be at once left alone. They obeyed.

Salme, who had the reputation of a Beduin beauty, was yellow and pale, and complained of pains in the stomach. The diagnosis did not take long. The symptoms pointed to colic, and our workwoman, with the help of one of Hassan's girls, gave the necessary alleviation. We meanwhile withdrew into the men's tent, where Hassan Bu Ismain played the host with all the grace and charm of the Arab. While we smoked cigarettes and sipped tea, suddenly a cry of joy came from the women's chamber. Salme was better. A stone fell from my heart. The medicine had done its duty, as was to be expected in the case of a young woman like Salme, and the normal course had followed.

I thought they would never cease shaking hands. I assured Hassan that he need not fear any recurrence of the illness, and he embraced me passionately. Repeated cries of joy continued to confirm the success of the cure.

When Hassan's servants left the tent and hastened to the herds, I urged our departure, and refused to stay, in spite of the Sheikh's request, though I should have been glad to let Eluâni and our workwoman share in the feast of joy. When we three were in the saddle, surrounded by the whole joyful family, Hassan came up to my horse with a fat sheep in his arms. "Take it : may God reward you!" he cried with tears of joy in his eyes. I stopped him : "You know, Hassan, that I haven't saved your wife on that account ; now grant me my wish." Then the broad-shouldered man went to my servant's horse, laid the sheep across the saddle-bows,

Joy and Sorrow

came back to me, and said: "Go in peace; as God wills, your wish shall be granted."

When we had reached our camp and I described our strange journey, and also mentioned that Hassan would come to-morrow to bring me his horse Ibrahîm, for which I had in vain been negotiating with him for months, they all thought it most unlikely.

But the next day Hassan Bu Ismain sent the horse by one of his servants, the horse whose eyes, as is said in a song of praise to the steed, resemble the souls of men, whose voice is like the roaring of the storm, and whose heart resembles the fire of the Samum.

The question is to be asked if the Effendi, amid all the disagreeables of the desert and the excavations, were never themselves in need of the Hakim. With the exception of ophthalmia, the return of which at its first entrance was guarded against by prophylactic means, we only suffered from touches of dysentery, and now and then perhaps a trace of what is generally called tropical fever. Heaven evidently protected us. For on an average one of us went to Alexandria once a fortnight, where we found a circle of compatriots eager to help us. We always lacked, however, two things, fresh bread and good water, the want of which we felt deeply. A few cases of Giesshübler were our own reserve in dire need, and were always with us. From April to November the daily quantum of water was, as far as possible, drunk in the form of tea or just coloured with red wine. A present from Hopkinson Pasha of two big earthen filters, holding together about 120 gallons, was a great comfort. Placed in the open air, they kept the liquid, even in the hot months, comparatively cool. In those months the water caravan, for which we had purchased three camels for about £5, went to Bir Eisêle, near Bahig, every other day, where as many as twelve large skins of water were obtained. As a rule, the quality of the water was good. Of course, it was never clear, but the Berkefeld filters were useless, since it was necessary to clean the filtering tubes every few minutes.

When the number of workmen was at or over one hundred, the water caravan had to go every day, and the two horses had to be added to it. The bay possessed a thirsty soul. At the time of the watering, two hours before sunset, he followed Mansûr, the guard, about, neighing for joy whenever he heard a pail rattle or the water caravan came in sight. The daily provision of water was stored in a large closed cask kept in a three-cornered wooden house. The daily giving out of it took place under my supervision, because no one was to be trusted with the precious liquid. Each tent received a pailful. While work was in progress, a tin can containing about 10 gallons was at the disposal of each larger group of workers; as a rule, it was only drunk during the pauses, and refilled three times according to need. Umm Sâd (Mother Sâd), who saved Monsignor Kaufmann's life, looked after this water service for a whole year; it included the filling and carrying of these cans over the whole extent of the excavations.

All attempts to make the cisterns and wells we dug out of service to us failed. For 22 yards down there was no water; to dig farther was not permitted by the statics of the limestone walls. Most likely, even so, we should only have come upon some salt liquid. But we found a benefit in a whole series of fine cisterns that, in the interests of archæology, had been cleared out, and were still in such good condition that from November to February, after a single tropical shower, the large underground reservoir was filled with excellent water, enough to last a fortnight. Such seasons of plenty made the friendly Beduin tribes bring their herds of camels to the city of Menas, where the beasts could drink to their hearts' content. Our own camels were, as a rule, watered every three days, and in the interval felt no thirst. In the interior of the desert the animals are taken to the wells every five days.

The assertion of our people that during the whole spring the camels would require no water was in reality greatly exceeded. From the beginning of January to April 10, 1907, for three months, the animals not only did not drink a drop of water, but refused a pailful if put before them. The succulent achdâr, the green weeds found in the desert in spring, sufficed them, and they grew well on the ancient mounds of the city of Menas. The apparently clumsy creatures sought out their favourite bits among the blocks of stone, and even the horses which pastured in the wadis—the old roads to the sacred city—at that season only drank a pailful of water every three days.

So, with the exception of a few days, the water question was a capital one, not only for life, but for general conditions. It needed the service almost continually of three camels and two men, and was hard work, for the filling of the deep cisterns of Eisêle, work for which every Beduin must bring his own large rope and implements for the wells, often took hours. How often when the water was being given out my cousin spoke to the people and showed them the material value of the gift. Then they used to say, thanking him, " Indeed, Effendi, the water is money!"

Joy and Sorrow

Quite rightly then did the leader of the excavations in his first official report praise the appearance of the water caravan at Karm Abu Mina in the beautiful poetical words of the Rufus epistle of Pope Leo XIII: "Candida Lympha! Datum vix quidquam hoc munere maius"—"Pure liquid, there is scarcely a greater gift than this!"

And so it is characteristic that the first attack of stranger Beduins on the excavators had evidently no other ground than a planned water-raid. It was on a dark spring evening, when Monsignor Kaufmann was working at the home-made writing-table, while I was already dreaming on the bed. Mansûr, the guard, knocked at the door, and said that he heard people approaching on the south who did not answer his challenge. Monsignor Kaufmann went to one of the windows looking south, opened the wooden shutters, and at the same moment two shots were heard and struck the mud wall. The lamp was quickly extinguished, for on the opening of the shutters it offered a mark. My cousin took his Winchester rifle, and kneeling down, fired in quick succession eleven sharp shots in the direction of the enemy, loaded again, and fired another eleven. The whole camp was, of course, alarmed, and our people plainly heard a troop fleeing. In their hurried flight a cask had struck against some firm object, probably the stirrups. The next morning the track, which pointed to several adults and two donkeys, was followed up, but without result. It was lucky that the hostile bullets had not hit any of the horses or camels, that were spending the night in rank and file in the open air close to the excavation buildings.

This night attack helped to spread the fame of our Winchester rifle. The rumour got abroad that it could be fired forty times without reloading, and the well‑preserved secret helped materially to our safety. No one lightly ventured near the camp by night, or even in the daytime, without the authorization of the guard, and Sheikh Sadaui set up a number of stone pyramids on the most distant Koms of the city of Menas, which usually form landmarks for wanderers in the desert, in order to draw the attention of strangers to certain perils : men and beasts, for instance, might, if they approached the undermined ground, sink into cisterns and tombs.

Three dogs counted among the lesser joys of our existence, presents from friends : a Beduin dog named Abiad, a young fellah dog whom we called Amenotep, and Siwi, the dog *par excellence*, one of the wonders of Bumna. Abiad, so called on account of his white colour, a wild Beduin Pomeranian, had been tamed by us with difficulty.

Joy and Sorrow

Entering the house was the hardest for him. He was accustomed to the desert and, like most Beduins, felt unsafe and unhappy within walls. All interest was concentrated on Siwi, whose brief earthly life will live in the legends of the Auladali when the epitaphs in the dogs' cemetery at Paris are long rotted away and destroyed. Siwi was given to me as a young pointer of Anglo-German cross-breed, an English pointer by a German hound of ancient descent, when I was travelling with the Khedive in Marmarika. The dog's arrival at Karm Abu Mina excited the greatest astonishment among those persons who had never been in the Nile valley and had never seen a European dog. In contrast to the wolf-hounds and pointers of the desert that guarded the tents of the Arabs, Siwi—the Beduins called him Siwaner, because they thought he came from the oasis—although only at most a year old, seemed a giant. When, eager to play, he approached them, they fled in terror. In the early days of his presence the cry "Come here, Effendi, and set us free!" was often heard. For the negroes and those dressed in dark apparel and the poor, Siwi was an object of continual fear, but no one ventured to illtreat him. Unfortunately we spoiled him, and the English officers and others of our guests made a pet of him. Only in that way can we account for the fact that, although by race he should have been a passionate sportsman, he refused the chase. Every chameleon or lizard put him off from his goal; he never ran to the booty at the sound of the shot, but away from the sand eddies caused by the bullet. At shooting matches he had to be chained up, for Siwi ran after each bullet. His only form of hunting consisted in dislodging the birds of passage, and still more in pursuing the edible djarbua. Siwi used to leave the building in the evening, and it was a delight to see him rush over the plain and watch how the swift runner gained on the little gazelle. On account of their swiftness, the Beduins call these delicacies, which I often ate, "gazal zughair." While the Beduin dog never left the wide region of the tent, Siwi, when he dared, accompanied all the rides and even the longer expeditions. When he felt tired, he howled until some one took him up on the camel, from which coign of vantage he surveyed the world, comfortable and well content.

In the evening ride which I took with my cousin, Siwi was useful as a protection against the dogs in the stranger tents, who were accustomed to bark dreadfully at every horseman. It was amusing to see the white and yellow troop in dozens rushing from the distance and then suddenly stopping:

they saw an animal such as they had never seen before. If Siwi ran up to them inquisitive and amiable, the foe turned on him, and then the dog, who was by nature a highly nervous creature, pursued the others in long leaps. But if we met a flock of sheep, then at the sight of Siwi there was a general stampede. It happened in Behêret, the north-west province of the delta, that a herd of steatopygous sheep, fleeing before Siwi, could find no other way than to swim across a little irrigation canal. In the environs of Ezbet el-Menchieh, a fellah village, situated half in the desert, Siwi was called "Effendi" by the terrified people, and there were peasants who actually believed that the Frankish dog had more intelligence than his Egyptian colleagues. Very characteristic, too, is a meeting I had on a journey to the Gulf of Sollum. Siwi was with us, and one day a strange caravan came in sight. It went by at a fair distance, but a man separated from it and came across the long way to me. He was sent to ask what sort of an animal Siwi was; they had been disputing, and some had said it was too active for a young calf, and others that it was much too big for a dog.

So Siwi, in contrast to his friends and excellent watchdogs, Abiad and Amenotep, was a show dog. When the others lay on guard out in the open in all weathers, if it was only slightly cold he asked to be let in. He also disliked the great heat. On the march he ran in the shade of the camels, among the excavations he sought out cool subterranean spaces. His greatest crime was that he would let no one have anything to eat until he was satisfied. Among the Beduins the dog is "unclean," and is not permitted to step on the mats on which the people sit, but Siwi quite unconcernedly lay down on them. He was later treacherously shot by a terrified fellah, and as the murder of a dog is reckoned a great crime among the natives, I offered a reward for information as to the perpetrator. Many came and announced that they were on the track, but nothing certain was established.

It was a great pleasure when visitors came to Karm Abu Mina, and in the second year of the excavations it was of frequent occurrence. Besides men of science, the officers of the English army formed a large contingent. Many people considered the expeditions into the desert among their pleasantest memories of Egypt. At the head of distinguished names stand the Duke of Connaught and Lord Cromer's successor, Sir Eldon Gorst, the uncrowned King of Egypt. High officials in the ministerial and diplomatic world also came, and, last but not least, compatriots.

Joy and Sorrow

The arrival of the great merchant of Alexandria, Heinrich Bindernagel, a warm patron of the excavations, with his wife and son was quite romantic. The man to whom Germanism in Egypt owes so much, in whose hospitable house science was always sure of a welcome, too early fell a victim to an insidious disease. One dark night they drew near—I had ridden out to meet them—the sacred city. A fire burnt in the desert for a guide; and on our arrival Monsignor Kaufmann had a salute fired in honour of the first German lady who visited us. We put our guests in the log-house, the son sharing our tent, and the Berber servants that of the Sheikh. After the usual sheep was slaughtered our people arranged a night improvisation by the big fire. We, with our guests, occupied folding chairs. The Beduins formed their large open semicircle, and began their greeting with rhythmical hand-clapping, which unexpectedly was transformed into pantomimic action. A veiled figure sprang forward in the light of the flames, and apparently apostrophized the assembly. Striding from one to the other, and swaying in time with the sound of the primitive orchestra of hands, he seemed to be looking for something. His manner made it clear that the something was his enemy. So he strode up and down, sometimes stopping longer at one, and then, in disappointment, turning to the next. He sought, and at last he found. He stopped in front of a young Beduin who, closely wrapped in his burnous, was almost unrecognizable. The seeker stretched out a dark hand and seized the folds of the burnous that were about the head. A young face looked out, angry and terrified; it is he, the foe who has enticed his love away. The seeker throws back his burnous, and stands disclosed, recognized by all as Haïn Makain of the tribe of the Harabi in Barca; opposite him stands the slender youth, an Auladali, the amiable Oâfi Sâle. Haïn's hands seize the dagger in his belt, but he restrains himself. Both step into the foreground, the action grows to a climax, the rest of the Beduins share the excitement of the disputants, and the clapping and psalm-like murmuring of the chorus grow faster every minute. Explanations are demanded. Oâfi, protesting, bares his breast as if he would say : "I will tear my heart out of my body before I can cease to love the brown maid." Haïn is in despair : the big, strong Harabi cannot hurt the weak boy; he must renounce, and go forth into other lands and strange tents. But the youth cannot do that, and does not flinch when Haïn flies at him and throttles him. He must give in, but the argument of force is in vain. He cannot, dare not give in. The chorus draws nearer, the

Joy and Sorrow

semicircle closes in, as if they would come to the rescue. The rhythmical clapping grows faster, as if to keep up with the course of the action, which goes forward unrestrained. Oâfi, who carries no weapon, protects himself as well as he can. Haïn swings his dagger, but often lets his hand fall. The youth has again shown him his bare breast; let him stab and then he will have rest. And again the torture of jealousy and love is renewed, until the victim falls with a horrible cry. Haïn's dagger has struck home, and Oâfi must die. He dies as only great actors die, too beautifully and too terribly to be true. His enemy sinks down by his side, covers the dead man with the burnous, and raises his arms to the dark heavens as if imploring Allah to hide the deed of blood.

Then suddenly the chorus stops. The play is over, and our guests were as much affected as we were, for the Sheikh had arranged the improvisation of his own accord, so that it was a pleasant surprise for us. The night quarters in the Kuschk, the box-like log-house, which included in its contents skulls and such things, did not wholly lack what was required in a bedroom, and was, of course, praised by our kind guests. They asked about the scratching noise that they heard under the floor in the middle of the night, and my cousin gave the good-humoured assurance that it was only rats, the charming and harmless djarbua of the desert. Soon after his return Herr Heinrich Bindernagel described his visit to the city of Menas in the *Egyptian Gazette* under the title of "The Shrine of St. Menas; a Modern Pilgrimage."

Original intermezzos were not lacking when visitors came to the city of Menas. A distinguished diplomatist, whom I accompanied later to Wadi Natrûn, spent a night with us in constant fear of attacks, because one of our sentries fired a shot to frighten off some one. The arrival of the first "homâr hadîd" was an amusing event. Hassan chanced to be on the tower of the Kasr, and came rushing down out of breath. "Effendi," he shouted in the distance, "the iron donkey is there." It was during the midday pause, and my cousin, very curious, hurried up at the strange news. Sheikh Sadaui explained that it was a bicycle. Soon after the glittering machine appeared, pushed by its owner, an English bank director, his ladies preferring real living donkeys, the strange cavalcade being completed by a black soldier on a tall white horse. The iron donkey was stabled in the Kuschk, which at that time served as kitchen, and Hassan, who had never before seen the creature that had often been described to him, did not dare to touch it. We amused ourselves by telling Hassan that if he

Joy and Sorrow

did it would cry out, and taking his black hand, we pressed it on the hooter. The consequence was that the man fled at great speed to his mother's tent. When work was over all the Beduins who did not know the mysterious machine filed past the iron donkey. Its owner is one of the most venturesome visitors to the Mariut Desert ; he often goes on his expeditions alone and unarmed, and does not object to spending the night in a Beduin tent. They were often anxious about him in Alexandria.

Another visitor to the city of Menas who used in the spring to wander alone through the desert was recognized by our Beduins. They designated him " root-seeker," and as they understood nothing of botany, regarded him as a madman. But the son of the desert respects a madman as a higher being, whose mind is with God.

CHAPTER IX

WITH THE VICEROY TO THE OASIS OF AMON—
AN HISTORIC PROGRESS THROUGH THE
DESERT IN THE STEPS OF ALEXANDER THE
GREAT

Abbas Hilmi II of Egypt—The royal caravan—Why the Viceroy
travels—The "crowned fellah" a title of honour—Table-
talk in the desert—The Sultan's road, the Alexander route
—Reception in the oasis of Siwa—The palm-grove men and
their life—The Egyptian Governor—The prison as dark-
room—Murder of the Mamûr of Siwa, 1910—Flora and
fauna—Mud towns and troglodytes—The Oracle Temple and
other classic ruins—Araschieh, the enchanted lake with
Solomon's crown—From the Fountain of the Sun—Kasr el-
Guraîschet—My ride to Zetûn—Return home—How Umm
Sâd saved my cousin's life

ON February 4, 1906, a mounted courier brought
a telegram containing an invitation from the
Khedive to take part in his great progress through
the desert to Amonium. So far neither of us had
seen the ruler of the country, nor had any intercourse with him, but we knew that our proceedings
in Mariut were regularly reported to him, and that
he purposed to visit the excavations at the first

INTERIOR OF AN ANCIENT TOMB.

ROCK FORMATION AT MENSCHIJE.

To face p. 262.

The Oasis of Amon

opportunity. The Viceroy's invitation was directed to Monsignor Kaufmann, and asked which of us would take the month's journey. It signified a very great honour for the two German explorers, and my cousin, who travelled back to Alexandria with the answer, was everywhere unreservedly congratulated. The thing was too great a sacrifice for him. Under no circumstances would he leave the excavations even for a week, for all the signs of the discovery of the tomb of St. Menas were at hand. But he enthusiastically urged it on me, as if that was necessary, and when he came back from Alexandria I had only three or four days in which to study the works of Minutoli, Rohlfs, and Robecchi-Brichetti, and to make preparations for the journey. The order to depart came as suddenly as the invitation from the Eastern potentate.

On February 9th I bade farewell to my cousin, who now remained in the desert alone with his Beduins. The viceregal train conveyed me to what was then the last station, whence an escort brought me in a ride of eight hours to the automobile garage, in the centre of Marmarika. When we reached it a square-built, cheerful-looking gentleman in khaki dress came to meet me, kindly assisted me to dismount, and held my horse's bridle. " How do you do, Herr Falls ? " he said in German ; " I am glad to make your acquaintance." The speaker was no other than Abbas Hilmi II, Khedive of Egypt. I was to have the good fortune to know him for some time more intimately than many who desired to enlist his favour. It was of practical advantage to us, in that his officials did us good service where it was not exactly their duty, and still more in respect to the natives. The intercourse with the "Effendine" was not unobserved by the Beduins, and contributed to our safety. During the progress through the desert the Khedive was accompanied by only four Europeans, among them his doctor, Kautzky Bey. The rest of the suite consisted of Egyptians and Arabs. I shared a double tent with a young French major, Vicomte de St. Exupéré, who was also travelling as a guest of the Khedive. The endless caravan was generally on the move the whole day, the commissariat division hurrying on some hours in advance, so that the camp was in order when we arrived, and after making onr toilette the four Europeans went to the large dining-tent. Here nothing was lacking, from table silver and fine damask tablecloths to the dishes which the Berber cook, Abu Balter, the "father of the hoe," knew how to prepare with exquisite art. As a good Moslem the Khedive drank no wine or spirits and did not smoke, but he placed no such prohibition on his guests, and was an excellent host.

ABBAS HILMI II, KHEDIVE OF EGYPT.

SCULPTURED LION FROM AMONIUM
(FRANKFORT MUSEUM).

THE OLDEST STATUETTE
OF THE MADONNA (CITY
OF MENAS).

To face p. 264.

The Oasis of Amon

Abbas Hilmi II was born July 14, 1874. At eighteen years of age, while studying at the Ritterakademie in Vienna, he was called to the throne at the death of his father, Tewfik Pasha, under whom Egypt was occupied by the English. The Khedive is directly descended from Mohammed Ali, the famous son of a Rumelian guard, the liberator of Egypt from the rule of the Mamelukes and the founder in 1841 of the new Khedivial dynasty. A rare sense of duty and hard industry have made Abbas Hilmi a ruler who serves as a brilliant example to all the officials of his country. At the great State ceremonies and on official occasions he appears in great pomp in his palaces, equipped with the luxury of East and West combined, and always with royal dignity. But he likes to lay all this aside whenever the business of State allows. It is not my purpose here to describe his political activity, which is, of course, much curtailed by the English occupation and which has evoked various verdicts according to the different parties and races. The Khedive does not keep a harem in the Oriental sense. He lives with two wives only. He has five children by the Khediva, of whom one is the Crown Prince, Mohammed Abd el-Monein, who is still a boy. He made a second marriage with an Austrian lady, who immediately before his journey to Mecca embraced Islamism.

Three Years in the Libyan Desert

During the whole of the long and interesting journey I very seldom saw Abbas Hilmi out of humour. If his people were awkward in pitching the tents or watering the beasts, or if any of the comforts he expected were lacking, he could thunder in Arabic and swing his kurbâsch in a threatening manner. But it should be observed that it was always more on his guests' account than on his own, for his frugality was exemplary for enterprises that need a sober, regular way of living. The evening talk was prolonged. Sometimes Abbas Hilmi spoke of the political situation of his country, and he did not conceal the deep discontent with which he regarded the autocratic—nay, the brusque —behaviour of Lord Cromer, who treated him as an executive official, not as an actual ruler. But his inclination to such frank speaking was unfortunately soon at an end. One day he said to me, "Haven't you noticed that Herr N. N. was coolly taking notes yesterday evening? I must keep guard on my words even here in the desert, so we won't talk about politics any more." As I often made digressions from the road in order to survey the route and because my cousin had laid on me the obligation of looking out for antiquities, the Khedive put at my disposal, besides my camel, which on account of his swiftness bore the name "Naâme" (ostrich), a horse and a mounted Arab,

The Oasis of Amon

a former slave-dealer, and, in case of need, a soldier. The Khedive himself sometimes rode and sometimes used a kind of light dog-cart, which he as a real Oriental prince took with him in the desert, and, as there never lacked fresh horses and men, in this exceptional case kept up his reputation. Sometimes I or one of the others took a place in this amazing vehicle, and his Highness liked to drive his "drag" himself through the sandy waste.

Abbas Hilmi takes a very great interest in the domestic economy of his country, especially in the cultivation of the soil, the breeding of cattle, and irrigation. He is the chief fellah, the crowned peasant, a name of honour to which he has full right and one which his foes in vain mention with a tinge of contempt. And in my opinion on two grounds. A true Pharaoh and a warm friend of his country can scarcely better testify his love for his subjects than by looking after the conditions of life on the land, the cultivation of the soil, by making improvements and laying down new canals and opening up fresh tracts of country; he who does this proves himself a son of the Nile, a fellah, in the sense in which the ancient Egyptians understood it, on whose heritage the Greeks and Romans were nourished, and to which they added scarcely anything essentially new. Secondly, Abbas Hilmi's decidedly businesslike methods—his speculations, as his adversaries put it—helped to exclude him from any political autocracy. Only since Lord Cromer's resignation in 1907—for Lord Cromer dominated the young ruler from the moment he left the Vienna Ritterakademie to ascend his father's throne—has Abbas Pasha had an opportunity to govern for himself, if only in a moderate measure. He was mistrusted by his own subjects, and his enormous purchases of land not only in Egypt, but especially on Turkish ground, increased their mistrust. His pilgrimage to Mecca in 1908 was suspected to be a political move, a speculation on the Caliphate; his marriage with the European baroness, whom I often saw with him in Mariut disguised as an officer, was taken in bad part, although the lady was converted to Islamism. It was said that the children of the first marriage, even the Khediva's eldest son, Prince Abd el-Moneïn, were to be excluded from the succession to the throne. And lately it has been insinuated that Abbas Hilmi's last purchase of land in South Caria points to his desire to abdicate. Land has been obtained for him there to the value of at least £2,000,000, land which with irrigation will be worth a hundredfold.

Thus the progress to Amonium, to the mysterious oasis of Siwa, on the western borders of his empire, was dictated chiefly by commercial interests. Two

The Oasis of Amon

questions occupied the chief place : first, is there in the region of that desert oasis land capable of cultivation ; and, second, would it be worth while to construct a branch line of railway from the Marmarika port, Mirsa Matru, to Siwa, which would sweep in the date exportation and a portion of the African oasis trade? It may be said at once that both questions for the present must be answered in the negative, but may be worth discussing in the not very distant future. That future will come nearer the quicker the incomparably easier and, for Egypt, more essential task of reclaiming the old north-west provinces of Mariut and Marmarika from the desert is successful, when they will again become the flourishing paradise of gardens they were formerly. On the other hand, the Viceroy's bold project of cultivating the Amon oasis will win greater importance in the course of time, the more profitable a similar undertaking in the south-west of his empire turns out to be—namely, the opening up of the oasis of El-Khargeh and Dachel. There the Government of Egypt shows great activity. It has built a railway from the Nile to the oasis, opened up wells and admirable cultivable land, and to all appearance mining and the working of minerals will play a part. It is hoped to come on coal, cobalt, sulphate of magnesium, ochre, phosphates ; beds of clay have already been found, and along the desert railway rich strata of marble. Monsignor Kaufmann has shown the important part played by this oasis in antiquity, especially in Christian times, in his interesting little book, "Ein alt-Christliches Pompeji in der Libyschen Wüste." [1]

That more elaborate desert railways are within the bounds of possibility in the future is further proved by the Mecca railway, that with the aid of Mohammedan money already goes as far as Medina, and the preparations that are gaining way for the project of the Sahara railway. For the latter three routes are proposed and partly tested : from Igli to the Niger, from the oasis of Biskra to Lake Tschad, and the shortest, from the military port of Biserta to Lake Tschad. The question is even being discussed of continuing it from Lake Tschad through Bilma to the French Congo and the Atlantic coast.

Abbas Hilmi is a direct contrast to his predecessor, Ismaïl Pasha, whose name modern Egypt has surrounded with all the magic splendour of the East, the opener-up of the sea route to India, the man to pay homage to whom men of science and explorers made a pilgrimage to the Nile. I need only mention the name of Rohlfs, the intrepid and thorough explorer of the Libyan Desert, the expenses of whose caravan were paid with viceregal

[1] Mainz, 1902.

The Oasis of Amon

money. The reigning Pharaoh has very little
time for scientific problems. Egyptologists know
something about that, for his first question in reference to our excavations—"What is Monsignor
Kaufmann paid for his work?"—tells everything.
He asked me whether we would not later excavate
at Siwa, where he alone could assist, and probably
the find would pay for the outlay. Although that
was very doubtful, the suggestion betrays the
tradesman rather than the patron of science. The
thing in itself was very risky, both on the score of
health and the hostility of the Siwa people, and
was anyway more in the domains of Egyptology.
His Highness told me later that M. M. von
Mathuiseulx purposed making use of the permission
to excavate. But I think that the distinguished
North African traveller seriously reconsidered
the matter when he paid a visit to the oasis.

So then it was for fairly prosaic reasons that the
Viceroy wished to learn something of the western
borders of his country, and was the first prince of
Egypt since the days of Alexander the Great to
traverse the route to the place of the oracle in the
heart of the desert.

The actual way through the desert was begun at
Mirsa Matru. The royal caravan consisted of a
vanguard of 62 camels and Arabs with 20 mounted
soldiers; in its chief division there were 288 camels,

Three Years in the Libyan Desert

22 horses, and 28 mounted men as a bodyguard, under the command of a dark-skinned Mameluke, a young officer always seen driving alone in a special carriage immediately behind the gala coach in the Khedive's ceremonial processions in Cairo. The chief part of the baggage was provisions and tents. We carried good Cairo water in 120 iron chests and 100 gheerbahs. Sixteen tents sufficed for his Highness and his suite, three more for the horse drivers, draught camel drivers, and servants. Large numbers of live sheep and fowls were stowed away, and an immense quantity of fodder for all the animals was carried.

It takes seven days to cross the desert from Mirsa Matru, the port of Marmarika, five of which are through a sea of sand absolutely without vegetation and with very few wells. It could be done more quickly without a caravan. Officers of the Egyptian coastguard have a record of doing the distance in four or four and a half days.

The route still bears the name of Sikke es-Sultani, the Sultan's route, by whom is meant no other than Alexander the Great, who marched along it twenty-two centuries before we did. I have described our march in detail in my book, "Siwa, die Oase des Sonnengottes in der Libyschen Wüste," and can only give a brief account of it here. From the mounds of ruins of ancient

VIEW OF SIWA, FROM THE HEIGHTS.

AÏN MÛSA (MOSES SPRING).

To face p. 272.

The Oasis of Amon

Parætonium (Mirsa Matru) we proceeded through Wadi Raml to Bir Goaiferi, past Dschebel Judar and Dschebel Taref into the stony desert. Then through the Pass of Kanaïs over diluvial oyster-beds and reefs to the four wells, Bir Lahafen, Bir Hakfet eggelâs, Bir hêlu, and Bir istable. Bir hêlu, the "freshwater" well, is the last station before Daffa and Hamraje, the region of heat and the red earth. Thence the road goes south in sight of the Coffin and Table Mountains to Ras el-Hamraje, and with seven steep ascents to Ghart el-Hanûn. We reached the borders of the oasis on the seventh day; the queen of African oases lay before us like enchanted ground, a depression exactly thirty yards below the level of the Mediterranean. Endless palm forests with shining silver lakes lie in the depression, and the strong rock walls of the Libyan plateau stand in a wide circle and under the burning sun look like high ranges of mountains. They are the high mountains of the west mentioned in the ancient temple inscriptions, and the oasis, to traverse which takes a day, is the country of the palm-grove men, the Sechet-am of the Egyptians.

Our entry at the head of the enormous caravan was an unforgettable sight. A living palm fence three miles in length marked the Via Triumphalis. Women enveloped in draperies, swinging palm-branches, and shouting their welcome with a thousand voices, stood on the dark, flat roofs of the capital, the serrated mud houses of which stretched up to the sky like a high-towered troglodyte citadel. The Khedive, escorted by his bodyguard in state uniform, rode first and we closely followed him. As we neared the town, plundered by Mohammed Ali in 1820, and the Senussi mosque that resembled a fortress, we found the native Sheikh, a deputation of Senussi, and the Egyptian Governor with his small garrison, forming a large square ready to receive us. The fluttering Arab banners, the wild native music, in which the drum and tom-tom prevailed, the chanting of the dark swaying figures on the roofs of Siwa, combined with the waving of palm-branches many yards in length, made a beautiful and harmonious picture. But discord was not lacking. The men in fluttering white burnous and narrow turbans, the bronze-coloured monks, greeted Effendine in silence and with ceremonious coldness. On their faces might be read curiosity and compulsion mingled with hatred, unconcealed hatred of the descendant of the plunderer whom no real native of Siwa unreservedly recognizes as master. I saw clearly that Abbas Hilmi could only make his position felt in this corner of his kingdom by display of an unusual kind, and that his bodyguard was

The Oasis of Amon

more than ornament here—it was a real defence
and protection.

The people of Siwa are a Semitic mixed race
of negro blood crossed with the light-coloured
ancient Libyan race. They number about six
thousand, and their cultivated land, much less
than in the times of antiquity, is rather more than
2 miles in extent, while the whole oasis measures
about 31 miles. Extensive salt lakes and salt
morasses occur in the fertile ground, which is
divided into fresh and salt earth, the value of which
depends on the number of springs by which each
property and the whole country is provided with
water.

The true native of Siwa is distinguished by
hatred of the foreigner and by laziness ; he leaves
the cultivation of the ground to the negro and the
freed slave. Slavery flourishes latently, but the
slave markets are no longer held in Siwa, but in
Dscharabub, close by. Sales from hand to hand,
however, go on as before. I was myself offered
a handsome negro at a comparatively low price.
The administration of the land, which has several
districts, is carried on by native notables, who also
collect the palm tax, the tribute for Egypt. The
Mamûr of Siwa, the Egyptian police officer, who
resides there as Governor and is changed every
four years, has to see that there is external peace,

and represents in some degree the Egyptian title
of possession. His post is by no means an easy
one, and with emotion he told me his troubles.
He only ventures in very rare cases to execute
justice, and the drugs in his medicine-chest go bad,
for no dweller in the oasis will let himself be
" poisoned "! When we asked him if he could
show us a suitable place for a dark-room for our
photographs, he at once set his prisoners free and
gave up the dungeon to us. The armed force consisted of fifty soldiers, who hold the fanatical natives
of the oasis in check. They had lately attempted
a rebellion and murdered the Mamûr. A general
rising was to follow the murder, but fortunately
the leader, Sheikh Suliman Habûn, and fifty
rebels were seized, put in irons and brought
to Alexandria for trial.

It goes without saying that during the days of
our stay in the oasis I never went out without a
guard, but I had the good fortune to meet a young
native who had for a short time been engaged in
our excavations at the city of Menas ; he spoke
favourably of me, and so I succeeded in discovering
some antiquities, among others a lion's head of the
Roman period, which the Viceroy presented to me
for the Frankfort Museum.

Siwa would be a paradise were it not for malaria,
which, except in the three or four winter months,

To face p. 276.

THE AUTHOR AT THE RUINS OF AMONIUM (UUM BÊDA.

The Oasis of Amon

renders a long sojourn impossible for Europeans. That disease, although the natives are unconscious of the fact, forms their best protection against civilization. No guns or cannons can do anything against the myriads of mosquitoes which disseminate the disease. But the natives themselves are by no means immune from attacks of malaria. Pale skins, dark-rimmed eyes, and the languid ways of many natives are symptoms not to be mistaken. Rohlfs thought that drainage and irrigation might be helpful.

The export of dates mentioned by Wanslebius, the humanist, forms the main part of the trade and exchange of the oasis. There are over 200,000 palms, 160,000 of which bear fruit and have an annual value of about £12,500. The exportation takes place in the winter months, and is entirely in the hands of the Auladali Beduins, whose caravans then number as many as one hundred camels. As the largest of the date caravans from Siwa to Alexandria used the route through the city of Menas, we were able to purchase our dates direct from the camels' backs. For a hundredweight of the finest, sweetest Abu Tauwîl, a sort scarcely ever seen in the European markets, as long as the forefinger, we paid at Karm Abu Mina rather less than five shillings; in Alexandria it would cost twelve shillings, and in Europe at least £2 or £2 10s.,

so fine a fruit is it. The date-tree also gives palm
wine and vinegar, and its bast serves for making
coarse and fine mats, baskets, and domestic utensils.
Not only human beings there feed on dates, but
the dry, poor sorts are used almost exclusively as
food for camels, horses, donkeys, and dogs. Other
products, like olives, maize, corn, sugar-cane,
haschisch, bersîm, pepper, and tobacco do not
supply one-half the consumption. But what could
be done with the ground is shown by the gardens
of rich Sheikhs, and especially those of the Senussi
monks, where, with figs, oranges, and apricots, even
the difficult African vine flourishes luxuriantly.
The chief articles brought back in exchange by the
date caravans from the valley of the Nile or from
Tripoli (Bengasi) are powder, arms, stuffs, tea,
sugar, and coffee. The chief caravan trade is in
the hands of the Auladali Beduins, who have to
deliver up their arms when they enter the oasis.

In the songs, Siwa is called a land rich in
donkeys, because other domestic animals, even
camels and oxen, flourish ill on a regime of dates.
These donkeys, whose ancestors belonged to the
Saïte, in their accomplishments rival the ships of
the desert. Who has ever climbed on the back of
a Cairo donkey up the rocky walls of Mokkatam
to the heights of the Arabian Desert, and then
ridden through the desert to the well of Moses,

The Oasis of Amon

must admire the security and endurance, the grace-
ful gait, and the cleverness of the Saïte breed. To
him it will not seem so incredible when I say that
a native of Siwa will at need make the week's
journey through the desert alone with his donkey.
A bag of dates forms their common food, and a
small gheerbah is refilled at the few springs met
with on the way. In far-off days of antiquity
extensive journeys were taken in the desert on the
back of a donkey. It is told in the Berlin hieratic
Papyrus 2 of an inhabitant of the Natrûn valley
who used to take salt and figs on his donkey to
the market of Chineu-Seteu (Heracleopolis) and
also to a town 68 miles south of Cairo! He
had no need to touch the capital, and could ride
in a south-easterly direction through the sporadically
cultivated Wadi Faregh. But even so it was a
very respectable journey, involving several days'
march.

As a rule the fauna of the oasis corresponds with
that of the north-east portion of the Libyan Desert.
The most important larger animals are hyenas,
gazelles, jackals, and farther in the interior of
the desert ostriches are found. Frogs inhabit
the waters of the oasis. The most remarkable
animal is a little fish, cyprinodon, which is so
plentiful that it is occasionally eaten as food by the
Beduins, but not by the natives of Siwa. Zittel,

a member of the Rohlfs expedition, diagnosed the
little creature as the same that is caught in the
streams of Algeria and in the Venetian lagoons, and
the distinguished Munich scholar was inclined to
regard the cyprinodon as a relic of the Sahara
ocean.

The caravan trade of the Auladali Beduins has
made the oasis accessible to the Arabs. But the
native idiom, the well-sounding Siwi language,
still prevails, and the office of interpreter, which is
hereditary in certain families, has, as formerly, a
certain importance. The Siwi language belongs
to the Berber dialects. Several European travellers have since Minutoli compiled Siwi voca-
bularies, but there is as yet no satisfactory
grammar.

The towns of Siwa are strong, almost inaccessible mud citadels, in which it is exceedingly
difficult to find one's way, for the streets are roofed
with palm-trunks on account of the sun, and are
dark on the brightest day. The towns stand on a
rock foundation, and when you come out again into
the open air you look over the many-storied flat sea
of roofs to the dark green beauty of the palm
forests, the silver and purple-red salt lakes, the
whole framed by the cliffs of the desert plateau.
Formerly there was only one gate or entrance into
a Siwa town. Even to-day the entrances are

THE CITADEL OF SIWA A HUNDRED YEARS AGO.

After Minutoli.

THE DSCHEBEL EL-BEBEL, THE CITADEL OF SIWA AT THE PRESENT TIME,

To face p. 280.

The Oasis of Amon

strictly guarded at night, and woe to the stranger, even if he be a son of the desert, who ventures to make his way in at night. The principal towns of the oasis are Siwa and Agermi; then come the smaller open towns, Sbûche, Edarra, and Menschije, and quite in the east, Zetûn. In the middle of summer the wealthier natives leave the town and exchange their mud house for an airier dwelling in the mountains. The "hill of the dead," with its ancient Egyptian necropolis, from which I abducted a collection of remarkable skulls for the Frankfort Museum, serves as a *villeggiatura*. The poorer natives and the foreigners who are suffered to take up their abode in the town dwell always in the tomb chambers of the Dschebel el-Beled belonging to Siwa. Although the furniture consists merely of a mat of palm-bast, they form by no means a bad place of residence. For excavators who do not prefer to live in the Governor's Mamurije, a thing that makes them many enemies, some large communicating tomb chambers were cleaned out, and they made an ideal dwelling-house.

The first question of the European who visits Siwa is for the famous sanctuary of the Sun-god, to whose oracle and fame the ancients, from Herodotus to the time of the sanctuaries of Menas— they have with more or less right been called the rival Christian foundation—have testified. The titular

god of the sanctuary was the ram-headed Amon-
Ra or Jupiter Amon, after whose temple the whole
oasis was named Amonium. Temple inscriptions
call him "existence in itself, whose legs are like
silver, whose skin is like gold, whose hair is like
sapphire, whose horns are like emerald," and praise
him as heaven and the creator of all things. The
oracle was famous throughout the world, the
words of the god were revealed to the priests,
who carried his statue on a golden bark, by the
swaying to and fro of the image. From Crœsus
onwards rulers and nations asked counsel of the
oracle of the desert. But the greatest of these
was Alexander the Great, who came in person at
the head of an enormous caravan, and whom the
chief of the eighty priests led into the Holy of
holies as the son of Amon-Ra, and there gave him
the still unknown answer of the god. That it
was favourable may be easily affirmed. It was
Alexander's wish to be buried in the oasis of
Jupiter Amon. But the adventurous convoy with
the magnificent funeral carriage only went as far
as Memphis, and even there the grave of the great
ruler was disturbed by Ptolemy Philadelphos and
the mummy taken to Alexandria.

The identity of the temple of the oracle with one
of the ancient buildings of the oasis is not absolutely certain. Since James Hamilton, the Scot-

The Oasis of Amon

tish traveller, saw in 1853 the ruins of a large
Egyptian temple on the chalk rocks of the town
of Agermi, that is pointed to as the sanctuary
of the oracle. Those ruins are so built in between
dwelling-houses that even Steindorff, the Leipzig
Egyptologist, who visited the oasis a few years
before us, did not succeed in determining the
ground plan of the smoke-coloured sanctuary with
its reliefs and hieroglyphics.

Other ruins too, like the limestone blocks of
Umm Bêda, were claimed to be the temple of Jupiter
Amon. We found only six of the columns with
hieroglyphics and pictures that were there sixty
years ago. Nearly all the ancient ruins in the
oasis are connected with the legend. So there is
a story of the subterranean "Christian houses,"
which means catacombs, in contrast to the underground tomb chambers of the heathens. But the
most extravagant is the tradition of the people
of Siwa about the Lake of Araschieh, in the north-
west of the oasis, now quite lost, the barren bank of
which no one could approach unharmed, until the
spell was accidentally removed through the conquest of Siwa by Mohammed Ali. Treasure was
said to be buried in the island of the lake, nothing
less than the Prophet's ring and sword and King
Solomon's crown. Butin, a French explorer, went
through the desert in 1813 with a portable boat in

order to discover this Nibelung treasure, and his rash enterprise nearly cost him his life.

The ancient world had its oasis miracle, the so-called Lake of Amon, or "Fountain of the Sun," about which Herodotus tells. In the morning the remarkable spring is tepid, at market time cooler, and at midday cold. In that stage of its temperature the water was used to irrigate the fields under cultivation. About evening the water became warmer again ; at sunset tepid, and at midnight boiling hot. The enigma, which both ancient and modern students of science have sought to explain, has never been solved, if the fairly modern tradition is followed which identifies a pretty spring of Siwa, surrounded by palms, Aïn Hamâm, the "Dove Spring," with the Lake of Amon. Aïn Hamâm, like other small bathing and irrigating pools, such as the Spring of Moses, Aïn Mûsa, Aïn Ben Lîf, was originally on the foundation of an ancient artificial tank. All those springs are to be reckoned among the fresh thermal waters of the oasis, which not only the inhabitants of the palm-groves but serious scholars of our day, among them Professor Schweinfurth, the Nestor of German African explorers, regard as a subterranean supply to the Nile. There were several hundreds of them in ancient times ; now there are about one hundred and fifty in the whole of the oasis. Abbas Hilmi specially desired to have

IN FRONT OF THE MOSQUE OF THE SENUSSI AT SIWA : THE HEAD OF THE SENUSSI MONKS
AND THE GOVERNOR WELCOME ABBAS HILMI.

To face p. 284.

The Oasis of Amon

these various springs analysed in order to determine their use for projects of irrigation. Dr. Bitter was to conduct the analyses at Cairo, and by desire of the Viceroy I myself assisted at the taking of the specimens. I also followed Monsignor Kaufmann's advice and registered the temperature at different times of the day and evening. At Aïn Hamâm and others of the same class I obtained nothing essentially different from what Rohlfs gave, an average of 84°–85° Fahr. for the different times. I inquired among the natives if no tradition or no particular spring came nearer the tales of the ancients than Aïn Hamâm, and learnt that a spring designated as "bigger" existed at some little distance from the capital, and as an ancient castle (Kasr) was named in the neighbourhood, an important new discovery seemed possible.

An extra expedition to Zetûn, which Rohlfs avoided on account of the fanaticism of its inhabitants, and which, but I did not know this at the time, Steindorff had visited on his return journey, took me to the mysterious castle called by the natives Kasr el-Guraîschet. The Khedive put soldiers, camels, and horses at my disposal, and after three and a half hours' ride in the direction which leads to Abu Schrûf we reached the Kasr, relics of a temple of the Græco-Egyptian period, with a large field of ruins bordering on it, where I found all sorts of minor antiquities. This biggest spring of Siwa was quite close to the temple. Surrounded by rushes and tall grass, it measured fifty paces in circumference and lost itself in the marshy ground. The chief stream feeds the large falls of Lake Magrari. The powerful spring of Kasr el-Guraîschet throws up water of an equal day and night temperature of 85° Fahr.; in the streams that flow off this sinks to 83° and 80°, and somewhat lower at night. As the ancients had no instruments for the absolute measuring of heat, they were relegated to subjective impressions. But in Siwa and the desert the difference between the day and night temperature is so great that the water of Kasr el-Guraîschet—and the other waters of the oasis in a less degree—although its temperature actually sinks several degrees at night, would feel quite extraordinarily warm. It would only be possible to determine if the thermal springs of Kasr el-Guraîschet were the real Sun springs by making excavations on the spot, just as excavation alone could identify the real sanctuary of the oracle of Amonium with some particular ruins of the oasis.

I had pitched my camp near the temple of Kasr el-Guraîschet, and my native guide was terribly alarmed when I ordered the military escort to encamp, while I myself, leaving the tents and camels, went in the night to Zetûn. He had to

yield and hazard the ride with me. Through fever-
engendering sebach, the marshy domains of mosquitoes, we reached the hamlet of Abu Schrûf and
after sunrise the cultivated district of Zetûn. Nearly
all the inhabitants are negroes, descendants of
slaves who belonged to the founder of the Senussi
brotherhood, whose local chief received me kindly,
and, as I brought the Khedive's greeting, entertained me with much ceremony. I was glad when
I could turn my back on the monastery. The
Sheikh of Senussia gave me his son to show me
everything, and here, as in other such surveys, a
large escort of curious hangers-on was not wanting.
The black faces watched me with the greatest suspicion, although for this expedition I had exchanged
the tropical helmet for the fez, and I confess that
more than once my heart beat faster when I took
specimens of water from the springs, for the fellows
might think I was mixing poison and witchcraft
with their precious gift of God in order to destroy
it. I spent half a day at Zetûn, and on the home-
ward ride had a most pleasant surprise. An
imposing troop of riders came towards us, and as
we could soon distinguish horses, we knew it to be
no hostile company. It was Abbas Hilmi himself
who had come out to fetch me, and I am still
uncertain whether some of my escort left behind at
Kasr el-Guraîschet had alarmed the Viceroy, for the

manner in which I carried out my visit to Zetûn was something of a risk.

During our sojourn in the oasis came royal couriers with letters for the Khedive and news from Karm Abu Mina. There my cousin had been in great danger, but at the same time he told me that all had gone well, and that there was no need for me to be anxious. All the same I was glad when news from the Government caused the Khedive to end the expedition sooner than he had originally intended. There is little fresh to record about our return, except that we passed the small uninhabited oasis of Gatara, and it so pleased Abbas Hilmi that he determined to settle it, and to instruct his engineers to make a road in the steep slopes of the plateau, in a depression of which it was sunk. When we reached Mirsa Matru, I could restrain myself no longer, and asked his Highness to allow me to travel as swiftly as possible to the city of Menas. But a Government yacht lay in the harbour, and as that would be quicker than the camels, thanks to the Viceroy's kindness, after taking a cordial farewell of him, I steamed off on the direct route to Alexandria, and to the surprise of all reached Karm Abu Mina unannounced and knocked at my cousin's door at midnight.

For the future, I always greeted the Khedive

To face p. 288.

THE MUD CITADELS OF THE CAPITAL OF THE OASIS.

The Oasis of Amon

whenever he came to Mariut or Marmarika. He stopped his train longer in Bahig in order to receive me, and I was also his guest in his little palace at Amriah, and read our occasional little publications to him, among which my ethnological articles in the *Frankfurter Zeitung* specially interested him.

During my long absence my cousin had made important discoveries, and above all had found the tomb of St. Menas. Smiling, he told me how on the day after my departure his Beduins revolted, and how thankful he was that in the excitement of the moment he had not given way to anger. A single shot, even if only fired to strike terror, would have sealed his fate. "Then you would have buried me in the great basilica," said the explorer, who owed his life to a Beduin woman. I will content myself with repeating here a brief account of the event which first appeared in 1906 in the report of the excavations published at Cairo. In describing the potter's ovens and furnaces then discovered, Monsignor Kaufmann writes as follows: "I must not neglect here to record the courage which a Beduin woman showed on the day of the wicked destruction of these ovens. Falls, my assistant, had on February 9th gone to the Khedive's camp in order to take part as his guest in his expedition to Siwa. Early the next day I observed Beduin horsemen and numerous persons with rifles in the distance, who, when the people set out for the works, barred the road, ostensibly on account of tribal disputes, but in truth in order to vent their anger on the Effendi who remained behind. The situation was made worse by the absence of a Sheikh whom we had dismissed a few weeks before, and through my threat to dismiss on the spot every workman who did not go to the basilica. Seventy refused and were dismissed; the rest went to work and we placed armed sentries. A stone flew past me occasionally, but the rebels remained at a respectful distance from my revolver. From the Kom I saw the only woman who had remained behind, wife of a spy, saddle my roan, and gallop off in the direction of Amriah, the seat of the Markaz. Scarcely four hours later she returned with a detachment of Sudanese on white horses, and later came the police officer from Bahig, who had been telephoned to, with his soldiers. As it was difficult to identify the attacking party (a Beduin never betrays a Beduin), the Sheikhs of the whole district were made personally responsible for the safety of the Effendi, and thus diplomatically peace was restored, The only victims of the whole affair were the three ovens. The four hours' ride of the Beduin woman to Amriah was doubly courageous when we learnt that shortly after she gave birth to a girl."

CHAPTER X

RELIGION AND CUSTOMS OF THE BEDUINS

Natural piety and superstition—The world of spirits—How I
caught an Afrîte—The ghost of the temple of Menas—
"Saints," of the Auladali—Dervish experiments—Primitive
serpents and scorpions—Mecca pilgrims—Mecca caravans
in the interior of Africa—The Senussi and Pan-Islamism—
Sidi el-Mahdi, the mysterious lord of the desert—Wedding
at Karm Abu Mina—Birth and death in the desert—Hospitality and vendetta—The Mâd—A nose for a nose—
Haschisch smuggling—Slavery.

THE son of the desert is deeply religious and
dependent almost unconsciously on certain pre-
scriptions of Islam in their outward forms. Most
of the people, on account of their nomad life and
their struggle with nature, are only acquainted with
the main features of the doctrine of their religion,
and so are inclined to place too much trust in the
few of them they learnt in a certain theological
grounding at school, and they use their knowledge
for reasons of business. Their ignorance makes
them too easily fanatical and the victims of exag-
geration, especially in respect to the belief in spirits,

a belief deeply planted in the hearts of Oriental and savage nations.

Prayer is the central point of the Beduin practice of religion ; it is decreed as a rule three times a day : at dawn, noon, and sunset. More prayer-times are only observed in the month Ramadhan. In the desert sand is often used for the prescribed ablutions. The person praying arranges an open circle of stones as his mosque, and, turning to the east, performs his devotions. Nothing hinders the believer from the practice of his religion. During the progress of a caravan, heedless of the others, he dismounts and prostrates himself ; Mecca pilgrims who pass through large towns are seen to spread their praying carpets in the streets and squares full of traffic. In order to prevent the disturbance of work, the head of the excavations at Karm Abu Mina ordered that prayers were only to be said in the pauses. The Beduins erected a round building of the height of a man out of fragments of limestone and marble, with a large rush mat inside, in the centre of a smooth piece of ground where once grew the vines of St. Menas. That was their mosque.

The Beduins and many Orientals put many Christians to shame as regards candour of confession and regularity of prayer and in their conduct during the fast of Ramadhan. During that month nothing may be eaten or drunk from dawn to sunset. Even smoking is forbidden. In the Nile valley the rulers make the thing easy, inasmuch that work is reduced as far as possible. The State shows consideration, and as the merchants close their business during a large part of the day, the officials, even the Ministers, have only a few hours' work. We excavators regarded the approach of the fast of Ramadhan with great anxiety. On the one hand nearly all the workpeople would absent themselves, and on the other, the fast always increased fanaticism. But most of our people remained industriously at work. On account of the heat and dust, thirst was more torturing than hunger, for which they compensated themselves at night. Towards evening the Beduin women began to cook the food and put the drinking-water ready. As the sun began to set some ascended the tower of the Kasr, the excavation buildings, in order to await the end of the twilight; the younger people stood below with paper or chips, ready at the first shout of "kalas!" from above—"The fast is over"—to light their cigarettes or take the first drink of water.

As a rule only the older ones prayed. Youths had no part in it, for in the desert prayer was regarded as a privilege of the men, a privilege in which women only share when they are old.

Three Years in the Libyan Desert

Spontaneous prayer took place during the excavations in the city of Menas when it was a question of dangerous undertakings. Before the setting up of heavy columns, when twenty to thirty men were occupied with the base and the ropes, the Fatha (the opening sentences of the Koran) were spoken in chorus with hands raised to heaven : "Praise be to God, Lord of the Worlds! The compassionate, the merciful! King on the day of reckoning! Thee only do we worship, and to Thee do we cry for help. Guide Thou us on the straight path, the path of those to whom Thou hast been gracious, with whom Thou art not angry, and who go not astray."

No workman descended into a subterranean vault or cistern without first kneeling in prayer. The behaviour of the people during the many years I observed them makes me believe in the real, strong, inborn piety of the Beduin, a piety which is shown in everyday life. If a man mounts his horse or camel, he does it in the name of God; every important action is accompanied by a "bism Allah." If the Beduin woman puts meat in the saucepan, feeds her child, hands a weapon, she does it in the name of the Most High. When I asked what the Beduin had in mind when he made that invocation, I was told: "God blesses everything, and every act only succeeds if it is Allah's will." And so it

results that in the desert at least faith in God is
strong and living, although the boundary line between faith and superstition is not always clear. For
there are many relations with the spirit world, and
especially the evil spirits and the devil, the Afrîte.
Those evil spirits form the chief source of income
of the Fiki, the man who can read the Koran and
exorcize spirits and heal the sick with verses from
it. The wise Fiki is summoned, he is told everything, entertained according to the means of his
host, writes a verse of the Koran on a scrap of
paper, which is sewed up in a little linen or leather
bag and worn as an amulet. The price of this
assistance is according to the possessions of the
seeker of it, a small sum of money or natural
produce.

The Fiki, a name by which the teacher of
the Koran is usually designated, is generally a
wanderer, a Maghrabi, an Arab from Tunis,
Algiers, or elsewhere in the West. His passage
from the Koran, which is sometimes written on a
stone or a fragment of pottery, is called Heschâb.
When he treats the sick or plays the Hakîm
(doctor), his first question is usually, "Who has
bewitched him?" or "Who has written anything
for him?" For the power of the Heschâb
influences even the absent.

Spirits and devils dwell in forsaken spots in the

desert and wherever ancient ruins of any extent are found. The magic lakes of the *fata Morgana* are "devil's water," and are generally called "sraf." Windspouts, which nearly always follow in the wake of the chamsin storm and make an impression of grandeur if they can be observed from the beginning throughout their progress (often in serpentine curves), as was possible from the excavation buildings in the city of Menas, are called "spirit winds." I was taken to half-ruined cisterns where I could "hear" the spirit. A stone was thrown down, and bats or pigeons buzzed or fluttered about in the depths.

I will only allude here to some among my many experiences which show the Beduin belief in spirits. One evening our cook, Eluâni, scared and pale, entered the summer tent we were then occupying, and reported that there was an Afrîte close by. We had sent him to make a round and see that no unauthorized person was loitering in the excavated city. I was desirous of at last making acquaintance with a ghost, and asked what he looked like. He said a shadow had just passed him and then a light shone in front of him, and that it remained fixed in one spot. I took down my gun, but Eluâni forbade me to take it, as an Afrîte must not be approached with a bunduk. As I always carried a revolver, there was not much

risk, and I followed him to the spot. It was in
the basilica of the Emperor Arcadius. As we
approached we really saw a little bright light in
the midst of the ruinous blocks of limestone. I
approached carefully, recognized what it was, and
boldly grasped it. The light instantly ceased, for
the lampyris, a fairly big firefly, was caught. I
had caught the ghost, went home in triumph, and
entered one of the tents where numerous persons
had assembled, all eagerly curious. Eluâni told
the story; I opened my hand, showed and explained
the creature, and asked : " Now, do you still believe
in your Afrîte?" But I withdrew, crestfallen, when
I was answered in all seriousness : " Effendi, the
Afrîte was actually there, but it changed itself into
an insect, and if you had tried to kill it you would
not have been sitting here with us in the tent."

The following story illustrates how it was with
the ghost of the city of Menas (Afrîte Bumna)
before our arrival, and before the discovery of
the sanctuaries. As we have seen above, a Beduin
Sheikh named Schuchân had pitched his tent near
the holy city. He and his sons avoided the sea of
stones under which the holy city of the desert lay
buried as far as possible. But during the winter
months fine herbage grew on the numerous mounds
of ruins, which Schuchân's camels eagerly sought
as food. It thus chanced that one evening the

Beduin unthinkingly took the shorter road through the stones in order to look after his herds. Suddenly, a few steps in front of him, he saw a bearded man with a pale face, who looked out motionless from among the fallen blocks of stone. The son of the desert managed to preserve his coolness when for the first time he saw the apparition so often talked of round the evening fire. He took up a stone with a threatening gesture, and called to his sons, who were looking after the camels near by. But before the help arrived he began to hurl big blocks of stone at the " devil of Bumna." And when the young men came up and assisted with all their might, the ghost vanished, and was seen neither the next morning nor ever again, at least until the day when Schuchân showed the memorable place to the Frankfort excavators, and with difficulty they made him understand that his Afrîte was a valuable white marble statue, which he had entirely destroyed. Later on we found the pieces.

If on that occasion the devil of Bumna played the future excavators a bad turn through the destruction of a marble statue, it once unconsciously did them a great favour. A " saint," Abd el-Kader, the same in whose honour the first station of the Mariut railway is named, came to Bumna soon after the rising of Arabi Pasha, and, induced by the splendid building material lying about, wanted

to erect a Zauja and a mosque. Naturally he
sought to procure water and to put an ancient
cistern into working order. Then one evening
the Bumna Afrite warned him not to dig further.
But Sidi Abd el-Kader did not heed the mysterious
voice, and the next day his slave was found dead
in the cistern. He was killed by a falling block
of stone, but everybody saw the hand of the Afrite
in the event. The slave was named Abd er-Rahman,
and came from Fessan. He was buried on a hill of
the city of Menas, and the inscription on his tomb
is now in the Frankfort Museum.

Abd el-Kader is honoured to-day as one of the
principal saints of the Beduins. I take for granted
that it is known that Islam has formed a cult of
saints and martyrs. Nearly every little town has
its Sheikh, a word that means elder, and also saint
as well as chief. It is mostly on the outskirts of
the desert that the little cupola of the tomb of a
saint is to be seen shining in the sun. Such a
tomb of a Sheikh, Sidi el-Fakir, honoured by
the Beduins, may be seen from the city of Menas
enthroned on a high ridge ; it forms a landmark
of the caravan route to Alexandria. When caravans or travellers approach the saint's tomb, they
all dismount in order to say a short prayer, and
if there is need for haste, it may be said from the
saddle. The chapel of the tomb is full of votive

offerings, weapons, etc. ; packed up tents and all sorts of implements and utensils lie around without guard, belonging to Beduins who have to wander afar, and who will find everything safe and in good order on their return. For the saint prevents robbery by enchanting the thieves so that they cannot stir from the spot. The people firmly believe this.

The principal saints of the Auladali are the Sheikhs Sidi Auen, Sidi Abd er-Rahman, Sidi Bu Driha, Sidi Bu Schaifa, and the still living Sheikh Sidi Achmêda. Great improvisations take place on their festivals : Beduins with their wives and children come in holiday attire, tents are pitched in the sacred district, and the sports and feasting, in which the descendants of the saint play the chief part, sometimes last for days. If the saint performs a miracle, thanksgivings and feasts are held. Such an event during the excavations once cost us a sheep. One of the men digging near the principal portal of the monastery suddenly sank in the ground before any one could help, and heavy blocks of limestone and pieces of marble fell on top of him and entirely buried him. Sheikh Sadaui saw the accident from an eminence, and loudly implored help from the Saint Abd er-Rahman. We hurried up, and it was a long time before the masses of stone could be removed, especially as a neighbouring wall threatened to fall down and had to be secured. Monsignor Kaufmann and I felt quite certain that the workman would be dead, and we too thanked God and providence that he was saved. The blocks of stone had fallen in such a way that they formed a roof over the head of the victim. He was extricated with great care and trouble not only alive, but absolutely unhurt. We gladly gave the customary sheep, which was slaughtered the same evening.

Miraculous powers of various sorts are ascribed to particular saints. Barren Beduin women make a pilgrimage to Sheikh Sidi Abd er-Rahman. The aid of other Sheikhs, when amulets or burning do not avail, is invoked in the diseases of camels, others again restore things that have been stolen or help in the vendetta. Sometimes a son inherits the "saintship" of his father, and the power which these persons exercise in their lifetime on the calm, silent Beduins must not be under-estimated. In connection with the particular activities of the Sheikh Sidi Abd er-Rahman, I may mention the remarkable custom of the Beduin women who walk three times round an antique statue in order to be cured of their sufferings. I confirmed it over and over again at Karm Abu Mina. But I was never so struck by it as in the Cairo Museum. I observed there some women, evidently fellahs, who made one of them walk three times round one of the Pharaoh mummies. It was doubtless due to the same superstition.

Next to saints, dervishes and lunatics play a special part, since they are regarded as the persons standing nearest to the Deity : the dervish or "penitent" because he renounces everything earthly, the madman because his spirit is already in Paradise with Allah. Examples of both were reckoned among our most assiduous visitors, and I need not say that they were well treated. We saw very little of the famous dervish arts. The brave, harmless folk did not understand the business of the Uled Ilwâns and Uled Sajds, the celebrated dervishes of the Nile valley of the Order of the Rifaje, who stick iron nails in their eyes, hurl stones at their chests and eat burning coals. We witnessed only two interesting experiments made by passing dervishes. One of our greatest troubles was the presence of scorpions and snakes, which endangered the lives of the Beduins working under the ground barefoot, and often naked. The scorpion that lived among the ruins of the city of Menas was a small dark yellow variety. It poisons children, who die from its sting unless an antidote is given without delay. The Beduins have such an antidote, which they prepare from the powdered tip of a snake's tail. With adults the symptoms of a scorpion's sting are sharp pain, a red and swollen place which often spreads to other parts of the body, then a feeling of cold, and sleeplessness. But they usually recover in two or three days.

Among the snakes the only real enemy was the uræus. Both the scorpions and this uræus, which may be seen in the royal badge of the Pharaohs, find their tamers. We became aware of this when we expressed a wish to preserve unblemished specimens of snakes, chameleons, and such-like. For as a rule the Beduins killed all such creatures with the axe or pick. A dervish who had spent some months in our workmen's colony brought a perfect specimen of a uræus in his turban, and put it through the tricks known to every traveller in the East. More taming was not to be thought of, since he delivered the creature up at once. But we received absolute security for his art when one day a uræus a yard long was disturbed. Monsignor Kaufmann, whose survey led him to the spot, summoned the dervish to tame the snake The dervish took off his turban, caught the reptile after a short pursuit (it tried to flee between the ruined blocks of stone) and wrapped it in his turban cloth. In the pause which immediately

Three Years in the Libyan Desert

followed he had his pipe fetched, placed the creature on his outspread burnous, and mastered it in
the usual manner. The Moses rod was only useful
on the ground : I mean the creature lay stretched
out like a stick, and as lifeless, until he let it free.
Two circumstances connected with the happy
presentation of other snakes of the same species
are worthy of mention : once the snake still
possessed its poisonous teeth and its poison : it
had no opportunity of biting stuff or any object.
In addition it had never been tamed. To the
question how he had learnt his art, the dervish
said it had been hereditary in his family for ages
without learning. He could offer no plausible
explanation, and concluded with " All rests with
God." The same dervish trained a scorpion to
follow the steps of a man moving in different
directions. He kept the creature in an empty
preserved-meat tin, and only let it work to the
accompaniment of his pipe. In that case the
training was done by means of a little stick. The
taming of scorpions is a much rarer art than
that of snakes. Significant of the powers ascribed
to the short-sighted creature is the tradition related by Makrizi about the history of the Emir
Taktabai, Governor of Kus. In order to escape
the attentions of a broken-in scorpion, he sat down
in a spot surrounded with water. The animal

crawled up the wall of the room to the ceiling and fell down. The Emir killed it, and had the tamer executed.

It is to be noted that the Beduin of Libya rarely observes the obligation of every Moslem once in his life to make a pilgrimage to Mecca. The cause lies in his attachment to the soil, at least of his particular desert. No one, however, is better suited to the fatigue of the pilgrimage, no one would feel more at home in it. To the Auladali Beduin, at any rate, a good example is not lacking. For centuries he has observed, or guided, the pilgrims of the West, from Morocco, Algiers, Tunis and Tripoli, whenever they chose the already mentioned caravan route through Marmarika and Mariut. Scarcely 2 per cent. of the Auladali could lay claim to the title of a Hadschi and had a right to wear the green turban. Those few had mostly taken the comfortable opportunity of joining the Machmal caravans. Every year, in token of their royal dignity and as a manifestation of faith, the rulers of Egypt send the Kiswe, a costly cover for the Kaaba, under a strong military escort to Mecca. The Kiswe is placed on a gold carrying-chair (Machmal) on one of the camels, and so the whole caravan is called "Machmal."

The route taken is via Suez and Dschidda

through the Arabian Desert, the Beduins of which are under the obligation, against a tribute of about £400, not to attack the caravan. For a year now an essential alteration has been carried out in Egypt with the purpose of always using as far as possible the new Mecca railway, and so diminishing the dangers and also the expense of the pilgrimage. Pilgrims who cannot or will not afford the luxury of the new method of transport will be at a disadvantage, and thus the number of western Beduins from the Libyan Desert and the more distant Sahara taking part in the pilgrimages is little likely to be increased.

In contrast to the holding back of the Libyan Beduins, the increase in the pilgrims from the interior of Africa is striking. For centuries the journey has been made in the most primitive fashion through Wadai and Kordofan to Khartum. Pilgrim caravans which formerly came from Bornu and passed the capital Dikoa, now prefer to go round the north of Lake Tschad in order to avoid the German customs. The caravans from those parts take on an average a year to do the journey. They take with them a strange article of exchange which guarantees their sustenance without special loads of provisions for the most difficult stages of the way, namely, boys and girls, who are readily sold on the way as slaves, but pay best if it is possible to take them as far as Mecca. Dr. Karl Kumm, the German African traveller, who explored the connections between the Niger and the Nile in those directions, two years ago met a caravan which was led by a son of the Sultan of Timbuctoo, a man who had studied in Fez and Kairuân. At Schari his caravan consisted of 150 persons, with 500 head of cattle, 50 donkeys, and 15 horses. When Dr. Kumm met the Prince again later, farther east at Keffi Genji, the men were decreased by a third and not a single animal remained.

The increase of the pilgrim traffic from the region of Lake Tschad is to be attributed to the influence of the Senussi, that power of Central Africa which for decades has embodied the great African peril. The spiritual influence of this Islamitish power is evident. The Senussi convert the heathen negro to Islamism, and compete too successfully with the Christian missions, since as a means to this conversion they introduce just the amount of civilization that the African can endure, and so impress the negroes. Thus the Senussi naturally gain in political importance. There is every sign that within a measurable space of time the Senussi will establish politically their Central African kingdom, and in a form which promises a longer duration than the bloody rule of the Mahdi of Omdurman. The last French reverse in Wadai, which entailed great sacrifice in November, 1910, in the district of Abescher, is to be placed wholly to the account of the Senussi, and it is significantly sounded in the proclamation made by the French when after the reverse they recognized the danger : the clearance of the land of Wadai is not desirable. It is an unfertile district, which can never be made into a colony useful for French interests. Later French news of victory over the Sultan of the Senussi refers to a vassal, not to the overlord and the chief power of the Senussi.

What is this mysterious political and spiritual power of the Senussi? How did it arise? Numerous Beduin tribes of the Libyan Desert, and more in the Sahara itself, even some in the Arabian Desert, adhere to it, and it unfurls the banner of Pan-Islamism in Central Africa itself.

The Senussi is a Mohammedan brotherhood of strict observance, so named after its founder, Sidi Mohammed ben Ali es-Senûsi, an Algerian, who died in 1859. But its influence only dates from the activities of his son, Sidi Mohammed el-Bedr. He was born in 1844 and died May 30, 1902, at Geru, and under the name of the Mahdi played a part in the east of North Africa, and especially in the desert. But for the Beduins the Mahdi is not dead. Although Lord Cromer and others proclaimed his death, he still lives. On a white horse, surrounded by white gazelles and antelopes, he wanders unseen through the desert, makes long journeys, and then suddenly appears among his adherents at fixed places, sometimes in two places at once. In May, 1906, it was officially announced that the Mahdi had returned from a secret journey to the oasis of Kufra. The seat of the master of the order of the "Jesuits of Islam," as the Senussi are called, was formerly the mosque and school of the oasis of Dscharabub, but it was removed in 1905 to the oasis of Kufra, and since 1902—since the supposed death of the Mahdi—it has been at Geru or Karu, situated between Kufra and Abescher, the capital of Wadai.

The return to the simple strict rule of Islam, its demand for abstemiousness, the prohibition of tobacco, coffee, dancing, and music, make its conquests in the desert and the oases easy for the apostle of the Senussi. The conduct of the order is admirable and the method of procedure perfect. In the Libyan Desert they began to send out envoys and preachers from the then central seat at Dscharabub. Then small convents, always with a school and a mosque, were established in the north-east coast region, especially in the district of Dschebel Achdar, ancient Cyrenaïca, and Marmarika. The oases and larger wadis (Wadi Natrûn) followed, and as the Beduins in the north-west and east were gained, so was the negro world on the southern borders of the great desert. A specially alluring rallying cry was the call to freedom from the dominion of those who had another faith. But this was to be accomplished by modern means. It is quite against the spirit of the Senussi (I was always told this in the oases as well as in the convents of the coast region) to take the life of the wise man, of the European when he makes no hostile attack. As far as possible the monks try to protect the traveller from robbery, but solely for diplomatic reasons. They wish to avoid every cause of friction with the Powers, especially with Turkey, which, although Mohammedan, is regarded as a hostile Power, since it repeatedly tried to gain over the new brotherhood, and with it, *de facto*, the hinterland of Cyrenaïca.

If it may be said that the desert has a ruler, a lord, then Sidi el-Mahdi, the living dead man of Geru, must be designated as the lord of the African desert, with whom individuals as well as the State must reckon. His disciples are not reformers, and have no quarrel with the rest of Islam. They desire to animate Islam. Therefore, whether a chance or a far-sighted purpose, it was a stroke of genius on the part of the founder to erect his three first convents in Mecca, Medina, and Dschidda, and then to go to Cyrenaïca and Dscharabub.

The circumstance that Sidi el-Mahdi still lives forms an ever-present latent danger. The Senussi, whose leader is now a relative of Sidi Achmed, the founder, will find an opportunity one day, when the stars appear favourable, to let the Mahdi reappear, and what that means in conjunction with the larger peril of Pan-Islamism may be seen in the assertion of Sali ben Said Omer el-Khalidi, a cultivated Senussi, made openly in 1907 in Egyptian newspapers : " The sole qualified representative of Pan-Islamism is the Sheikh Senussi." That man was driven out of Tangier and Tunis in 1906 as an envoy of the Senussi, was expelled from Malta and fled to Bengasi on Turkish ground, whence he travelled through Dscharabub to Barca, and through the Auladali district to the Nile valley. I hear that he now occupies the position of a chief delegate of the Central Committee of the Islamitish Union, and will perhaps be more disagreeably known.

The Senussi work systematically, even among the Beduins, for the rising generation. The monk who can gain a talented boy provides free maintenance in the Koran school of a convent, and I have met Beduins who allowed their sons to join a caravan to Dscharabub in order to spend some years in the chief school of the Senussi in that distant oasis, which is a fortnight's journey. Educated Senussi are occasionally sent to the most famous of all Mohammedan universities, the el-Ahzar at Cairo, which is the oldest in the world, for in 1907 it celebrated its millenary.

The hard rough conditions of life, the continual struggle with nature, together with—except so far as the Auladali are concerned—a corresponding purity of race, place the son of the desert in all that is connected with morality higher than other Orientals. So that it will be his good fortune if civilization with its modern ideas of morality keeps away from him. If circumstances permit, he marries at the age of seventeen or eighteen. The bride is sometimes not more than fourteen or fifteen, and as the women are not veiled, she is not so strange to the bridegroom as in towns and villages.

As a general rule monogamy is preferred. Where polygamy is practised there are seldom more than two wives—Islam allows four—and generally the second wife is taken for material motives. Perhaps she brought fine herds, tents, or other possessions, or it was an advantage for the man

Religion and Customs of the Beduins

to be allied with the clan or family. An important Arab Sheikh, who is a friend of mine, has two wives, one in Mariut, the other on the borders of the desert, where he holds the post of Ghaffir, or guard, on the estate of a pasha. He told me he had married in order to have a home in Mariut, and to plant there in favourable circumstances, or make good purchases of camels, and also to keep his chief wife better in check. At need he rode to the Gebel and appeared there suddenly with his second establishment. " I never have it better," he said, " than when the two tents stand side by side; jealousy makes each surpass herself." But it chanced that we saw the other side of the shield at Karm Abu Mina. The second wife, of whose existence we knew nothing, came to one of our workmen from a great distance with bag and baggage, and wanted to pitch her tent by the side of that of her rival. The latter tried to prevent it, and a regular duel between the women ensued. As the wife who had come from so far was left by her husband without support, it seemed just to divide his wages, ten or twelve shillings, between the two tents; therefore both were compelled to suffer, and so they departed.

In many cases the young Beduin looks out for his bride himself. Then he returns home and tells of the " noble young horse" that dwells yonder in the tents of a tribe, and that he desires to possess. Or else the father goes about and in his own interest seeks a good match for one of his sons. There is seldom a refusal, and the marriages are nearly always fairly happy. The girls, of course, are not consulted. According to Mohammed the wife is a subordinate being, whom the man may at any time get rid of with the words "I send you away," a means of which the husband rarely avails himself. She lives with her children in the harem, the women's part of the tent, cut off by a perpendicular curtain, and takes no part in the counsels, or the meals, or the conversation of the men, if relatives are not concerned. Yet she easily understands how to influence the men without their knowing it, to exhort them, and compel them to her will. Such a woman, especially if she is older and experienced, takes the place of a real matriarch. Resolute and proud, she pursues great aims, and we had proof of this when, in the first year of the excavations, such a Beduin woman, who possessed three tents and a herd of forty camels, wished to dispute with Monsignor Kaufmann his right to excavate in the city of Menas. That was the ground and soil of her race; there lay the tombs of her ancestors. She carried it so far that Mamûr Markaz, the chief official of Mariut, had to come with a troop of police and make it clear to her that the desert belonged to the Egyptian Government. The negotiations were dramatic and excited. The Mamûr and the excavators sat on chairs, the forty-year-old Matrije on a mat between us, and near her, as a helper, the same Sheikh Schuchân who had first shown us hospitality in the city of Menas. But the handsome bearded man was merely for show: Matrije, adorned with her valuable silver bracelets, necklaces, and beautiful blue-green tattooings, conducted the proceedings. In our hearts we thought the brave woman was right, and were glad it was not our hearts but the representative of the Government that had to decide. Matrije and her adherents had to undertake to pitch their tents at a suitable distance from us, and to let their camels pasture in the early Christian city only with express permission. We separated in perfect amity, and when Halime, the old lady's daughter, drove her camels to the Karm, she brought every day a large wooden bowl of precious fresh camel's milk as a welcome tribute. And later Matrije married her former " counsel," our friend Schuchân.

The long duration of the excavations allowed us to assist at a Beduin wedding, and in order that all might take part in it we had to sacrifice a whole working day. The event was announced

some weeks before. During the time of preparation
an improvisation was given in front of one of the
tents every evening, the rhythmical hand-clapping
continuing until late in the night. At length the
eve of the wedding arrived. As heavy tropical
rains had filled the cisterns, every one when they
had finished work performed their ablutions
thoroughly. Then they put on their best white
garments and cleaned their guns. The two
Effendi gave several pounds of powder, carefully
divided into the right portions, by way of backschish.
The next morning sunrise was saluted with the
firing of guns, and the men prayed in front of their
tents. In front of the bridegroom's tent big copper
pots were boiling, in which rice and machrûta,
a sort of polenta, were cooking, while other big
pots for meat stood in readiness. The bridegroom,
one of our workmen named Abd el-Schuard, sat
nicely dressed on his mat, feeling himself the
centre of everything, and received the congratulations of stranger Beduins who were permitted to
come to-day. The man had come to us very
poor, and had now saved up £4 and a tent.
" What should I do with much money?" he said.
" I want to marry." My cousin had taken him
to task weeks before, and made it clear to him
that if he was dismissed, or the excavations given
up, he would possess nothing, and would be left

in poverty with his wife. But it was of no avail ; he always replied : " I shall eat bread."

The slaughtering of a sheep was the first great ceremony. The men sat round our Sheikh Sadaui in a wide circle, who in the name of Allah cut the creature's throat, not quickly, but out of love for the animal slowly, with several cuts. The Auladali regard swift killing as the sign of a hard heart, and the victim's head must never be quite cut off. The animal must lose all blood. One dips his hand in the blood, goes to the bridegroom's tent, and smears the tent-peg with it. The fellahs do the same, and press the bloody hand several times on the wooden door of the courtyard.

After the meat is cut up (even the intestines find approval) the caravan is prepared which is to fetch the bride. The tents of her tribe were in the desert, a journey of a couple of hours. All available horses and camels were decorated. An especially fine camel bore on its back a karmût made out of tent-poles, over which hung rugs, like a pretty miniature tent. There the bride would take her place. Women relatives, on this occasion entirely veiled, sat on the other camels, which were draped with gay-coloured rugs. At short intervals they uttered the chant of joy (sarlûl), louder when the men fired their guns, only ceasing when the bride entered the tent of her future husband. Accompanied by Beduins on horseback and on foot, the procession marched to the desert to the tent of the bride's father. Without any ceremony the bride in her fine attire was taken to the karmût, and an elderly relative sat beside her on the camel. The procession then went through the neighbouring desert from tent to tent to receive wedding gifts. At last, after an absence of six hours, the caravan again approached the city of Menas. The youths and boys who had stayed behind clapped hands and danced in front of the bridegroom's tent, and amid sarlûl and shouts of joy the bride went seven times round the tent. Then the camel knelt down, the girl entered the tent with her relatives, and it was closed. The young people outside continued to sing and dance, and at the moment when Abd el-Schuard came out of his wedding tent and showed the crowd his bloody fingers the noise increased, all the guns were let off, and the old people shouted their good wishes, in which the words "God is good" continually recurred. A universal feast closed the proceedings. A devout stillness and the loud breaking of bones proclaimed the gratitude of the guests, and the following night the Beduin dogs from ever so far round scented that there was something for them to fetch from Karm Abu Mina. Our own dogs, Siwi, Abiad, and Amenotep were so generous, and well satisfied, that they let their wild colleagues come undisturbed.

We also had a birth in the city of Menas. Umm Sâd, who, as related in Chapter IX, saved my cousin's life, soon after my return from the oasis gave birth to a girl. She received the name of Bumna, *i.e.*, Father Menas. The mother went about her hard work the same day. If it had been a boy, shots of joy would have been fired. Oil plays a great part at a birth, and the mother remains standing, for she fears she would die if she lay down. According to the assertions of the people miscarriages are very few. The child is wrapped in rugs, and the name, which is often hereditary in the family, decided on immediately. Some who come to congratulate bring a few pence as a present, "milk money" for the child. For the first three days salt and bread are placed beside the infant as a protection against the devil and evil spirits. If he cries too much a Heschâb is written for him. I was much struck by the general custom among the Auladali and also in the Nile valley of suckling the children for two or three years. In contrast to the fellahs, girls are not circumcised, and boys not until the age of fourteen or fifteen. From his sixth year the boy does not live exclusively in the tents, but makes himself useful as herd-boy. Little fellows in the desert know as well how to look after the camels as the naked little fellah boys the dangerous and fierce-looking Nile buffaloes.

We were always thankful that, in spite of all the dangers connected with the excavation works, death never came during our proceedings in the city of St. Menas. We often heard in the neighbourhood the terrible Beduin death-wail when one of their loved ones died. They begin it before death has actually occurred. It reaches its climax after death and during burial, and is sounded for a week every night in memory of the dead person. After death the relatives wash the body and stop up all the openings with camel's or sheep's wool, rags, or even grass. The corpse is then wrapped in cloths, and the wealthier Beduins sometimes possess a green shroud, in which it is rolled up like a mummy. The funeral follows the day of death, and if possible the corpse is buried where its ancestors lie, and that is often on a hill on the caravan route. Sheikhs and prominent men are distinguished by a tomb on a height. Some Sheikhs' tombs were found in the east of the temple of Menas, over the choir end of the great basilica of the Emperor Arcadius. We spared the spot, especially as near relatives of the dead still lived. The corpse, borne on an improvised bier, is accompanied by all the tent companions and friends to the monotonous

TOMB OF ABD ER-RAHMAN ON AN EMINENCE OF THE CITY OF MENAS
(THE INSCRIPTION IS IN THE FRANKFORT MUSEUM).

To face p. 320.

sound of " La ilâha ill' Allah, we Mohammed er rasûl' Allah." Friends are the bearers, then come the men, and lastly the women, who swing their black transparent head-cloths towards the bier and utter their wailing chant. The grave is not deep, and the face of the dead must look towards the east. The Auladali have the idea that only Moslems are so buried, and that the corpses of Christians are buried with the faces to the ground. The grave is covered with earth and the low mound with the heaviest stones possible, on account of the hyenas and jackals. Ruins are particularly preferred as burial-places on account of the stones. Sometimes the Simi or tribal badge is scratched on one of the stones. Inscriptions on Beduin tombs are very rare. There was one on the tomb of a Beduin slave from Fessan buried in the city of Menas.[1]

After the burial, all who had come in contact with the dead man perform ablutions, for they had become unclean. Then the funeral feast takes place, which consists of the usual rice, machrûta, and mutton. At twilight the women form a semicircle in front of the dead person's tent—if a man with two wives, in front of the two tents—set up wailing, and between whiles praise the virtues of the dead. On the seventh evening the ceremonies are concluded by another funeral banquet.

[1] See p. 299.

Three Years in the Libyan Desert

Among the customs and unwritten laws of the desert, which are of the age of the Bible, the law of hospitality and the law of the vendetta hold the chief place. Hospitality from Beduin to Beduin, even to an enemy, is compulsory. It includes the coming night also, and the wanderer must often enough put up with poverty. If any one passes by a tent at dinner-time, a repeated " fátal, ja fátal!" ("Please come!") invites him to stay and dine. A refusal would be an offence. The law of hospitality applies also to the foreigner, to the European, but when the person and his purpose are unknown, and the haunts of civilization are not far off, it is combined with a wholesome suspicion. The Beduin expects corresponding little gifts from the European. The Oriental phrases : " This tent is thy house"; " I am thy slave "; " Take my wife and my daughters and my sons," are mere flowers of speech and politeness.

In the course of three years I saw all possible regions and came in contact with the most various tribes of north-west Egypt, and I never found the great law of hospitality neglected. Poor Beduins offered milk, bread, or water. Wealthy Beduins made it a point of honour, directly after my arrival, to choose out the finest sheep from the flock, to kill it in my presence, and to say: "It is thine, Effendi."

The law of blood for blood lives tenaciously in the desert, although some alleviation of it is accepted among the Auladali, since the payment of a ransom for the debt of blood is permitted more often than formerly. For instance, a Mariut Beduin killed another in a dispute. The murderer fled out of the country to Barca, just as the Barca Beduin finds the safest protection against his enemies on Egyptian soil. A council, the Mâd, is held, to which the parties send their representatives. Finally a large sum of money is agreed on as ransom. It is often so large that the whole tribe must contribute in order to produce the two hundred Egyptian pounds and more.

During the excavations there were, however, cases in which no money in the world could have made the old right yield. Once during a wedding improvisation at Hawarieh, the bridegroom was shot when the salute of joy was given. The murderer fled into the Nile valley, but fell into the hands of the Egyptian police and was condemned to eighteen years' imprisonment. He was taken to the Sudan to undergo his punishment, since the danger of the vendetta was known. But the murdered man's brother procured satisfaction by shooting the prisoner's brother. He was hanged. It is worthy of note that the vendetta is also powerful when it is a question of interference with girls. On the other hand, I know two cases where girls were murdered because they had transgressed.

Three Years in the Libyan Desert

We sometimes had a very difficult position with the Beduins, and the suspicion aroused by the frequent visits of officers of the mounted police patrols, who came solely on account of our safety, added to our troubles. Of course we learned much that could not without the greatest danger be used for the advantage of our own lives; we sometimes employed fugitives and men whose crimes, when they were later discovered, filled us with as much horror as a duel in our own country. And now and again there were complications. One day a woman came crying and calling for help: her husband was shot. On account of a love affair the son had shot his own father, and the son was one of our workmen. He had fled with the corpse. The Mariut police were at once informed and patrols searched everything in the environs of Schakâne, the place where the murder was committed, an hour from the excavation buildings, in order to find the corpse, which the son had hidden. As no Beduin would come forward as witness, there was no testimony except the father's corpse. The search was continued in an entirely opposite direction, at Abu Machlûf, as I started the hypothesis that the son might perhaps have thrown the corpse into an ancient cistern which was in the ridge of hills to the west of the city of Menas. In fact, some broken metnan bushes gave a clue, and the corpse was found at Abu Machlûf, but buried in the sand. The young murderer had fled into the Nile valley and so forfeited his life. Hopkinson Pasha, the president of the police, remembered the photograph of the group of our workpeople that he had seen in one of his visits to the excavation buildings, and asked if the fugitive was in it. He was there—at least, his head and bust ; it was enlarged, and led to his capture at Gezireh. He was eventually hanged.

Among the Auladali, as with all other Beduins of the Libyan Desert, administration of justice is in the hands of the Mâd, the Council of Elders. In the family Mâd, as well as in the tribal Mâd, the oldest and most worthy are considered to be the most impartial. The men assemble in a tent, and tea or coffee introduces the proceedings. Each side in turn lays the matter before the president of the Mâd. The adversaries of course come to blows, abuse and threaten each other, and burst into fearful oaths. Then one of the elders intervenes with the magic words, " Pray to the Prophet," and the surging waves are stilled. " A thousand times," is the reply. This is repeated for hours, even for a whole day. I have often assisted at a Mâd, mostly by chance, when during a journey in the desert I came to tents where I knew the inhabitants. The Effendi, to whom much wisdom was ascribed, must be the impartial judge, a proceeding that only helped in the way of patience and tea-drinking. Sometimes a calming influence was produced by clearly setting forth the matter in dispute and strictly proving that right or wrong lay on this side or that. But very often the question of a stupid person or of an unexpected arrival would set the whole debate going again, and then there was no end to it. Attempt was made to prevent war between single clans and tribes by the intervention of the Mâd, or if the Barûfa was already proceeding, to settle the quarrel.

If a fight occurred near the city of Menas the people were with difficulty restrained from taking a side. We were obliged to let workmen go who belonged to either of the clans involved. As the Beduins knew that we ourselves would never take sides, and so long as no obstacle was put in our way we should not give the alarm to the Egyptian authorities, in time the wounded sought help at the Kasr Abu Mina. In periods of unrest we made our workmen deliver up their weapons and ammunition. The strict but just procedure of the chief of the excavations was respected by all reasonable persons: "The Effendi el-Kebir, the old Effendi, is as just as the Koran," they used to say in commendation.

When a Barûfa has once broken out a Mâd can

only have authority after there has been some decisive victory, however temporary. The weapons are not often very dangerous, since the men seldom have much ammunition and use the old muzzle-loading guns or long thin bayonets. Those who have neither guns nor steel use the nabût or the hebl. The nabût is a thick stick or cudgel of the height of a man, the hebl a bludgeon fastened to the arm by a sling. Pictures and inscriptions are scratched on such weapons. The terrible war-cry shows that the fight, which usually starts with stone-throwing, has begun. In tribal feuds and family quarrels it is generally the women who egg on the men : women even sometimes themselves take up weapons, and with warlike courage rush on the enemy. The cries of these black furies in their fluttering garments vastly add to the irritation of the combatants on both sides.

I remember a scene that took place at Christmas, which we celebrated shortly after beginning the excavations in the desert, that shows how quickly we won friends. We had had guests all day long, and had invited Beduins from the near neighbour-hood besides our workpeople. Late in the evening we determined to light up a Christmas-tree and to make a big bonfire on one of the high Koms of the city of Menas. Old chests, packing material, and such-like were piled up high and saturated with oil,

Three Years in the Libyan Desert

It soon burned up, and looked gigantic against the dark sky of the quiet desert. Hardly a quarter of an hour had passed when armed men came pouring in from all directions, even horsemen, all of them persons who had been our guests. They thought that the Kuschk, our first log-house, was in flames, that a Barûfa had broken out, and came to defend us with their arms. We were immensely pleased.

The police avail themselves very cleverly of the institution of the Mâd in the coast region and round about the new Khedivial desert railway ; when it is not a question of a heavy crime, they hand over the person concerned to a Beduin Mâd. And on the other hand Beduins who are established settlers, and therefore under control, turn to the native police in cases where the Mâd cannot come to a successful decision. I remember a tragi-comical affair of the kind. During a Barûfa, a seventy-year-old Beduin had his nose bitten off. His adversary offered compensation, but the old man refused it : he would have nothing but his enemy's nose. He was offered a large sum, to which the whole clan contributed ; but the Mâd sat for days without result. He would have no money, only his enemy's nose. At last it was decided to call in the aid of the police, and after fresh and long negotiations the old man agreed to take a compensation of £120. The matter certainly gave a new reason for our accident insurance, the value of a lost European nose.

Robberies of camels and smuggling of haschisch often led to severe fighting when the thieves could be verified or the capture of a smugglers' caravan took place. The smugglers are mostly Greeks, who carry the contraband in little sailing-boats from Greece, land on the shores of Marmarika, and make use of the Beduins as forwarding agents. They choose dark nights for the transport into the Nile valley, because then the mounted black soldiers of the Egyptian coastguard cannot venture into the desert. The haschisch, on the capture of which a premium of many times its value is set, lies ready in small waterproof packets, often sunk in the sea, marked for those who know the shore by a red wooden buoy or something similar. The conductors of the smuggling enterprises through the desert are Beduins; they mostly travel in couples, and well armed. They go half a day in advance of the smugglers' caravan in order to spy out the land. The holes of the city of Menas were formerly their best hiding-places, but during the excavation these were destroyed. The haschisch caravans rarely consisted of more than three camels, the drivers being a few boys. The animals were laden with tiny sacks, which the boys could at any moment hide or throw away. They marched only at nights, so that the smugglers ran little risk, and a golden harvest would be won by all concerned in the business.

I may say here a few more words about slavery, a subject I have incidentally touched elsewhere. The slaves of the Auladali are nearly all freed persons who prefer to remain with their masters, and are treated as members of the family. It is in the hinterland, and especially in the oases, that slaves are still found. The slave trade is only openly carried on in Northern Egypt, in the oasis of Dscharabub. It is essentially the Turkish market which is provided with slaves from Dscharabub, although officially it is usual to deny this. The price of a girl or boy between twelve and twenty years of age is from £4 upwards. Wadai and Bagirmi are the original lands of these human goods. The great caravan routes from Tripoli to Fessan, Lake Tschad, etc., are—according to the assertion of Hans Vischer, the English resident at Lake Tschad, who lately crossed the hinterland of Tripoli, little frequented since the days of the German African explorers, Vogel and Nachtigal—no longer to be recognized by the white bones of the slaves who were unable to endure the long journey to the north. The oasis of Kufra is a place connected with the slave caravans. It is a prominent seat of the Senussi monks, who keep there a complete arsenal of modern weapons and ammunition in the centre of the Sahara. Turkish ships touch at night on the shores of Tripoli, usually once a month, in order to take the finest slaves to their place of destination.

CHAPTER XI

BEDUIN AND FELLAH—THE RECLAIMING OF THE DESERT

The "ostraka" of the city of Menas—The lessons of the excavations at Karm Abu Mina—The outlook for Mariut —A far-reaching attempt of the Khedive—Agriculture and Beduin trade—Success on the borders of the delta—How the Nile mud changes the desert into a paradise—Fellah villages—The rôle of the Beduins in the borderland—The awakening of the Egyptian peasants.

IN 1909 Rowland Snelling, the well-known Egyptian journalist, set on foot the question of reclaiming the Libyan Desert. He had visited the city of Menas and the western desert, and then accepted an invitation from the corporation of Western Egypt to the "great oasis," and published the results of his journey in an article in the *Egyptian Gazette.* He entitled it " Ostraka." The term means the inscribed tablets, generally of clay, which are found in the mounds of ruins in the Nile valley, and which with the papyri that have been discovered provide us with a library of works on the history of ancient Egyptian

THE NABÛT AS FLAIL.

To face p. 332.

civilization. The ostraka of which Rowland
Snelling treated were the inscribed tablets of the
city of Menas. We found a great many,- and
those in question show by the depth of the layer
in which they were that they are fifth-century
documents. They were the oldest Christian
ostraka in the Greek language, and among other
things their contents throw light on the cultivation of the vine in the domains of the sanctuary
of Menas. The labourers in the vineyard, the
owners, the crop, the divisions of the clergy of
the sanctuary, the wages, the invalids, and so
forth are recorded. The coco-nut palm is also
mentioned, a tree now almost unknown in Northern
Egypt. The wine-presses that we found might
be called the supplement to these orders, letters,
and receipts, of which only a small portion can
be deciphered ; in the deepest layers of the cisterns
further evidence was found in the guise of the
wood of date-palms, remains of vine-poles as thick
as an arm which had slumbered for a thousand
years in the mud crust beside well-preserved
portions of a wooden plough, the make of which
corresponds exactly with that now used by the
Beduins. Ten, even twenty, yards of rubbish
had to be removed before we got to the hard
mud crust in which those relics lay hermetically
sealed to prove the former wealth and fertility of

the land that had since become desert. It was the general opinion that the ancient cultivation of Mareotis had only extended to the actual coast region and had only had sporadic settlements in the desert.

The results of the Kaufmann Menas Expedition proved the contrary, and its leader was right to draw attention to the lessons that these conclusive instances might teach for the reclaiming of Mariut. "The whole of the northern Auladali Desert could to-day be restored to its ancient flourishing condition," writes Monsignor Kaufmann in his often-mentioned "Guide" to the excavations, "and, indeed, by employing the ancient foundations." He refers to the cisterns of the city of Menas, which "are sufficient for the cultivation of productive fruit gardens and arable land of a square mile in extent"; to the irrigation canals that might be continued far into the desert; to Karm Abu Mina as "a central point for the irrigation system of Mareotis," and the corresponding ruins at Haschm-el-Aisch, Hamam, Haschm-el-Äschel, Kasr el-Gettajeh, Abu Machlûf, Schakâne, etc. "Their ancient wells and reservoirs are only buried—in many cases purposely buried—for it lies (and lay) in the express interests of the Beduins to have as few watering-places as possible within the boundaries of civilization."

Beduin and Fellah

We have seen how the Khedive, Abbas Hilmi II, in beginning the construction of the North-Western Egyptian Railway at his own expense, made a decisive step towards reclaiming at least the coast region of the western desert of the ancient provinces of Mariut and Marmarika. The expectations bound up with the railway for acquiring new land capable of cultivation were, through lack of water, not quite fulfilled. I refer here, of course, to the settler, to the training of the natives in agriculture, not to the royal master, for whom the railway is a profitable means of transport and source of income. Settlements and fine tracts of cultivated land are to be found alongside the new railway line, chiefly in the part of Mariut near Alexandria. The Beduin markets of Hamam, Bahig, and Amriah do an enormous trade. Amriah and the environs of Kingi Mariut have palm gardens and vineyards, and the cultivated land of a German, Herr Winterstein, of Alexandria, offers a model as the most important attempt at new cultivation. Nut gardens, barley, palms, and other trees all flourish there; Beduins who live in their tents close by are the labourers, and they claim part of the harvest as a reward.

An Egyptian land company attempted to found a large agricultural colony in Hamam during the excavations in Mariut, and settled Russian Jews

335

there. I often visited the colony, and register here the opinion of the Beduins who accompanied me: "The old Effendi (my cousin) wouldn't employ these people a week at Bumna." Bad work was the quintessence, but in any case much might be gained at Hamam and in the surrounding plain if labourers less skilful but better accustomed to the climate could be brought there, and if the water conditions were improved. As long as fresh-water canals are not laid down, cisterns and large tanks have to be relied on for storing the annual rain-water. Progress in that direction must be admitted, but it is small. It is also questionable if the large expense is justified unless the desert can be included. It is, of course, not suited for the so-called larger cultivation, for the soil is not right for cotton, rice, or sugar-cane. But all that flourished there in times of antiquity, palms, fruit-trees—in the city of Menas there grew, among others, carob-trees and almond-trees—vines, and barley. The Beduins sow barley sporadically in the wadis of the rain zone. As a good rain year can only be reckoned on every four years, they seldom stand to gain much. But a rain year produces eighty times the seed sown. In order to get fodder for the camels and horses, we made a trial and sowed scheïr in the plain, the ancient garden land of the city of Menas, which had been ploughed Beduin fashion with the light

IN THE OASIS OF THE FAYÛM : DRINKING AT THE JOSEPH SPRING.

To face p. 336.

Beduin and Fellah

camel plough. Although 1907 was not a good year, we reaped eight times the seed sowed. The barley, where it is best, is seldom more than 15 to 20 inches high in the desert. The Beduins reap it with the hands, breaking off the stalk, and thrash it in primitive fashion with a pole.

During the excavations, when the attention of the Egyptians was turned more eagerly to the desert in the north-west, agricultural experts under the direction of MM. Simond Bey and Leopold Jullien examined the land of Mariut, and declared that without an extensive system of irrigation, in other words, without the assistance of the Government, only sporadic small farming was possible. This meant that they had no idea of the skill of the Beduin labourer; the costly European hand must stand at the plough; they even considered the fellah, remarkable to say, unsuited to small cultivation in the north-west. Larger undertakings are condemned to failure beforehand. The conclusion of their report was : " On the whole the experts advise against the business." Whether any attempt will be made to profit by the lessons of the Menas expedition, which I have given above in Kaufmann's words, seems doubtful.

The opening up of the country would, of course, also reveal mineral resources. The stone-quarries of Dschebel Baten have for a long while yielded serviceable building material for Alexandria, and that it possesses hidden treasure is proved by the stratum of gypsum discovered near the city of Menas at Gherbanieh. It was known in ancient times. An Alexandrian building company has meanwhile begun to work it : an easy matter, since gypsum of the quality of Cyprus gypsum lies a very little below the surface of the ground—indeed, shows itself above in places—and with a thickness of three yards will yield an annual output of more than a million tons of raw material. If we consider that the island of Cyprus had, so to speak, a monopoly of gypsum for Egypt,[1] the importance of the discovery is recognized, and the increasing profit of the Khedivial desert railway is clearly understood.

The Auladali Beduin only concerns himself with agriculture for his own needs and those of his animals. He seeks his gains in the buying and selling of animals and in the increase of his herds. What sums pass through his hands may be computed, since a sheep which in Barca and Marmarika is sold at eight shillings, outside the gates of Alexandria and in the Beduin markets of Bahig and Amriah, according to the season, fetches double and treble (sixteen to twenty-four shillings), which is the normal Egyptian price.

I knew a poor Beduin whose commercial genius

[1] 20,494 tons in 1908.

338

RELIC OF ANCIENT LIBYAN CULTIVATION : THE JOSEPH CANAL.

AULADALI REAPING WITH THEIR HANDS.

To face p. 338.

brought him a large fortune. He lay in wait on
the chief caravan route of Derb-el-Hagg for the
Barca caravans, not to attack them—a thing
scarcely to be feared in the region of Mariut,
especially near the coast—but to purchase tired-
out camels for a trifle. The caravans, of course,
would only part with such camels as could not
endure more than a few days' further journeying,
and the owner was glad to get two or three pounds
for them. My Beduin acquired these animals with
borrowed money, fed them for a month on barley
and chopped straw, and then let them run loose in
the hattje, feed there and get rested, and afterwards sold them at every larger market for five
or six times the price he had given for them.
Systematic camel-rearing is very profitable, because
it needs scarcely any outlay. Many young Beduins
who possess at least one good camel at the time
of the cotton harvest wander into the delta and hire
out the animal, a proceeding that brings in about
three shillings a day for a few weeks. They return
home with a sum that maintains them for a long
while. The Beduins enter also into direct agricultural relations with the fellahs.

There could be no greater contrast than that
which exists between the fellah, who for centuries
has been oppressed, who was bound to the soil,
whose lot was harder than that of a slave, and

whose life was worth less than that of a cow, and the free son of the desert with his commanding eye and unbounded belief in himself. The position of the fellah has, however, improved since the English came into the valley of the Nile, yet the contrast still holds good, and is most striking on the western borders of the delta of the Nile. As the Auladali desert is there extremely flat, there is a greater chance of rendering it once again capable of cultivation. It was only a question of getting a drop of the source of all blessing in Egypt, the Bacher en-Nil. In the first century of our era Rufus of Ephesus wrote that no river water was drinkable without sterilization—he naturally said boiling—except the water of the Nile. And contemporary science confirms this. The Nile mud, which acts as its own filter, when brought into the desert makes it a Garden of Eden. The annual inundation of the Nile, which is increased by the mountain torrents of Abyssinia and the rain - spouts of equatorial Africa, has long been utilized, inasmuch as the surplus water is kept together by coffer-dams and only drained off methodically. The enormous dams of Cairo, Assuan, Siut, and Kaljub allow the precious drops of the sea of yellow mud to be so distributed, that not only in the months in which water is scarce, from March to July, the lands of the delta are watered by numerous branch

DESERT AND METROPOLIS. THE ARAB CEMETERY OF CAIRO AT THE EDGE OF THE
DESERT. THE ALABASTER MOSQUE OF MOHAMMED ALI IN THE DISTANCE.

To face p. 340.

canals, a thing impossible in ancient times through the former low position of the Nile, but the smaller canals can be carried right into the desert. Millions of square miles of land are thus made capable of cultivation, and are worked every year. Where twenty years ago the Auladali Beduins lay in wait for the traveller, white snowfields of cotton-trees and palm-shaded villages are now to be seen. A perfectly organized land speculation has set in. One day the Hukûma appears on unenclosed ground, hattje or desert; the authorities intervene and make the owner's title safe. Such and such a Beduin tribe can perhaps prove certain ancient rights, and is then compensated with money. Until then the land had no value. For a feddan, or Egyptian acre, £3, £4, or £5 is paid, an enormous sum for worthless land. A year later the drainage of the ground is begun by making little trenches, the network of which is drawn closer and closer. The Bey or the company that bought the land has only to wait for the connection with the neighbouring canal to be made for the gold to flow in streams. The company itself cultivates half of it; cotton, rice, durrha are planted and attended to by fellahs, who obtain cattle and implements and a fifth of the harvest by way of wages. The rest is offered for sale, at £15 to £40 and more an acre, according to its quality and its propinquity to water. The owner, supposing that he is no poor speculator, is a millionaire pasha in ten years, but the fellahs toil and moil as before for their Bey or their "compania," and the Beduins see with astonishment what is lured forth out of the land.

The Beduins play a twofold part in the fellah villages built of bricks of Nile mud. At the edge of the desert they live in those villages in large numbers and carry on agriculture themselves ; ten Arabs are easily equal to a village of fifty fellahs. They live absolutely separate from each other, the Beduins in tents, the fellahs in their dêrs. Even in the absolute peasant villages the visitor sees at least one Beduin tent, mostly so situated that the only road to it can be surveyed from it. It is the Ghaffir's or guard's tent, the local police, an office filled by Beduins throughout the frontier district, and even under the big farmers, the companies, or the Government itself. Their pay consists, according to circumstances, of a bare sum of one or two pounds a month or of a share of the agriculture, the profit on the harvest.

The circumstance that the whole of the western part of the province of Behêret, which extends from the Rosetta arm of the Nile to the Libyan Desert, the chief town of which is the ancient Horus town, Time en-Hor, the picturesque Damanhur, consists of reclaimed desert land, sufficiently explains the

Beduin and Fellah

large number of Beduins found there, some of whom are settlers and others only partly so. The insecurity of Behêret is proverbial and a great anxiety for the Government. The mixture of the two elements, the Beduins and the fellahs, by no means tends to diminish the insecurity. If the fellah songs compare Mariut to hell, to which the unbeliever is banished, the land of Behêret in contrast is the land " Seidne Jussuf," Paradise, but the Paradise of the Arab, whose intelligence combined with his political liberty gives him everywhere the upper hand of the fellah. The Arab, notwithstanding that he looks after the policing of the frontier, is a source of anxiety to the fellah, and especially to the Government, which loses greatly in prestige through carrying on the business of recruiting. The Beduin is exempt from military service and from taxation, and he extends the exemption to the children of mixed marriages. For a money bribe responsible Government Sheikhs enter them in the lists of the tribes. Wearisome inquiries have to be made, and if the Government enlists the young men by force they flee into the desert. The fellah, who is not free, sees this with envy, but is powerless, for he dares not give information, lest he should have his Beduin competitors and the whole Kabyle against him. So in the whole of the west of the delta the Beduin is master of the situation. Only rarely and under special precautions do the police venture into the outlying fellah villages, which in consequence of the thick mesh of canals are only accessible by long roundabout ways, and for months during the irrigation of the cotton plants rise like green hamlets from an immense lagoon, and are only connected by the canal dams. Both fellah and Beduin regard the Government police as their common enemy. Wherever possible serious disputes are settled in the Mâd, but nothing prevents the Auladali Beduins from practising their law of vendetta in those districts.

Besides a common enemy both sides have a common interest : the protection of their possessions, the cotton, worth its weight in gold during the protracted harvest weeks, and the punctual arrival of the water. The success of the work of many months depends on the latter ; if the engineers or their subordinates make a fault in any spot in the delta, the desired fertilization of the soil by the mud is interrupted and everything rendered uncertain. Then either the "Mohantez" is bribed to open the sluices for a night or Beduins and fellahs open the supply together one dark night and defend it by force of arms. Single villages fight veritable battles for their water privileges. But thanks to the English surveillance, conditions are improving, and where the system leads to injustice and preferences,

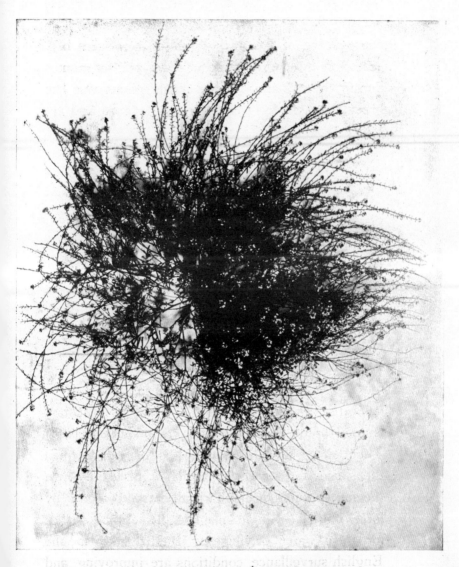

FLORA OF THE DESERT.   NUÂR OF THE HATTJE.

To face p. 344.

it is only with the subordinate corruptible officials. Those improvements, combined with the making of new canals, will, quite apart from the maintenance of the land already laid out, be the chief task for the country for a very long time to come. It must not be forgotten that our time, with all its civilization, stands far behind that of the ancients. Who now thinks of so gigantic a possibility as that of building a canal from the Central Nile right across the desert to the Red Sea, as the Pharaohs planned it, and who remembers that the most important of the boasted waterways, filled with " the tears which Isis wept for her husband," rest on ancient foundations or were surpassed by similar constructions ! I remember the fresh-water canal 45 yards deep that connected Bubastis with the eastern salt lakes, and so fertilized the land of Goshen, to traverse which, according to Herodotus, took a period of four days. It was built in the fourteenth century before Christ. I remember, too, the Joseph Canal, the Bacher Jussuf, about 207 miles in length, which runs north from Siut into the Libyan Desert and opens up the wonderful "land of roses," the oasis of Fayûm. There oranges and olives, peaches and figs, rice and sugar grow as they did thousands of years ago, the same fruits which once grew in the sandy oasis of the Auladali Desert.

We have seen how the progress of civilization, at

Three Years in the Libyan Desert

least in the western region of the Delta, does not quite oust the Beduin. But unfortunately, on the other hand, it leads only very slowly to improvement in the position of the fellah. His statute labour is the same, although the taxes are juster and the share of the profits more secure. But the fellah is not yet sufficiently awakened to understand how to get wealth at the fountain-head. I have seen with horror how the profits of the richest harvests have been squandered, how the old grounded mistrust— partly on religious considerations—of banks, of securing the money that has been gained, is rather increasing than diminishing. The Beduin buys herds with his gold ; the fellah buries it in a pot, and it happens that he cannot find the place, that he dies and no one knows where it is, that he is watched and robbed. As before, he is dependent on his employer or on the company, to whom house, cattle and all belong, and who can dismiss him at any moment. Therefore the people when they help each other with money demand enormous interest. A single guinea is doubled in a year. They borrow durrha and other victuals, lend money in the hope of good harvests, and so tie the rope about their necks.

346

INDEX

Abbas Hilmi II, Khedive of Egypt, 13, 204, 215, 216, 217, 232, 233 ; 262–89 *passim* ; 335

Abd el-Al, 29, 33, 36, 54, 59, 62, 72, 112, 113, 114, 116, 125, 126, 141, 142, 144

Abd el-Alim, 155, 156

Abd el-Kader, 142, 210, 298, 299

Abd el-Moneïn, Prince, 268

Abd el-Schuard, 244

Abd er-Rahman, 213, 214, 221, 299, 300, 301

Abd-errâsi Abu Reïm, 216

Abescher, 308, 309

Abma Gabriel, Abbot of Dêr Baramûs, 76, 77

Abu Hanesch, Sheikh, tomb of the, 215

Abu Machlûf, 174, 324, 325, 334

Abu Musa, 78, 91

Abu Rîch, Sheikh, 71, 72

Abu Roâsch, pyramids of, 63

Abu Schasar, 216

Abu Schrûf, 285, 287

Abu Sêf, 29, 54, 58, 59, 60,

Abu Zet el-Hilâl, tales of, 123, 133

Abukir, 206

Abusir, 132, 175, 185, 197, 200, 212, 215

Abyssinia, 340

Achmed ibn Dinar, 180

Adickes, Dr. Franz, 183, 184

Africa, Central, 1, 179, 306, 307, 308, 340

Africa, fauna of, 65, 66

Africa, North, 1, 4, 197, 308

Agermi, 281, 283

Agûbe (Katabathmos), 193, 201, 202, 203, 213, 214, 219, 229

Aïn Ben Lîf, 284

Aïn Hamâm, 284, 285

Aïn Mûsa, 284

Alexander the Great, 271, 272, 282 ; tomb of, 15–17

Alexandria, 3 *ff.*

Algeria, 280

Algiers, 197, 229, 295, 305

Ali Abu el-Nûr el-Gherbi, Sheikh, 231, 232, 233

Almaida, 212

America, 217

Amon, Lake of, 284

Amon, oasis of, 269

Index

Amon-Ra, 282
Amonium, 194, 198, 262, 268, 282, 286
Amonius, 67
Amr ibn el'-As, General, 68
Amriah, 141, 149, 155, 157, 175, 193, 198, 206, 211, 217, 289, 290, 335, 338
Anfûchi, bay of, 17
Antony the Hermit, 67
Appenzell, canton of, 22
Arabi Pasha, 19, 230, 231, 298
Arabian Desert, 278, 306, 308
" Arabian Nights," the, 122
Araschieh, Lake of, 283
Arcadius, basilica of the Emperor, 131, 140, 177, 178, 223, 297
Arcadius, the Emperor, 105, 179
Arians, the, 103
Armenia, 217
Asia Minor, 10
Assemani, keeper of Vatican Library, 86
Assuan, 340
Athanasius the Great, 136, 139, 176, 223
Athens, 9
Audschile, oasis of, 201
Augustus, the Emperor, 17
Auladali Desert, 31, 64, 113, 118, 119, 123, 125, 132, 191, 192, 194, 200, 334, 340, 345
Auladali, tribe of the, 185–92

Bab-Frankenfurt, 49, 56, 198
Bacharije, oasis of, 55, 198, 237
Bacher en-Nil, 230, 340

Bagirmi, 330
Bahig, 156, 160, 193, 211, 225, 232, 248, 289, 290, 335, 338
Barca, 1, 5, 134, 143, 175, 185, 186, 188, 194, 198, 238, 311, 338
Barth, Heinrich, 192, 193, 220
Bary, Herr von, Consul-General at Tunis, 6
Basle, 22
Beduin funeral customs, 320, 321
Beduin hospitality, 322
Beduin Mâd (council), 323, 325, 326, 328, 344
Beduin marriage customs, 312–18
Beduin slave-trade, 330, 331
Beduin smugglers, 329, 330
Beduin superstitions, 295, 296, 297
Beduin vendetta, 322–5
Behêret, 205, 206, 207, 210, 255, 342, 343
Bengasi, 3, 4, 5, 6, 204, 278, 311
Berkefeld filters, 248
Berlin, 22
Berne, 22
Bilma, 270
Bindernagel, Heinrich, merchant of Alexandria, 257, 260
Bir Abu Batta, 216
Bir Abu Zister, 216
Bir Bakusch, 215
Bir Beta, 214, 215
Bir Eiséle, 126, 127, 248, 250
Bir El Maddar, 216
Bir Emselich, 56, 57, 58

Index

Bir Geraule, 215, 216, 217
Bir Goaiferi, 273
Bir Hakfet eggelâs, 273
Bir Hamam, 34, 37, 42, 197, 212, 334, 335, 336
Bir Haschm-el-Aisch, 35 *ff.*, 58, 63, 200, 212, 334
Bir hêlu, 273
Bir Hooker, 72, 98, 100, 113, 114
Bir istable, 273
Bir Lahafen, 273
Biserta, port of, 270
Biskra, 270
Bitter, Dr., 285
Blanckenhorn, 64, 65
Bode, Dr., Director of the Berlin Museum, 149, 183, 184
Bomba, 188
Bornu, 306
Bosphorus, the, 4
Botti, G., 17
Breccia, E., 17
Brindisi, 14
British Museum, 86
Browne, 216
Brugsch Pasha, 146, 200
Bu Schaifa, Gulf of, 215, 217
Bubastis, 345
Butin, 283
Butler, J., 78
Byzantium, 139, 178, 180

Cairo, 13, 23, 99, 156, 197, 198, 199, 204, 279, 285, 340
Cairo Museum, 128, 302
Camperio, 2
Caria, South, 268

Chêr, family of, 159, 222, 241, 242
Chineu-Seteu, 279
Christmas in the desert, 221–8
"Church of the Sheikhs," Macarius Monastery, 105–8
Coffin Mountains, 273
Cologne Cathedral, 13
Congo, French, 270
Connaught, Duke of, 256
Constantine, the Emperor, 84, 136, 139, 176, 179
Constantinople, 4
Crawford, Earl of, 91
Crete, 10, 22
Crœsus, 282
Cromer, Lord, 203, 213, 230, 256, 266, 268, 309
Curzon, Lord, 86
Cyprus, island of, 338
Cyrenaïca, 132, 139, 185, 190, 201, 203, 310, 311
Cyrenaïca expedition, 1–7
Cyrene, 3

Dachel, 269
Daffa, 273
Damanhur, 342
Dar-Fur, 222
Date caravans, 277, 278
Decius, the Emperor, 66
Denischwai, 230
Dêr Amba Bischâi, monastery of, 67 ; visit to, 91–7
Dêr Baramûs, monastery of, 67 ; visit to, 73–86 ; 87, 90, 92, 102
Dêr es-Surjani, monastery of, 67, 86, 87, 90, 91

349

Index

Derb el-Hagg el Maghrabe, 196, 197, 339
Derna, 6
Dervishes, 302, 303
Dikoa, 306
Diocletian, 136
Dioskoros, patriarch, 89
Don Pedro, Emperor of Brazil, 40
Dörpfeld, Professor Wilhelm, of Athens, 3
Dscharabub, oasis of, 194, 198, 201, 202, 203, 309, 311, 312, 330
Dschebel Achdar, 4, 7, 310
Dschebel Baten, 211, 337
Dschebel ed-Dara, 49
Dschebel el-Beled, 281
Dschebel el-Boheb, 46
Dschebel el-Farr, 56
Dschebel el-Laban, 56
Dschebel Hadîd, 70
Dschebel Judar, 273
Dschebel Scharraff, 57
Dschebel Somâra, 56
Dschebel Taref, 273
Dschidda, 305, 311

Edarra, 281
Edfu, temple of, 66
Egypt, 1, 7, 178, 179, 197, 203, 217, 218
El-Ahzar University, Cairo, 312
El-Almaida, ruins of, 41, 42
El-Gara, 201
El-Hadra, 18, 19
El-Halfa, 43, 44, 47
El-Hamam, 175, 201

El-Khargeh, oasis of, 269
El-Lischa, 57
El-Nêd, mountain of, 118
Elpis Melenas, Baroness von Schwartz, 22
Eluâni, 29 ff.; 228, 240, 241, 243, 296, 297
England, 229
En-Hêd, mountain of, 72
Epiphanius of Aschumneïn, 174
Eratosthenes, 65
Ezbet el-Menchieh, village of, 255

Farafrah (El-wa), 198, 229
Faregh, Valley of, 63
Fashoda, 230
Fayûm, the, 145, 345
Fessan, 330
Fez, 229, 307
Fort Napoleon, signal station of, 25
France, 229
Frankfort-on-Main, 63
Frankfort Museum, 276, 281, 299
Fritsch, 22
Furtwängler, Professor, of Munich, 2, 3

Gara, oasis of, 198, 216
Gared el-Laban, 46, 48, 57
Gared Saadêh, 49
Gatara, oasis of, 194, 216, 288
Gaul, 179
Gerah, 194
Gerbanieh, 200, 338
Germany, 7, 179, 214

Index

Germany, Emperor of, 229, 230
Geru (Karu), 308, 309, 310
Ghart el-Hanûn, 273
Gorst, Sir Eldon, 256
Goshen, land of, 345
Gotschlick, Dr., of Alexandria, 59
Greece, 7, 9, 179
Green Mountains, the, 4, 5

Haimann, 2
Hamilton, James, 282
Harami, the, 128
Harnack, Professor, of Berlin, 3
Hartmann, Professor, of Berlin, 132
Haschm-el-Aschel, 334
Hassan Bu Ismain, 244, 245, 246, 247
Hauran, the, 238
Haydn, Amadeus, 40, 41
Heisterbach, legend of the monk of, 167
Heliopolis, temple of the sun at, 15
Heracleopolis, 279
Herisau, 22
Herodotus, 201, 281, 284, 345
Hieracites, the, 103
Hitalije cycle of Arabic legends, 133
Hopkinson Pasha, 24, 149, 161, 231, 248, 325

Igli, 270
India, 230
Ischaïla, island of, 218, 219
Ischynon, martyr of Alexandria, 108

Ismail Pasha, 15, 270
Italy, 6

Jerusalem, 179
Joseph, Patriarch, 180
Joseph Canal, 345
Jullien, Leopold, 337
Junker, Dr. Wilhelm, 37, 102, 118, 132, 193
Jupiter-Amon, 16, 201, 216, 282, 283

Kairuân, 7, 307
Kaljub, 340
Kanaïs, 216; gulf of, 213, 214; pass of, 273
Karm Abu Mina, 131 ff.
Karm Abûm, 123, 126
Karm Medar, 215
Kasr Dschedîd, 202
Kasr el-Adschebia, 203
Kasr el-Garaîschet, 285, 286
Kasr el-Gettajeh, 58, 59, 63, 118, 132, 334
Kasr Schama el-Gherbie, 212, 219
Kaufmann, Heinrich, father of Monsignor Kaufmann, 183
Kaufmann, Monsignor, 1 ff.
Kautzky Bey, 264
Kayser, Gustav, 25, 204
Keffi Genji, 307
Khartum, 15, 306
Khediva, the, 268
Khedive, the, and Schiess Pasha, 20, 22, 23
Khedivial railway, 27, 156, 191, 194, 328

Index

Kiepert, Richard, of Berlin, 3
Kingi Mariut, 211
Kirsch, Professor, of Freiberg, 3
Koch, 22
Kom esch Schugâfa, Greek catacombs of, 17
Kom Marghab, 120, 121, 123, 125
Kordofan, 306
Kossuth, 137
Kufra, oasis of, 309, 330
Kumm, Dr. Karl, 307

Leontius, the Greek Emperor, 82
Liturgy, the Coptic, 95, 96
London, 15
Lotos-eaters, land of the, 196
Loxonetae, 175
Lycus Fluvius, 64

Macarius, monastery of, 63; visit to, 100-11
Madagascar, 65
Mádani, sect of, 210
Magrari, falls of Lake, 286
Mahmud Pasha Sidky, Governor of Alexandria, 23, 27
Makrizi, mediæval Arab writer, 67, 304
Malta, 7, 311
Mamûr Markaz, 27, 28, 29, 59, 123, 149, 150, 151, 152, 153, 156, 157, 211, 308, 309, 310, 311, 314, 315
Mâr Baseleios, patriarch, 89
Mâr Gabriel, patriarch, 89
Mâr Joannes, patriarch, 89

Mâr Kosmas, patriarch, 89
Marea, town of, 199, 205
Mareotis, Lake, 120, 139, 205
Mareotis, province of, 39, 64, 193, 199, 334
Mariut, desert of, 199, 261, 262
Mariut, Lake of, 142, 210
Mariut, province of, 24, 42, 119, 151, 161; 186-220; 231, 262, 269, 289, 305, 334, 335, 337, 339, 343
Marmarika, 3, 30, 39, 42, 64; 186-220; 237, 263, 269, 272, 289, 305, 310, 335, 338
Maspero, Sir Gaston, 146
Mathuiseulx, M. von, 271
Mecca, 307, 311
Mecca pilgrims, 237, 292, 305
Mecca railway, 270, 306
Medina, 311
Medina Kiffari, ruins of, 118, 119, 132
Mediterranean, the, 1, 19, 38, 63, 212, 214
Memphis, 16, 282
Menas, bath of, 182, 183
Menas, city of, 65, 133, 139, 156, 159, 195 *ff.*, 223, 226, 227, 249, 250, 252, 276, 288, 294, 296, 297, 299, 302, 314 *ff.*, 334, 336, 338
Menas, excavation of, 18, 159-84; 186, 204
Menas, temple of, 7, 30, 119, 129, 130, 134, 135, 140, 145, 146, 205, 281, 333
Menschije, 281

Index

Mex, Lake of, 206, 207 ; quarries of, 205 ; suburb of Alexandria, 140, 141, 142, 207

Minutoli, General von, 192, 193, 217, 263, 280

Mirage, 120, 121

Miralai Kelham, 30

Mirsa Berek, 217

Mirsa Matru, 196, 201, 202, 204, 212, 215, 216, 217, 218, 219, 269, 271, 272, 288

Mohammed Ali, 19, 137, 206, 211, 265, 274, 283

Mokkatam, 278

Monophysitism, heresy of, 95

Morocco, 197, 229, 237, 305

Moses of Nisibis, 87, 88, 89, 90

Muftah Dabûn, Sheikh, 28–155 *passim*

Muharak, Central Egypt, monastary of, 92

Mycenæ, 9

Nachtigal, 330

Natrûn Lakes, 66

Natrûn Valley, 56, 58, 62, 63, 194, 197, 198, 279

Nebi Daniel mosque, 15, 16

New York, 15

Nicæa, holy fathers of, 104

Niger, the, 270, 307

Nile, the, 13, *passim*; delta of, 19 *passim*; Rosetta arm of, 342 ; valley of, 67, 76, 77, 92, 192, 278, 293, 311, 340

Nitrian Desert, 67, 74, 174

Nubia, 178

Omdurman, victory of, 15

Ostrom, the Emperor of, 223

Pacho, J. R., 2, 59, 131, 132, 193

Paraetonium (El-Baratûn), 201, 217, 273

Paris, 22

Patras, 9

Pensilum, M., 72

Pentapolis, the Cyrenaïcan, 2

Persia, 230

Piræus, the, 9

Pliny, 7

Port Said, 147

Porte, the, 4

Porto Rio Soloma, 202

Procopius, 2

Ptolemy Philadelphos, 282

Pyramids, the Great, of Ghizeh, 186, 194, 199

Quatremer, French archæologist, 133

Ramadhan, fast of, 292, 293

Ramleh, 13, 21

Ras Alam Rûm, 216, 217

Ras el-Bakar, the cow-mountain 55

Ras el-Hamraje, 273

Ras el-Kanaïs, 216

Ravenna, 178

Red Sea, 117

Robecchi-Brichetti, 263

Rohlfs, 2, 263, 270, 277, 280, 285

Rücker-Jenisch, Freiherr von, 4

Index

Ruelberg, Georg, 26
Rufus of Ephesus, 340
Russia, 179, 229

Sahara Desert, the, 1, 195, 230,
  306, 308, 331 ; railway, 270
St. Antony, monastery of, Pet-
  ræa, 92
St. Dometius, 78, 82–4
St. Elias, monastery of, 67, 91
St. Ephraim, tree of, 87
St. Exupéré, Vicomte de, 264
St. John of Kolobos, monastery
  of, 67, 68
St. Macarius, 67, 82, 83, 84, 91,
  102, 103
St. Maximus, 78, 82–4
St. Menas, 130 ; legend of, 136–
  9 ; tomb of, 263, 289
St. Nub, monastery of, 68, 91
St. Paul, monastery of, Petræa,
  92
St. Paul's Church (outside the
  gates), Rome, 177
St. Peter's, Rome, 177 ; ancient
  basilica of, 88
Saïte donkeys, 278, 279
Sali ben Said Omer el-Khalidi,
  311
Salt, extraction of, 97–100
Sbûche, 281
Schakâne, 324, 334
Schiess Pasha, 14, 15, 17, 19, 20,
  21, 22, 23, 24, 26, 28, 33, 41,
  59, 114, 128, 145
Schillizzi, 16
Schliemann, Heinrich, tomb of,
  9, 15

Schorp, the Horus town, 66,
  342
Schuâbi, the, 62, 69, 70
Schuchân, Sheikh, 129, 130, 154,
  155, 164, 297, 315
Schuêre, 31
Schultze, Professor Viktor, of
  Greifswald, 2
Schweinfurth, Professor Georg,
  2, 22, 284
Sebel Hills, 19
Sechet-am, 273
Sechmet, the lion-headed war
  goddess, 14, 15
Senckenberg Physical Research
  Society, treatises of the, 63
Senussi monks, the, 198, 213,
  215, 230, 274, 307 ff.
Septimus Severus, 17
Serapeum, ruins of, at Alexan-
  dria, 14
Sfax, 7
Sicard, Père, French missionary,
  110
Sidi Achmêda, 300
Sidi Auen, 300
Sidi Barani, 203, 204
Sidi Bu Driha, 300
Sidi Bu Schaifa, 300
Sidi el-Fakir, Sheikh, tomb of,
  299, 300
Sidi Gaber, 18
Sidi Jadem, basilica of, 175
"Sidi Melûnte," mystery of, 122,
  123
Sidi Mohammed ben Ali es-
  Senûse, founder of the Senussi
  brotherhood, 308

Index

Sidi Sadaui, Sheikh, overseer of the Menas excavations, 151 *ff.*; 225 *ff.*; 260, 300

Simond Bey, 337

Siut, 340, 345

Siwa, oasis of, 49, 65, 194, 196, 198, 201, 203, 216, 217, 229, 237, 268 *ff.*, 286, 289; people of the, 275; towns of the, 280, 281

Siwi language, 280

Smith-Porcher, 2

Snake-charmers, 302, 303, 304

Snelling, Rowland, 173, 332, 333

Sohâg, monasteries of, 92

Sollum, 29, 188, 218; 301 *ff.*; 255

Somara, wadis of, 79

Sophronius, 135

Sponge-fishing, 217, 218

Steindorff, 283, 285

Stendel, Dr., 26

Stradonitz, Kekule von, 3

Stromer, Professor, of Reichenbach, 63

Strzygovski, Professor Joseph, of Vienna, 3, 89

Suez, 305

Suez Canal, 22, 148; opening of, 99

Suliman Habûn, Sheikh, 276

Sun-god, sanctuary of the, 281

Supan, Professor, of Gotha, 3

Synesius, 2

Syria, 217

Syrte, Little, 196

Table Mountains, 273

Tangier, 311

Tattam, Henry, 87

Taunus, the, 225

Terenouli, 134

Terraneh, 99, 199

Tewfik Pasha, 16, 205

Theodosius, the Emperor, 14, 15, 105, 179

Thiersch, Professor, of Freiburg, 16

Timbuctoo, Sultan of, 307

Tiryns, 9

Transcaucasia, 230

Tripoli, 3, 4, 5, 6, 7, 12, 25, 197, 237, 278, 305, 330, 331

Troy, 9

Tschad, Lake, 270, 307, 320

Tucher, Freiherr von, 149

Tunis, 6, 7, 26, 197, 229, 295, 305, 311

Turkestan, 230

Turkey, 310

Tussûn, Prince, 17

Umm Bêda, 283

Unnofer, mountain of, 66

Val, Monsignor de, of Rome, 3

Venetian lagoons, 280

Virchow, 22

Vischer, Hans, 330

Vogel, 330

Wadai, 306, 308, 309, 330

Wadi Dafne, 29, 203

Wadi Djeffer, 102

Wadi el-Habîb, 61

Wadi Faregh, 56, 62, 63, 194, 279

Index

Wadi Halfa, 64

Wadi Moghara, 47, 50, 56, 58, 64, 102, 186, 194, 198

Wadi Natrûn, 30, 31, 56, 57, 61, 118, 174, 188, 211, 260, 310

Wadi Raml, 216, 273

Wanslebius, 277

Wardian, 204, 205

Water difficulties in the desert, 25, 26, 37, 47, 53, 54, 124, 125, 218, 219, 247, 248, 249, 250, 251

"Waterless river" (Bacher bela mâ), the, 64, 96, 97

Winterstein, Herr, of Alexandria, 335

Zeno, the Emperor, 140, 180, 182

Zetûn, 281, 282, 286, 287

Zittel, 279